A New
World of
Words

A New World of Words

Redefining

Early

American

Literature

William C.
Spengemann

Yale University Press
New Haven and London

Designed by Deborah Dutton.
Set in Trump Mediæval text and Birch
display type by The Composing Room of
Michigan.

Printed in the United States of America by
Edwards Brothers, Inc., Ann Arbor,
Michigan.

**Library of Congress Cataloging-in-
Publication Data**

Spengemann, William C.
A new world of words : redefining early
American literature /
William C. Spengemann.
p.   cm.
Includes bibliographical references and
index.
ISBN 0-300-05794-6
1. American literature—Colonial period, ca.
1600–1775—History and criticism—Theory,
etc.   2. Franklin, Benjamin, 1706–1790—
Criticism and interpretation.   3. Milton,
John, 1608–1674. Paradise lost.   4. Smith,
John, 1580–1631. True relation.
5. Columbus, Christopher.   6. Canon
(Literature)   I. Title.
PS185.S67   1994
810.9'001—dc20   93-21015
CIP

A catalogue record for this book is available
from the British Library.

The paper in this book meets the guidelines
for permanence and durability of the
Committee on Production Guidelines for
Book Longevity of the Council on Library
Resources.

10   9   8   7   6   5   4   3   2   1

For Joaquin
and Pascal

Contents

Preface

Early American Literature has never been a subject to make the heart leap. As Michael Colacurccio once observed, there isn't much there that can be called literature, and what little there is isn't very good (111). The justice of this harsh but by no means uncommon judgment rests entirely on the way the subject has always been defined, as writings in English by sometime residents of those British colonies that later became the United States, and the failure of those writings to meet the literary criteria of still later times. The definition mocks history. No one wrote in what has been called "the future United States," a future that did not exist until it was a past; and *literature* did not mean to William Byrd what it would to Matthew Arnold. Worse yet, this definition of Early American Literature reflects a number of nineteenth-century assumptions regarding America, literature, and history that we no longer share. The Early American Literature invented by Samuel Lorenzo Knapp and improved by Moses Coit Tyler may have been *their* past, but it is certainly not ours; and until we contrive to see the subject from our own historical and critical vantage point, it will remain less than American, less than literary, and early in some history that does not include us.

A primary aim of this book, accordingly, is to reclaim the subject by redefining its constituent terms—*early, American,* and *literature*—in ways more respectful of the historical circumstances in which English writings were produced before 1800 and the critical circumstances in which such writings are now received. If Early American Literature could be seen not as the least American, least literary phase of American literary history but as an important phase in the evolution of the language that conditions all of our literary and historical judgments, the subject might undergo a renaissance. It might even come to rival the English Renaissance and its American namesake as a past especially responsible for, and to, the present, and so become, like them, a subject that, automatically shedding lustre rather than derision upon their practitioners, is attractive to scholars capable of enhancing that lustre.

These pages are not addressed solely to Early Americanists, however. Although the book draws its materials largely from writings before 1800, there is no contention here that is not equally applicable to the subject of American literature as a whole or to any other of the periods commonly supposed to constitute its history. It is as true of *Moby-Dick* and *North of Boston* as it is of John Smith's *True Relation* that the Americanness of a piece of writing has nothing necessarily to do with the citizenship of the writer. In this respect, the particular period chosen for remark here is merely a polemical convenience, a time that highlights the problems, historical and critical, that attend the nationalistic idea of American literature and the benefits, also historical and critical, of replacing that idea with one grounded in language.

Were someone to ask for my credentials as an inspector of Early American Literature, I would have little to show. I came to the subject rather late in my career and, having never penetrated very far into its dense interior, cannot pretend to know it inside out. Inexpertness, however, has not kept me from issuing periodic critiques of expert work in the field, along with suggestions for its reformation. That my unsolicited advice has been more often seriously considered than dismissed out of hand testifies less to any authority I can claim than to the uncommon willingness of Early Americanists to entertain other ideas, however uninformed or intemperately expressed, regarding their own business.

The institution of Early American Literature, in short, has been very good to me, both professionally and personally—far better, I'm afraid, than my manners have sometimes deserved—and I want to announce my gratitude right here, in case it should fail to announce itself in the pages to come. Were I to list in the order of their importance to me those scholars who have encouraged and aided my work, they would all have to come first. In the interests of legibility, I name them here in alphabetical order: Nina Baym, Peter Carafiol, Greg Comnes, Richard De Prospo, Everett Emerson, Norman Grabo, Philip Gura, William Hedges, Annette Kolodny, David Laurence, Leo Lemay, David Levin, Michael Lofaro, Donald Pease, Karen Rowe, John Seelye, David Shields, and Larzer Ziff.

Ellen Graham, my longtime editor and friend, contracted for this book. Kathy Harp prepared the copy. Richard Miller edited it with gleeful exactitude, and Jonathan Brent, Ellen Graham's successor, steered it through the press.

According to convention, these people, having been duly if inadequately thanked, should now be absolved of all responsibility for whatever ensues. That, however, would be disingenuous as well as ungrateful. Were it not for them, this book would never have appeared. Except for the two young men named in the dedication, it would never have been written.

A New
World of
Words

1

Early American Literature as a Period of Literary History

The idea of Early American Literature necessarily involves an idea of history. The word *early* posits a historical relation, at once chronological and organic, between the texts so designated and American literature proper, which comes later and, presumably, constitutes a more advanced stage in the development of that entity. *American*, similarly, defines the literature in question primarily in historical, as opposed to what we normally consider literary, terms, having less to do with the way it is written than with where it was written, or who wrote it, or what it is about. Even the word *literature*, as employed here, has a historical dimension in that its meaning has changed radically over the centuries since the texts we think of as Early American Literature were written. Sarah Kemble Knight would not have called her journal literature, but Early Americanists do, thus acknowledging that a piece of writing not so intended can become literature in time, given the right historical circumstances.

History has been an essential element of Early American Literature from the very beginning. The subject came into being, in the decades following the American Revolution, in response to avowedly political, rather than to literary, demands. That is, it was not the perceived literariness of colonial writings that recommended their inclusion in the ranks of American literature. On the contrary, virtually everyone involved in discovering or creating the national literature agreed that even the best colonial writings were literarily deficient, while the mill run were bereft of literary qualities altogether. Among the several anthologies of American verse that appeared between James Rivington's aborted *Specimens of American Poetry*, in 1773, and Samuel Kettell's collection of the same name, more than a half-century later, not one included the work of any pre-Revolutionary writer. The few commentators on American literature who even mentioned colonial writings did so only to say that no literature could be found there. In what may be the earliest recorded suggestion that American literature has its origins in the colonies, Robert Southey opened a review of Abiel Holmes's *American Annals*, in 1809, with a brief survey of colonial writers—most of them poets—in order to show that "[n]o work of distinguished merit in any branch [of literature] has yet been produced among" the Anglo-Americans (Ruland, ed., *Native Muse* 70). Nine years later, William Cullen Bryant implied a similar kinship between contemporary and colonial poetry by way of rendering a similar judgment: "For the first century after the settlement of this country, the few quaint and unskillful specimens of poetry which yet remain to us are looked upon merely as objects of curiosity, are preserved only in the cabinet of the antiquary, and give little pleasure if read without reference to the age and people which produced them" (100).

What motivated the invention of an Early American Literature where none seemed to exist was a felt need among patriots of the new nation at once to reinforce its claims to political independence and to demonstrate its right to be counted among the civilized nations of the world. Noah Webster expressed a sentiment widely shared when he maintained that American independence required a distinct literature as well as a separate politics (Spencer 27). Proof of that independence, according to the idea of national literatures then being promulgated in Europe, lay in the discovery of an autochthonous history behind current literary productions; and that history, coupled with the impulse to recover it, proclaimed a nation's arrival at cultural maturity. "All civilized nations," Samuel Knapp wrote in 1829, "have made great exertions, in some period of their history, to discover the origins of their literature" (30). His own *Lectures on*

American Literature, with Remarks on Some Passages of American History, aimed, therefore, "to establish the claims of the United States to that intellectual, literary, and scientific eminence, which we say, she deserves to have" (3).

Knapp fully realized that the writings of the colonists did not readily lend themselves to this nationalistic project. In order even to think of them as literature, he had to strip the term of its recently acquired connotations of imaginativeness and formal artistry and reclothe it in Dr. Johnson's definition as learned writing in any form or field. In this "extended sense" (29), which is in fact its "proper sense," Knapp maintains, literature constitutes "the transcript of the head and heart of man . . . in every age of his existence." To be sure, "even his imaginings belong to the literature of the world." But still "more" do the "descriptions of his country" (31). All together, these various documents make up the "national literature," which, "thoroughly studied, affords the best criterion by which may be judged the principles and powers of a people, as well as their rank in the scale of a civilization" (29).

Knapp's efforts to supply American literature with a respectably long history by including the colonies in it were redoubled by Samuel Kettell's anthology of American poems, published in the same year. Like Knapp, Kettell was sensitive to the low critical repute of pre-national writings. "The literary productions of our fathers," he notes in his preface, "have been held in unwarrantable disesteem by their descendants" (iii). And like Knapp, he finesses the problem of artistic deficiency by shifting his emphasis from recognized literary value, the exhibition of artistic genius, to historical value, the expression of national character. "What though our early literature cannot boast of a Dante or a Chaucer," Kettell asks with a perceptible sinking of the heart, "it can furnish such testimonials of talent and mental cultivation as are highly creditable to the country." Furthermore, "everything published among us must have some value, if not on account of its intrinsic merits, at least as affording some insight into the spirit and temper of the times" (iii–iv). If American literary history wanted what Knapp called "previous ages of heroic virtue and gigantic labors" (4), colonial writings, however inelegant, would have to fill the gap.

Having been cobbled together from the historical archives in order to fill out a historical outline and to meet political demands, Early American Literature has always depended for its identity, justification, and value far more upon historical than upon literary considerations. During the first half-century of its existence, from its christening in the volumes of Knapp and Kettell until its entry into college at the close of the 1800s, virtually every claim for the historical importance of the subject came accompanied by an admission of its literary failings. As James Freeman Clarke so bluntly put the case in 1843, every American should know the Puritan poets, even though they "ne'er traced a tolerable line in verse" (qtd. Spencer 185–86). Rufus Griswold felt obliged to precede his anthologies of American prose and American poetry (1842 and 1846) with narrative surveys of what had already come to be called the Colonial Period. But since he also felt that "little poetry had been written in this country" (*Poets* xvii) before Philip Freneau's time, he spared his readers unnecessary transcriptions of the texts themselves. John S. Hart's idea that "American literature dates from the first settlement of the American colonies" (*Manual* 25) informs all the historical studies of the subject published between Griswold's anthologies and Moses Coit Tyler's *History of American Literature:* those of Henry T. Tuckerman, Samuel G. Allibone, the Duyckincks, Hart himself, and John Nichol. And all of these take evident pains to define literature in such a way as to admit colonial writings without demanding of them the imaginativeness, sensitivity to nature, privacy of purpose, and sublimity of expression that were agreed to distinguish literary from utilitarian writings.

Even Tyler, the reputed patriarch of Early American Literature, grounded the importance of colonial writing principally in the proposition that "the history of American literature" begins "with the earliest English settlements in this country" (1.v) rather than in any literary virtues of the writings themselves. While he includes in his history only texts that "have some noteworthy value as literature" (1.vi), even these fare poorly when judged against "modern" standards (1.252). "Anne Bradstreet and . . . the other American verse writers of the seventeenth century" are virtually unreadable (1.282). If the early settlers in general had "little skill in and regard for [literature] as a fine art, . . . as the ministress of aesthetic delight" (1.8), the Puritans in particular were actively "at war with the beautiful" (1.264). That Michael Wigglesworth's "verse is quite lacking in art" could have mattered very little to his audience, since "all sensitive-ness to literary form [was] torpid in New England" (2.25, 27). "Upon the whole, the 'Poetical Mediations' of Roger Wolcott are sad rubbish," the poems of John Seecomb "metrical balderdash," making us only thankful that no more early New England verse has survived (2.46,47). Were it not for the evidence of a certain penchant for versification and for the measure of progress that these writings afford the literary historian, they would hardly warrant our attention at all.

Since the pioneer historians of American literature generally agreed that colonial writing was not really literary, they tended to differ only in their judgment of whether it was really American, and therefore historically admissible. Were the colonists really Americans? Not at all, thought George Barrell Cheever, whose *American Commonplace Book of Prose* (1828) featured "specimens of American literature from its earliest period to the present day" (3) but nothing written before the Revolution. To W. B. O. Peabody, the colonial poets represented in Kettell's volumes did seem typically American, not least in their unhappily utilitarian attitude toward the art of verse (Ruland, ed., *Native Muse* 231–32). Orestes Brownson, on the other hand, found the colonists, just as unfortunately, un-American—"They gloried in calling themselves Englishmen; and whatever was English was right in their eyes" (280)—whereas for James Russell Lowell, who opined metaphorically that "the first furrow drawn by an English plough in the thin soil of Plymouth was the first line in our Declaration of Independence" (123), an instinctive Americanness was the colonists' happiest trait. Thomas Wentworth Higginson and Henry W. Boynton took Brownson's side: the colonists were English; they considered England their home; and these conditions persisted until the Revolution, the earliest date to which American literature can be traced (3–4, 7). William B. Otis, on the other hand, agreed with Lowell: "in subject-matter, in thought, and in spirit, early American verse is, as a whole, characteristic of the broad, fresh, original, and liberty-loving land which gave it birth" (ix).

Emerging as the subject had, in the twilight of a declining Enlightenment rationalism and an emerging Romantic aestheticism, Early American Literature tended from the outset to fall between two critical stools. To the rational taste, the colonists—the Puritans especially—produced too much that was stylistically outré and intellectually unbalanced, while the aesthetes found the same writers excessively utilitarian. Both of these critical inclinations may be seen at work in Tyler's history. On the one hand, his prodigious efforts to recover the artifacts of the seventeenth century and to make them available in extensive transcriptions bespeaks something of that disillusionment with rational optimism and that nostalgia for the baroque that we associate with Carlyle and Melville. On the other hand, Tyler's allegiance to the Enlightenment values of uniformity and progress shows in his Johnsonian distaste for what he calls "the Fantastic school of Literature," with its "strained analogies, unexpected images, pedantries, indelicacies, freaks of allusion, monstrosities of phrase" (2.87–88), as well as in his clear preference for prose over verse, his insistence that the succession of period styles in literary history marks a steady improvement in character and taste, and his habit of judging the work of all periods by universal standards of "naturalness" and "truth." The "worst lines" of the colonial poets, Tyler avers, "can be readily matched for fantastic perversion, and for total absence of beauty, by passages from the poems of John Donne, George Herbert, Crashaw, . . . and even of Herrick, Cowley, and Dryden" (1.282–83). It is Franklin, in Tyler's view, who is America's first true man of letters; his "mastery of style—that pure, pithy, racy, and delightful diction— . . . makes him still one of the great exemplars of English prose" (2.251–52).

If the value of the colonial period lay in its socially interested, forward-looking, businesslike prose—an opinion Tyler was neither the first nor the last to hold—that value still could not rightly be called literary. *Literature* denotes that writing which "raises the mind and hurries it to sublimity," according to Thomas Higginson and H. W. Boynton (5), or, as Fred Louis Pattee would have it, "the class of writings distinguished for beauty of style or expression" (1). In order to consider colonial writings literature, Pattee maintained, we must construe the term historically, as "the entire body of [nonscientific] productions that emanated from a nation during its history" (3). Under that rubric, Bradstreet's verses and Bradford's annals will qualify, despite their patent unloveliness.

That colonial writing was able to maintain, even to improve, its grip on American readers over the course of the nineteenth century must, given its widely acknowledged unliterariness, be laid primarily to historical interests. For literary historians, these interests arose from the need to distinguish current American writings in English by discovering for them non-British sources and a separate line of development. Like the *Mayflower* descendants and the First Families of Virginia, American literature needed a local ancestry in order to proclaim its national identity—something by no means evident in the writings of people like Irving and Bryant, upon which patriotic critics tended to dote—as well as to avoid potentially unflattering comparisons between the poems of, say, Longfellow or Lowell and those of Tennyson and Arnold. "Perceiving that America has produced much that is creditable during the past century," Higginson and Boynton scoffed, the literary historians "have set about finding a direct American pedigree for it"—just like the upstart Irishman who, finding himself the owner of a castle, ordered portraits of the ancestors he should have had (2). Had this literary genealogy been what was wanted, it would have led back to a Homeric age of epic and song. But, as Henry Beers and many of his colleagues lamented, "That engaging naivete and that heroic rudeness which gave a charm to the popular tales and songs of Europe find . . . no counterpart on our soil. Instead of emerging from the twilight of the past, the first American writings were produced under the garish noon of a modern and learned age. Decrepitude rather than youthfulness is the mark of a colonial literature" (9). As a result, even the most patriotic historians of America's literature had no choice but to view it, as W. P. Trent sighed, "in the light, or if one will, the darkness of the no-literature that is represented by the far from cosmopolitan names of Mrs. Bradstreet, Michael Wigglesworth, and Cotton Mather" (*A History* 2).

Historiographical necessity, however, will not fully account for the appearance, in the last quarter of the century, of eight studies devoted entirely to colonial writings. Whereas Samuel Knapp, look-

ing back from 1829, had repaired to the colonies perforce, his counterparts in the closing decades of the century agreed almost without
reservation that their own time offered an embarrassment of riches
for the literary scholar. And while the rules of "evolutionary philosophy," as Trent conceded, might require the historian to approach
this promised land by way of the colonial desert, they certainly did
not oblige anyone to remain there. That so many chose to do so must
strike us the way Urbain de Bellegarde's politics did Christopher
Newman: as displaying "a taste for certain oddities of diet; . . . . an
appetite . . . for fishbones or nutshells" (167). The explanation for a
relish so seemingly perverse must be sought elsewhere than in its
objects.

Paramount among the circumstances contributing to this
awakened interest in colonial writings is the unprecedented concern
of the nineteenth century, triggered by the perception of accelerating
changes in every aspect of modern life, with discovering points of
relation between the runaway present and the rapidly vanishing
past. In America, as everywhere else in the industrializing West, this
contemplation of the receding agrarian shore from the pitching deck
of the modern steamship evoked mingled sensations of liberation
and anxiety, anticipation and nostalgia. If the past could serve as a
fixed point from which to measure political and economic progress,
it could also stand as a reminder of something lost—the family, the
village, the church, the timeless rituals of the seasons. In either case,
the past had to be kept in sight, as a basis for present self-
congratulation or as a repository of sustaining values—or, better
still, as a complex image of the ambivalence most people felt about
their giddy modern condition. The Centennial Exposition of 1876 in
Philadelphia celebrated a century of progress since the Revolution
by including among its displays a collection of colonial mem-
orabilia. The colonists portrayed in such popular artifacts as George
Boughton's *The Puritans Going to Church* (1867), Francis David
Millet's *At the Inn* (1886), Augustus Saint-Gaudens's *The Puritan*
(1887), and the magazine illustrations of Edwin Austin Abbey and
Howard Pyle manage simultaneously to flatter and rebuke the
viewer with their stern and simple pieties. And in the popular histories of colonial fashions, manners, and customs published around

the turn of the century by Alice M. Earle and her many imitators, condescension and wistfulness coalesce in a fascination with the quaint that is not fundamentally different from the attitude of late nineteenth-century American literary historians toward the writings of the colonists.

When purely literary considerations came into play, however, no amount of historical interest would serve to rescue the colonists from Trent's judgment that they are "the property of the antiquary, not the student of literature" (A History 30). Until the last quarter of the century, anthologists of American literature, being concerned more to celebrate than to retrace the nation's arrival at literary excellence, found nothing to their purpose in the colonial records. The schoolroom texts of Webster and McGuffey, The Atlantic Clubbook (1834), Lyman Cobb's North American Reader (1835), Bryant's Selections from the American Poets (1840), John Keese's The Poets of America (1842), and Thomas Buchanan Read's The Female Poets of America (1848) devoted most, if not all, of their pages to living writers. Among the anthologists of the first half-century, Caroline May alone let her special interests lead her back beyond the nation's birthday for examples of American female poets (1848). This exclusionary rule held throughout the postbellum years. For the anthologist in search of American contributions to poetry in English—even one like Whittier, who had written on colonial subjects and had edited John Woolman's journal (1871)—critical values made Early American Literature seem a contradiction in terms. Neither Whittier's Songs of Three Centuries (1876) nor Emerson's Parnassus (1874) finds room for a Bradstreet or a Barlow, let alone a Wigglesworth. "The poetical literature of our country," Whittier rather unpatriotically proclaimed, "can scarcely be said to have a longer date than that of a single generation. As a matter of fact, the fathers of it are still living" (iv).

Tyler's history marks a significant passage in the development of Early American Literature as a subject of study, its transformation from amateur to professional status. Although Tyler's audience now consists almost entirely of academic specialists in the field, the History itself addresses a far more various "public" (x). Comprising "working brother[s] in the guild of letters" (xi), "students of the

9

subject" (viii), and general readers interested in "the literary unfolding of the American mind" (vi), this intended readership points, at once, back to the fifty years since Knapp's *Lectures*, when the subject was studied altogether outside the university, and ahead to the time when it would be studied almost nowhere else. Knapp alludes to the circumstances—wonderfully documented in our own time by Frederick Rudolph's history of the American college curriculum—that kept his materials out of the lecture hall, as well as to the interests that would eventually alter those circumstances beyond recognition, when he notes that "[t]he English language has not with us, generally speaking, been deeply studied by those who use it, either for the common business of life, or by those who make it a vehicle of matters of high import in enlightening, and directing their countrymen" (10).

To be sure, the signs of coming change were already evident. The College of William and Mary had appointed the first American professor of a modern language (French) as early as 1780. In the same year, Harvard had allowed undergraduates to substitute French for Hebrew. Timothy Dwight had agitated, albeit unsuccessfully, for the inclusion of English language and belles lettres in the Yale curriculum in the 1790s. Noah Webster and W.H. McGuffey had succeeded in introducing English readings into American schoolrooms by 1800, and the first courses in English composition were taught in American colleges in 1823. By the time the volumes of Knapp and Kettell appeared, however, the curricular modernization that might have made space for texts in English like those of the colonists had been thwarted by the Yale *Report* of 1828, which reaffirmed the centrality of the classics in higher education and would constitute academic dogma for another fifty years.

The situation out of which Tyler's history arose was altogether different. Looking back, in 1873, on the thirty years that had passed since the publication of his *Class Book of Poetry* and *Class Book of Prose*, John S. Hart marveled at the growth of English studies during that period: "Hardly a school of any standing is now to be found that does not include the systematic study of English Literature in its ordinary curriculum" (viii). Although characteristically slower, the progress of English studies in the colleges had been no less remarkable. The 1850s saw the first undergraduate course in English, at Michigan; the first modern curriculum based on English literature, foreign languages, history, and science, at Amherst; and the first course on "American Authors," at Heidelberg College, in Ohio. Within ten years after Appomattox, some twenty-six colleges were offering courses in American literature; President Eliot's elective plan at Harvard had freed undergraduates from classical requirements to take courses in English; and, most important of all, Yale had published *The Needs of the University* (1871), reversing the decisions of its 1828 *Report* and removing the center of its curriculum from the classics to the modern languages, history, and the sciences. Hart's own *Manual* (1873) had originated in his required course in American literature at Princeton, and its publication alongside two similar volumes—Francis H. Underwood's *Handbook of English Literature: American Authors* and N. K. Royse's *Manual of American Literature* (both 1872)—indicates the spread of such courses from the schools throughout the colleges.

With the displacement of the classics by the modern curriculum and the consequent rise of English studies, including courses in American writers, Early American Literature became an academic subject, amidst circumstances perfectly conducive to its historical character. Whereas the other modern languages had recommended themselves on largely practical grounds, English, as a presumably known tongue, had to associate itself with science and historiography in order to overcome traditional objections to the study of subjects, like Shakespeare and contemporary writings, already in the students' possession. It was, therefore, as a historical science, as philology, that English entered the university, leaving scant room for literature, except as an ethical component of moral philosophy, and none for American writers, except as an aspect of American history. Tyler's own career fairly illustrates the division. He began as a minister, abandoned the pulpit for a professorship in English at the University of Michigan, and resigned that post to write the *History of American Literature* that earned him the nation's first professorship of history, at Cornell. Although removed from the precincts of literary morality by quirks of Puritan creed and Virginian caste, as well as from philology by its irrelevance to Grimm's law and the great vowel shift, Early American Literature found itself welcome in American history, where its already long career as a corpus of documents reflecting America's march toward nationhood fitted the subject nicely for service as the first phase of undergraduate survey courses and as a respectably antique topic of graduate study and professional research.

Once inside the university, Early American Literature underwent gradually the metamorphosis of all academically adopted subjects: let something, however popular, become assigned matter, and it will cease to exist outside the classroom. And, as a primarily historical subject, the more exclusively an academic property colonial writing became, the more heavily its fortunes there depended upon the changing status of history in the production of literary knowledge. During what may be called the golden age of American literary history, from Hart's 1873 *Manual* to the *Cambridge History* of 1917, colonial writing benefited from several of the institutional developments that Lawrence Veysey has described. The creation of English departments, to impose bureaucratic control upon the plethora of courses spawned by the elective system, drew American writings from historical studies on the one side and from moral philosophy on the other and united these two strains, the ethical-aesthetic and the national-historical, to produce courses in American literary history that were at once sufficiently patriotic to please trustees, scientific enough to satisfy professional scholars, and literary enough to generate the enrollments upon which departmental power depended. A triple threat despite the contempt of departmental Anglophiles, American literary history assisted the gradual displacement of philology by literary studies in the English curriculum; and the colonial period, despite the condescensions of progressive Americanists, shared the spoils.

With every inch of curricular ground that literature wrested from philology, however, the position of colonial writings, so aesthetically vulnerable, became increasingly exposed to critical attack. The idea of American literature had always been variously understood as comprising, on the one hand, writings of all sorts and qualities that demonstrated Americanness and, on the other hand, writings by Americans that met cosmopolitan standards of literariness; and the widely perceived failure of early texts to meet the latter criterion had forced even its staunchest exponents to make their case in primarily historical terms and to flash their own critical credentials by lamenting its lack of artistry. Very seldom did a historian overtly challenge the reigning conception of literariness, as did the editors of the first volume of the *Cambridge History* in proposing a peculiarly American definition of literature that would accommodate colonial documents. "To write the intellectual history of America from the modern aesthetic standpoint," insisted the Cambridge editors, is not only to misrepresent the colonial period but to miss precisely what makes American literature as a whole unique: "namely, that for two centuries the main energy of Americans went into exploration, settlement, labour for subsistence and state craft," rather than into the production of "art for art" (x).

This view of American literature as a body of "prose competently recording . . . practical activities and expressing . . . moral, religious, and political ideas," rather than as "poetry and fiction," enabled the Cambridge editors to devote to the colonial period ten full chapters and parts of two more, where self-consciously critical historians like Stedman had tended to dismiss the subject in a few introductory pages. The editors' repeated references to the "modern aesthetic standpoint" and to "current finical and transitory definitions of literature" (x), however, bespeak a siege mentality, a consciousness that the historical values that made colonial texts worth studying were being imperiled by what Charles F. Richardson called the "well-known laws of criticism." "If we think of Shakespeare, Bunyan, Milton, the seventeenth-century choir of lyrists, Sir Thomas Browne, Jeremy Taylor, Addison, Swift, Dryden, Gray, Goldsmith, and the eighteenth-century novelists," Richardson had asked without waiting for an answer, "what shall we say of the intrinsic worth of most of the books written on American soil" before the Revolution? (xvii–xviii). When the laws of criticism were less "well-known," Early American Literature could pass literary inspection under the cloak of historical significance. But with the spread of "current finical" tastes and their codification into "laws," Early Americanness was coming to seem, even to apologists like the Cambridge historians, less a compensation, or even an excuse, for the admitted unliterariness of colonial writing than its sufficient cause.

The gap opened here between literature and American history widened steadily in the years following the First World War. At the very moment when American literature, thanks in part to its association with scientific historiography, was securing a foothold in the academy, H. L. Mencken culminated a long-standing debate over the importance of Puritanism in the formation of American art and character by attaching that word to everything pinched and unlovely in the national life. With the publication of "Puritanism as a Literary Force" in 1917, the term entered the popular vocabulary as an antonym for art.

The idea was anything but new. Anthologists of America's contributions to world literature had held it since the Revolution, and progressive historians had routinely denied the importance of the Puritans in the development of American literature, considering their productions little more than a sort of zero-point from which to measure the rise of the national letters. Mencken's essay, however, added to these reservations an element of cosmopolitan modernism that scoffed at moral aestheticism and progressive historicism alike, associating both with a genteel American culture that had stifled and alienated the nation's most promising artists. Never mind that Mencken used "Puritanism" to signify rather vague ideas of repressive respectability and moral idealism that had little or nothing to do with seventeenth-century New England and might just as well have been called Victorian. His popularization of the term and its subsequent adoption by critics like Van Wyck Brooks and Ludwig Lewisohn helped to detach the concept of American literature from that of American history and to connect it instead with an idea of radical departure from American traditions.

As long as salvos like Mencken's were fired from outside the university walls, historicism and the colonial studies it supported were safe in their academic redoubt. Journalism had always cared more for the latest than for the earliest American writings, which it left pretty much to antiquarian professors; and with increasing professionalization the scholars had come to regard journalists as altogether too unscientifically impressionistic, too fashionably presentist, to carry much weight in serious matters. American literature, however, had begun life as a journalistic idea imbued with a spirit of modernity. Indeed, the struggle to establish the subject in the university may be viewed as a late skirmish in the protracted war of the moderns against the ancients. The progressive young men responsible were merely continuing the revolution that had replaced the classics with English, and philology with the history of modern literature. The historical method itself appealed to Americanists in part because it was modern, and they had used it primarily to explain the literary present, which they valued far above the nation's comparatively unliterary past. While a professionally respectable antiquarianism continued to characterize graduate studies in literature well into the 1950s, the first undergraduate courses in American literature had routinely dealt with living writers, just as the earliest undergraduate offerings in English literature had featured the Victorians. The inertia of American studies tended powerfully toward the present; and if criticism could ever acquire an air of scientific rigor like that which dignified philology and history, professors of American literature would be among the first to take it up.

The systematization of critical analysis necessary to its adoption by the academy arrived in the 1920s with I. A. Richards's *Principles of Literary Criticism* (1924) and *Practical Criticism* (1929), two books that, along with successors like Cleanth Brooks and Robert Penn Warren's *Understanding Poetry* (1938) and John Crowe Ransom's *The New Criticism* (1941), helped to shift the emphasis of English studies as a whole from historical context to literary text. This shift was to have especially grave consequences for the subject of American literature, which had been founded on the principles of national history and whose past, compared to England's, offered few writings deemed literary enough to warrant formalistic explication.

The effects of the change from historical to literary concerns appear most vividly in a movement toward what is now called *canonization*, the singling out for special attention of texts that, although perhaps historically unrepresentative, perhaps even unread in their own time, recommended themselves to present tastes and to the analytic techniques of modern criticism. This critical sifting of the American past, announced in Carl Van Doren's "Toward a New Canon" (1932), can be seen already at work in Henry Seidel Canby's *Classic Americans* (1931). Its effect upon the status of what literary history had called the colonial period can be readily discerned in Canby's subtitle: *A Study of Eminent American Writers, with an Introductory Survey of the Colonial Background of Our National Literature.* Undergraduate textbooks, once concerned to trace America's history as reflected in writings of all sorts, became anthologies of presently esteemed masterworks—which is to say "poems," whether in verse or in prose—by "major writers." A lingering obeisance to the historical values implicit in the very idea of American literature, along with the literary historians' habit of discovering in Anne Bradstreet's "Contemplations" or the "Epitaph" for Nathaniel Bacon a saving remnant of poetical sensibility in the colonial wilderness, helped to enshrine a few writers like Bradstreet, Edwards, Franklin, and, above all, the recently unearthed Edward Taylor among the anthologized "masters." But the predations of ahistorical criticism upon Early American Literature were to prove severe. When Floyd Stovall set out in 1956 to review the scholarship published since the appearance of Robert E. Spiller's compendious *Literary History of the United States* (1948), he called his survey *Eight American Authors* and included none earlier than Poe.

How gravely criticism threatened the historical foundations of American literature in general and of Early American Literature in particular can be seen in the reactions of Americanists published throughout these years. A command of "social, economic, and political history," Norman Foerster maintained in the introduction to his *Reinterpretations,* "is peculiarly important in the case of American literature" (xii). In order to preserve its national identity, Fred Louis Pattee insisted in the same volume, American literature must be seen "against the background of American history" (11). The contribution to Foerster's collection by Arthur Schlesinger, Sr., predicted that "[u]ntil the historian frees himself from the domination of literary critics, his work is certain to fall short of its highest promise" (164); and in an essay published the same year in the *Yale Review,* Schlesinger questioned the value of literary masterpieces for the study of American history, advocating instead the use of less unique materials and more of them.

As critical pressures increased with essays like Cleanth Brooks's "Literary History vs. Criticism" (1940) and W. K. Wimsatt's "History and Criticism: A Problematic Relationship" (1954), which argued the incompatibility of the two disciplines, Americanists felt obliged to respond. A few bucked the tide; Louis B. Wright's plan for a "New History of American Literature" (1940) proposed defining literature as "the total output of the printing press" (284). Some sought to hold their ground, maintaining with Robert Spiller (1959) that the "literary" and "social" approaches to American studies could be reconciled. The majority went downstream with Clarence Gohdes, who had argued in 1938 that American literature should select its materials primarily on the basis of literariness. But however an Americanist might answer the question, Is American literature really literature? an answer was clearly required. Criticism had begun to set the standards for English studies and would no more brook denial than history had once, or than theory will now.

It was amidst this climate of literary presentism that the American studies movement began at Harvard in 1938 to make a place for literary scholars who retained an interest in the critically proscribed subject of national history. But even in this halfway house, criticism would exert its influence, producing literary histories that, instead of proceeding from an idea of America to whatever writings reflected it, started with an idea of literature and extrapolated America from the texts that manifested that idea. This present-centered historicism had been advocated as early as 1918, in Van Wyck Brooks's "On Creating a Usable Past." D. H. Lawrence had inadvertently provided its model in *Studies in Classic American Literature* (1923), and Lionel Trilling gave it its classical formulation in "Reality in America" (1946), his attack upon the unliterary historicism of V. L. Parrington. Combined with the New England tradition of thinking the Puritans responsible for the creation of American culture as a whole, it produced histories like Charles Feidelson's *Symbolism and American Literature* (1953), Harry Levin's *The Power of Blackness* (1958), Roy Harvey Pearce's *The Continuity of American Poetry* (1961), and Hyatt Waggoner's *The American Poets* (1968), in which colonial writers, especially the Puritans, figured more prominently perhaps than ever before as the progenitors of themes and styles that came to maturity in the classics of later centuries.

The removal of the Puritans from the murky byways of American literary history to its point of origin was owing largely to the scholarship of Perry Miller, who, along with his Harvard colleagues Samuel Eliot Morrison and Kenneth Murdock, developed a species of intellectual history capable of mediating the conflict between unliterary national history and ahistorical criticism. Instead of viewing American history through whatever writings happened to open upon it, or deriving a history from a canon of recognized classics, the intellectual historians posited between the historical and literary poles an abstract middle ground called "the American mind," which expressed itself most clearly in writings of particular formal complexity and connected the writings of very different times and places in a continuous historical development, from the Bay Colony to Concord and on—given a historian afoot with his vision—to Paris and West Egg.

Once formulated, this scheme revealed its own predecessors: the Puritanizing of American writers by Stuart Pratt Sherman and by Paul Elmer More, whose essay "The Origins of Poe and Hawthorne" (1904) said in nineteen pages virtually everything that would be said on the subject of Puritan influence for the next seventy years; and the work of George Woodbridge Riley, whose *American Philosophy, from Puritanism to Pragmatism* (1915) appeared in a revised edition eight years later under the title *American Thought from Puritanism to Pragmatism and Beyond* (1923). These two strains, the Puritan and the intellectual, moved closer together in the first volume of Parrington's *Main Currents of American Thought,* which he called *The Colonial Mind* (1927), and in the essays by Norman Foerster and Kenneth Murdock for *The Reinterpretation of American Literature* (1928), where "the Puritan tradition" heads the agenda of topics for research in the field. They converge in Russell Blankenship's *American Literature as an Expression of the National Mind* (1931), forming a single stream that runs through Miller's "From Edwards to Emerson" (1940), Murdock's *Literature and Theology in Colonial New England* (1949), Miller's *The New England Mind* (1939, 1953), and straight to Sacvan Bercovitch's *The Puritan Origins of the American Self* (1975).

Even here, however, the inclusion of colonial writings in American literature said less about their own literariness than about their historical relations to later, more evidently literary texts. Cotton Mather's hard work on behalf of the American Renaissance did not make him a Melville. The heavy dependence of Early American Literature on such historical connections—whether to later writings or to colonial culture—made the subject particularly vulnerable to formalist animadversions against all such extraneous concerns in the identification, analysis, and judgment of literature. To counter these attacks, Early Americanists adopted the various strategies of their colleagues in later periods: repairing to American studies, where historical "backgrounds" and continuities were not simply anathema and literary distinction was less insisted upon; canonizing a select number of ostensibly major writers; and subjecting to formalistic analysis whichever texts could bear the weight. As early as 1920, Thomas G. Wright, discerning the drift of English studies toward literariness, had revised Tyler's unflattering comparison between the Puritans and the Metaphysicals in the light of recent critical revaluations of seventeenth-century English poetry to improve the colonists' literary standing. Ten years later, Perry Miller and Thomas H. Johnson included in their anthology *The Puritans* (1938) a section on these writers as "literary artists" (64), by way of counterbalancing, at least somewhat, the historical emphasis of that volume. For the most part, however, Early American Literature waited out the reign of the New Criticism in American studies, under the dispensation of intellectual and cultural history, whose very concepts of intellect and culture tended to favor literature without defining the category so narrowly as to disqualify sermons and theological disquisitions.

Not until the early 1970s, when formalism itself was beginning to draw theoretical fire from abroad and political fire at home, did Early Americanists presume to confront the critics on their own ground. In "Teaching Early American Literature" (1970), J. M. Garrison took up on behalf of his subject Clarence Gohdes's arguments of three decades earlier: that the methods of literary history commonly employed in the field were not really literary and that the texts for study should be chosen on the basis of conscious artistry, rather than historical representativeness. A year later, Taylor, Edwards, and Franklin solidified their position in the literary canon among the likes of Henry Adams, Cooper, Dickinson, and Howells, when Robert Rees and Earl Harbert compiled *Fifteen American Authors Before 1900* (1971) to augment Floyd Stovall's big eight. And the canon expanded still further with Everett Emerson's collection of essays on the major writers of early America (1972), which added Bradford, Bradstreet, Cotton Mather, William Byrd, Freneau, and Charles Brockden Brown to the roster.

These somewhat belated efforts at repairing the critical reputation of Early American Literature owe something, doubtless, to perceived instabilities in the authority of the New Criticism to dictate the materials of literary study. The movement owes a good deal more, however, to the work of certain Early Americanists who grasped the possibility of applying formalist criticism to the reputedly unliterary texts thrust upon them by their field. In "The Veiled Vision" (1962) and "Puritan Devotion and American Literary Theory" (1969), Norman Grabo argued the value of aesthetic criticism as an instrument of knowledge concerning the place of the Puritans in American literary history. David Levin's essays *In Defense of Historical Writing* (1967) applied to colonial historiography the formalist methods he had devised eight years earlier to treat nineteenth-century historians as Romantic artists. And in 1968, Daniel Shea discovered a textual hospitality to essentially the same techniques in the extraliterary precincts of colonial autobiography. In order to turn their texts into literature, the colonialists were beginning to realize, they had only to deal with them in acceptably literary ways.

All together, these various reactions to the indictments and condescensions of ahistorical criticism reflect a general movement of Early American Literature away from the source of its troubles in English studies, American as well as British, and toward the reconstitution of itself as a distinct field of study grounded in history and governed by literary criteria of its own. In 1966, the Early Americanists launched their own journal to encourage scholarship in the period and to publish work whose historical interests and quasi-literary subjects the journal *American Literature* had come to regard with a certain chilly hauteur. The rapid expansion of junior faculty throughout the 1960s swelled the ranks of colonialists with young scholars on the lookout for less-studied subjects in which to earn tenure. These new specialists, in turn, produced increasing numbers of essays and monographs that, addressed to like-minded readers, could discuss colonial writing without either apology for its literary quality or much concern for its bearing on the American classics. In 1967, Rex Burbank and Jack B. Moore compiled *The Literature of Early America*, the first anthology devoted entirely to the subject since 1917; and in 1970, Russell Nye published his *American Literary History, 1607–1830*, the first separate survey of the field since Tyler's. To the tune of articles in Early American Literature decrying the subordination of colonial studies to the concerns of later periods, "American Literature 1: Seventeenth and Eighteenth Centuries" secured its own place on the MLA program in 1969, about the same time that Everett Emerson's volume of essays on major colonial writers established a separate canon for the field.

Just when Early American Literature was making a separate peace with aesthetic criticism in order to preserve its own indispensable historical ground, a new generation of theorists was busily revising the meaning and function of history itself along lines calculated to unseat ahistorical formalism and restore history on a new footing to its former power in the conduct of literary studies. The journal *New Literary History* had been founded in 1968 to air these theoretical reconsiderations, and its editor, Ralph Cohen, collected a volume of essays from the magazine in 1974 under the title *New Directions in Literary History*. One of the contributors to that volume, Robert Weimann, assembled his own essays on the subject in *Structure and Society in Literary History* (1976), including in the collection a specific analysis of American literary history and its struggles, former and present, with the New Criticism (89–145). Americanists proper can be said to have got up on the new wave of historicism when Leslie Fiedler attacked the national canon at the English Institute, in 1979, and when, in 1980, a festschrift for Arlin Turner came out bearing the title *Toward a New American Literary*

History. Although both Fiedler and the contributors to Turner's fest-schrift tended to hug the history and let the theory go, their unblushing regard for the circumstances of textual production, as opposed to those of critical reception, for the materials of popular culture, and for writings other than poetry and fiction, betokens a change in the climate of literary studies quite agreeable to the historical interests of Early American Literature. History soi-disant was back in favor, and in shifting its emphasis from diachronic continuities among canonized texts to synchronic relations between texts of virtually any sort and their generating circumstances, the new historicisms comported nicely both with the sort of texts Early American Literature mainly comprised and with its inclination to assert its identity as a distinct field.

After long rustication in American studies and in the opening chapters of books about the American Renaissance, the inartistic colonists found themselves, rather suddenly, at home again among the critics, who, increasingly concerned with such matters as gender, race, and class, as well as professionally driven to find new texts to analyze, had come to regard best-sellers like *Wide, Wide World* and autobiographical narratives like those written by slaves as no less deserving of critical attention than *The Scarlet Letter* or "Song of Myself." The proponents of a distinct American literature had always included those who found that idea realized in the unconventional expressions of printers, carpenters, steamboat pilots, and other ostensible nonwriters, rather than in the masterpieces of American Dantes and Chaucers; and the removal of the cosmopolitan New Criticism left the road once again clear for this vehicle of nationalist sentiment.

Nowhere is the regained footing of the colonial period in the rehistoricized field of American literature more visible than in the choice of two colonial scholars, Emory Elliott and Sacvan Bercovitch, to edit the first two comprehensive histories of the subject to appear in some forty years. True, the conception of history had changed since its last appearance, recognizing the diversity of American things where it had once emphasized national uniformity, finding discontinuities where (and with as much apparent gratification as) it had previously uncovered signs of organic development.

Equally true, there lurk beneath the celebrations of "dissensus" in these new histories residual elements of the old nationalistic idea of a proleptic colonial period. Nonetheless, history was back in the game, and Early American Literature would be allowed to play, at least until another generation came along and, in order to nullify the advantages of veteran players, changed the rules yet again.

If Early American Literature has always depended on some idea of history, that dependence is probably unavoidable, given that its materials were all written a long time ago, amidst circumstances radically different from any in which they are apt ever to be read, and also given the unlikelihood of anyone's ever reinstituting an essential idea of literature that would include colonial writings. At the same time, the particular idea of history upon which Early American Literature has always relied for its identity and significance as a subject raises so many problems—and such blatant ones—that, unlike the inventors of the internal combustion engine when faced with the problem of excess heat, we should ask ourselves whether the basic concept itself may not be flawed.

By restricting Early American Literature to writings from the British colonies that would one day become states, scholars seriously misconceive the very thing their historical interests purport to value: the actual situation in which these texts were written and which they are supposed to reflect. Although it seems odd to have to say anything so obvious, the colonies were not united states during the two hundred years when what we call Early American Literature was being written. They were British colonies, populated by British subjects who, whatever their attitudes toward the colonial administration and the Crown, thought of themselves and their places of residence in that light. To regard colonial Virginia, Massachusetts, Pennsylvania, and the rest as united states, even in posse, is to view them from a historical point radically different from their own, lending them a unity they did not possess, separating them as a whole from the nation that owned and governed them, abstracting them from the rest of British America, and severing some of them from nearby colonies in the Caribbean or in Canada with which they shared important features. Defined as the "future United States," in the words of Howard Mumford Jones (25), or "what is now the United States," as Everett Emerson has it ("John Smith" 1333), Early America becomes a phase in a history whose center lies elsewhere, a seedbed or cradle of as yet unrealized maturations, situated on the eastern shore of a continent whose very existence remained largely unknown throughout much of the period in question.

Scholars interested in colonial culture and literature have been grumbling about these problems for generations, and the history of colonial studies is punctuated by attempts to break the hold of nationalism upon the subject. In the early decades of this century, Imperialist historians like George Beer, H. L. Osgood, Charles Andrews, and Lawrence Gipson labored mightily to remove the thirteen charter colonies from the history of the United States to that of European expansion, beginning in the Renaissance. Led by the work of Herbert E. Bolton in the 1930s, a group of Pan-American historians, including such Latin Americans as Edmundo O'Gorman, Germán Arciniegas, and Silvio Zavala, campaigned for the inclusion of Britain's North American settlements in a single hemispheric scheme of New World development. Reminders that England and her American colonies formed a coherent transatlantic community extend from the work of Michael Kraus in the 1940s to that of Norman Fiering (1976) and Ian K. Steele (1986). Beginning at least as early as 1928, with Howard Mumford Jones's essay "The European Backgrounds" (for Norman Foerster's *Reinterpretations*), comparatists—both literary, like John McCormick, Wayne Falke, and Owen Aldridge, and historical, like the several contributors to C. Vann Woodward's *The Comparative Approach to American History*—have repeatedly advised Americanists to look beyond national boundaries, real and imaginary, for the context of their subject. And with the theoretical Great Awakening of the past few years, traditional assumptions regarding national evolution have undergone a battering from such colonial historians as Jack P. Greene and from literary scholars like David Laurence and Richard DeProspo.

Although each of these alternative constructions of the subject has proved its worth by revealing aspects of colonial literature and culture that nationalism obscures, none of them has managed so far to supplant the nationalist model, which remains clearly visible even in the arguments of some of its most forceful critics. As Greene and J. R. Pole observe in the introduction to their volume of essays, even the resolute antinationalism of the Imperialists "was strongly conditioned by the knowledge that the colonial period had been followed by the American Revolution and the founding of the American nation" (2). And despite their penetrating critiques of nationalist assumptions, most proponents of the new methods of literary history continue to select their texts from the writings—usually canonized ones—of colonists who resided in places that would one day lie inside the boundaries of the United States.

In spite of its evident flaws, the nationalist model appears to offer the specialist in Early American Literature something that its various alternatives do not. The sources of that appeal, I think, can be discerned in the preferred title of the subject itself. By calling certain colonial writings Early American Literature, devotees of the subject seem bent upon registering an impression, an experience of reading, that led them to concentrate on these texts in the first place: a perception that they come early in a historical scheme that somehow includes the modern reader; that they are in some sense American, in spite of having been written in English by British subjects long before such a thing as the United States was even dreamed of; and that, for all their apparent want of poetic genius, they ask to be thought of and treated as literature.

The alternative approaches, on the other hand, all seem to throw the Early American Literary baby out with the nationalist bath. When colonial writings are situated within the history of European imperialism or of the transatlantic English community, the impression of their Americanness tends to fade. Placed by comparatists alongside the plays of Shakespeare and Milton's poems, their literariness evaporates. The Pan-Americanists' insistence upon lumping together the writers of New England and Mexico ignores the sense of Early Americanists, all but a very few of whom are professors of English, that Edward Taylor speaks to them in a way that Sor Juana, writing in Spanish, simply does not. And by impugning the authority of the reader's critical judgments, the new historicisms deny any value to the impression that some colonial writings are more literary than the rest. Better the ignis fatuus of nationalism, says the student of Early American Literature, than no illume at all.

But then, no sooner does the colonialist restore colonial writings to the context of national literary history than they lose a good deal of the experienced value this situation was chosen to preserve. Replaced at the beginning of historical development in which true Americanness and true literariness would not emerge until the colonists were all dead and gone, Early American Literature can only seem, by virtue of its earliness, less American and less literary than *Uncle Tom's Cabin*, let alone *Huckleberry Finn*. American literary history, it appears, is a thing Early American Literature can neither do with nor do without, a sort of iron lung that keeps the subject alive only by keeping it flat on its back.

If the subject demands an idea of history but cannot prosper under the nationalist program and cannot survive under any of the alternative schemes that have so far been proposed for it, then it wants a different idea of American literary history: one that will construe the word *early* to mean something other than "less," *American* to denote something more literary than the citizenship conferred retroactively upon colonial authors, and *literature* to designate something at once more historical than "timeless beauty," less prejudicial to colonial documents than "poetry" or "fiction," and more alert to discriminations than just plain "writing." What this new idea might look like we can perhaps begin to see by examining the nationalist model itself to determine just where it goes wrong.

The concept of national literary history, Claudio Guillén reminds us, arose late in the eighteenth century, consequent upon the development of modern theories of history in general. At that time, Guillén argues, the classical idea of literature as a timeless whole grounded in a universal poetics and rhetoric gave way before erupting interests in individuality, which emphasized the differences among writers, and in temporal change, which highlighted the differences among periods and places. "The main consequence" of this upheaval in historical thought, Guillén continues, "was a serial view of literature as a chronological succession of works and writers. To counteract this seriality and compensate for the loss of an independent focus found in poetics or poetry itself, literary historians were forced to form new alliances and seek outside means of support. The concept of the nation, regarded by definition as an organic whole, growing and developing in history, became an all-embracing principle of unity" (5–6).

Joseph Femia describes the alliance somewhat less dramatically as a foregone conclusion of emergent historicism, which viewed "all ideas and values [as] products of a given historical epoch, of a specific civilization, or even of a definite national collectivity" and held that all "forms of human experience, including works of art or philosophy, must be understood and assessed not in terms of eternal principles, valid for all men in all circumstances, but (essentially) in relation to the scales of values and rules of thought appropriate to their own specific time and environment" (115–16). But however the alliance between literature and the nation is described, the results remain the same: literature came to be seen as a product of national cultures and therefore as evidence of national identity and a measure of national worth.

The first literary histories to employ this nationalist scheme, Girolamo Tirasboschi's *Storia della letteratura italiana* and Thomas Warton's *History of English Poetry*, were completed in the same year as the Articles of Confederation. A flurry of such histories, including Jean Sismondi's on Italian literature and Friedrich Bouterwek's on the literature of Spain, gave rise in the United States to the idea that this new nation too should have a literature of its own and, hence, to a rising chorus of demands for the speedy furnishing of the as yet empty apartments of American literature and then for a confirmation of its fulfillment in a national literary history. This is the patriotic charge taken up rather limply by John Neal's essays on American writers for *Blackwood's Magazine* (1824–25) and more resolutely by Knapp's *Lectures* in 1829. Not to be behindhand in the lengthening parade of nations, the new country would underscore its political independence and declare its cultural identity with a history of its literary origins, growth, and apotheosis.

The nationalist model of literary history devised by Tiraboschi and his European contemporaries, however, did not really suit the literature of the United States. Those historians had defined the "nation" as an essentially linguistic culture evolving organically toward political self-consciousness. Indeed, Tiraboschi's Italy had not yet arrived at this state of political realization when he wrote its history, and his many European imitators have generally made the language of the writing, rather than the political citizenship of the writer, the test of literary nationality. As Brander Matthews once pointed out, histories of German literature routinely include the writings of Friedrich Hebbel, a Dane, and Johann Hebel, who was Swiss, alongside Goethe's and date its origins long before the political unification of Germany. According to the same linguistic criterion, histories of French literature include the writings of Madame de Staël, who was born a Swiss and became a Scandinavian; Saint Francis de Sales, a Savoyard who refused to become a Frenchman; the Scot Anthony Hamilton, the Swiss Jean-Jacques Rousseau, the German Melchior von Grimm, and the Italian Ferdinando Galiani; as well as the brothers de Maistre, of Savoy; Maeterlinck, a Belgian; the Canadian Louis Frechette; and, most remarkable of all in this context, the American Francis Viélé-Griffin, whose father was a native of New York, a graduate of West Point, and a Union general in the Civil War. On the other hand, Peter Abelard, Saint Bernard de Thou, and Isaac Casaubon never appear in French literary history because, although themselves French, they wrote in Latin.

The materials available for a literary history of the United States, however, had no such linguistic nationality. Although everyone who yearned for an American literature supposed that, whatever form it might take, it would all be written in English, not in any of the several other languages Americans used, that supposedly common language was not also peculiar to it. In order to claim the sort of uniqueness that came automatically to Italian literature along with its language, American literature had to be defined politically, as literature written by Americans. But in shifting its basis of nationality from language to authorial citizenship, American literature deprived itself of the identity, coherence, and historical continuity that national literary history required and that language alone could provide.

Thanks solely to its language, French literature is immediately recognizable: all of it is written in French. But if American literature

is literature written by Americans, then it can presumably appear in
whatever language an American writer happens to use. What is
more, French literature is unmistakable: it alone is written in
French. But unless we know that Poe was an American, we cannot
tell that "The Cask of Amontillado" is. Nor, merely by reading it,
could we be certain that Blake's "America" is not. And French literature is historically continuous: although widely dispersed in time,
Le chanson de Roland, Phèdre, and L'étranger are connected by a
single enduring grammar that informs all three and identifies them
as episodes in its stylistic development. Apart from the citizenship
of their respective authors, however, Emerson's essays and Ole
Rölvaag's novels have nothing inherently in common that locates
them both in a single historical development, rather than in two
mutually independent ones: English and Norwegian.

Defined politically rather than linguistically, the American literature taken up by its earliest historians resembled not those of
Tiraboschi's Italy or Bouterwek's Spain but that of Switzerland. Unfortunately, the Swiss had never produced a national literary history
for the United States to imitate. Apparently secure in the national
identity and stature afforded by geography and political longevity,
they contented themselves with celebrating Swiss contributions to
French, German, and Italian literature. But even if some Swiss had
recorded all those literary contributions in print, that volume would
not have satisfied the demand of a fledgling, insecure nation for a
literary history of its very own. Although the United States had no
national language—indeed, because it lacked one—it would have a
history of American literature to wave like a flag in the face of
scoffing Europe. Knapp supplied the first one. Succeeding decades
produced a great many more, every one of them concerned above all
to lend the writings of Americans some semblance of the identity,
coherence, and historical continuity that they necessarily lacked
but that the prototypes of nationalist literary history, equating nation with tongue, had been able to take for granted.

In order to alleviate the problems of indistinctness, incoher-
ence, and historical discontinuity that inhere in the political definition of American literature and to preserve at least some of the
benefits enjoyed by national literatures that define themselves lin-

guistically, American literary histories have tended, almost without exception, to restrict their attention to one of the many languages American writers have used. For a number of complicated reasons (none of them very American in any ideal sense), the language of choice in American literary history has been English. But no matter which language the historians had picked, that choice would have misrepresented the subject no less, reducing American literature to literature in that tongue by Americans and thus missing from the outset one of the more striking features of American literature defined as writings by Americans, its linguistic variety.

Equally disastrous, since none of the languages that American writers have used is peculiar to them, any concentration by American literary history upon writings in a single tongue automatically robs the subject of that self-evident uniqueness which makes it unnecessary for historians of French and Spanish literature to spend their time, as Americanists must, defining the thing whose development they mean to trace. Because whatever language an American literary history may choose will have been used by non-American writers as well, that history must avoid calling undue attention to that language, for fear of arousing people like Matthews, who insist that writings in English by Americans belong, by definition, to English literature, just as writings in German by Czechs belong to German literature. By placing language off-limits as an object of analysis, however, American literary history automatically deprives itself not only of the information that language alone can afford but of the very benefits that concentration upon a single language was supposed to provide: the identity, coherence, and historical continuity of the subject.

Of all the deprivations caused by this linguistic paranoia, surely the most important to the literary historian is the loss of that ground of temporal continuity which the nationalist model locates in language. Shy of a ground that, in connecting American writings with each other, connects them with British writings as well, historians of American literature have had a notoriously hard time linking earlier American writers to later ones. Because such connections are at once indispensable to the national literary historian and invisible apart from language, they have been more often merely asserted or assumed than demonstrated in American literary history. Samuel Knapp, a pioneer in this as in so many other aspects of the genre, located the value of colonial writers partly in "the influence which they undoubtedly exercised upon the writers who succeeded them" (xvii), leaving the word *undoubtedly* to do the work of demonstration all by itself. With a degree of justice now almost unimaginable, Knapp also called the early settlers the "ancestors" and "forefathers" (4) of his readers. But he offered no explanation of how Americanness is genetically transmitted from one text to another, any more than do the many scholars who use these same metaphors today to connect Thomas Hooker and Norman Mailer in an American genealogy.

Whether or not Melville was in fact the heir of John Winthrop, Knapp certainly bequeathed to later American literary historians this problem of explaining the principles of continuity and change that make Bradford and Irving, Wigglesworth and Bryant, figures in the same historical frieze. Under the harshest possible construction, the colonies might represent an absolute nullity, a point either of non-Americanness, from which to measure "the growth of [our] letters . . . from cultural dependence to autonomy" (Sears vii), or of nonliterariness, from which to trace the "Rise of Poetry" in America (Stedman, *Poets* 1). Somewhat less dismissively, the historian might find value in colonial as well as in later writings, but value of different sorts, so that the progress of American literature could pass from writings "whose interest is historical rather than literary" to works of "intrinsic aesthetic value" (Bronson iii; Trent, *A History* 1).

Changes of a related sort might be seen in a generic movement from the historical narrative through the sermon and the political pamphlet to poetry and fiction; or in a succession of subjects, beginning with history and topography, moving on to theology and politics and arriving at last at nature. If such abrupt changes seemed to belie historical continuity, one might simply assert, as Trent and Wells did, that what is manifest in present American literature was latent in the colonial writers, who "were building better than they knew for the future of America" (2.vi); or, as James L. Onderdonk had it, that "amid so much that was worthless may still be discerned a few germs of that poetic spirit that was to bear fruit in . . . the golden

era of American song" (117–18); or, in another version of this botani-
cal figure, that Jonathan Edwards bore the "fruit of Cotton Mather
and Wigglesworth" as well as "the seed of Emerson and Channing"
(Trent and Wells 3.ix).

In tracing these continuities, some literary historians argued
that literary changes merely reflect "the different stages in American history" (Stedman and Hutchinson 5), or "the thought which
has molded this nation" (Hallek 6), or "the development of national
culture" (Trent and Wells 1.iii), thus allowing colonial writings to
serve "as a valuable supplement to the direct study of American
history and society" (Newcomer iii). A few granted literature a development of its own, either one running parallel to political and
cultural history, so that "a knowledge of each" is "essential . . . in
order to interpret the other" (White iv), or one intersecting the history of "riches, knowledge, and power" to contribute its own mite to
the "formation of the national sentiment" (Stedman, *Poets* 1). Those
historians who located the development of literature in literature
itself might discover the continuity between early and later American writings, as Stedman did, in "the feeling and vision" of "American song" (5, 2) or, as the *Cambridge History* did, in the "energetic,"
"masculine" tradition of American prose (1.x).

Exactly how these "traditions" were transmitted, however, few
historians were prepared to say. Although indifferent craftsmen
themselves, C. F. Richardson maintained, "The Puritans of Massachusetts Bay were direct precursors and the actual founders of most
that is good in American letters. [Their writings] were the index
fingers pointing to future triumphs. Bradford and Winthrop were the
intellectual ancestors of Emerson and Hawthorne" (1.xvi–xvii).
James Onderdonk set out to "trace the influence of colonial literature upon the development of genuine poetry" (16–17). But neither
of these historians went beyond noting an improvement in American writing after 1800 to explain exactly how the admitted defi-
ciencies of colonial writings "pointed to" or "influenced" that
improvement. Only those who saw the links between the American
literary present and the colonial past as having been forged in the
present—by the modern writer's use of colonial subjects or by the
contemporary reader's interest in colonial records (Bronson iv,

White 2, Pattee 16)—managed to explain the historical connection with any precision. Such skeptical empiricism, however, was hardly calculated to satisfy the prevailing need to distinguish American literature by granting objective status to its historical evolution.

At once inclined by its nationalist models to stick to writings in one language and forbidden by its peculiar linguistic situation from attending to that language, American literary history has necessarily failed to do the very things that the model was invented to make possible: characterize the nation's literature as a whole, distinguish it from the literatures of other nations, and chart its development over time. In order to perform these tasks, American literary history has had to seek its grounds of identity and continuity somewhere other than in language—in the citizenship of its authors, in some extraliterary history that literature is supposed to reflect, in recurring themes or genres supposed to be uniquely American. But no matter where it has looked for this ground of nationality, the thing discovered has invariably proved neither common nor unique to the works of American writers, but either peculiar to an unrepresentative few or else evident in the writings of non-Americans, or both.

As a result, American literary history has turned out to be little more than a chronology of texts written in the language of another nation by citizens, actual or imputed, of the United States, with little apparent reason for its existence beyond the wishful thinking and largely political designs of certain nineteenth-century American patriots and twentieth-century English professors. By trying to have it both ways—treating writings in only one language without admitting that they are written in that language—American literary history has ended up with an idea of Americanness that is political rather than literary, an idea of literature that is aesthetic or generic rather than American, and, hence, a history that must choose between America and literature, with no way to integrate the two in a historical conception of American literature.

Whatever their incidental virtues, the histories of American literature that this evasive thinking has produced hardly warrant its continuance. If the texts that concern us are written in English, then they belong first of all to the category of writings in that language, no matter who wrote them, or where they were written, or what they are about; and no subdivision of that category along political or geographical or chronological lines will remove them from it. As writings in English, they are conditioned by the character of that language before they are conditioned by authorial nationality, subject matter, place of composition, or anything else. Consequently, we cannot hope to understand them if, afraid of compromising their Americanness, we deny ourselves free access to information about the history, structure, and variety of the language from which they are entirely made.

Because the texts we call Early American Literature are, with few if any exceptions, written in English, they are automatically related to everything ever written in that language, no matter how far removed in time and space. By that essential measure, they are distinct from every text written in another language, no matter how temporally or physically adjacent. Anyone who can read English can read Thomas Malory, John Smith, and Salman Rushdie with about equal facility. But someone who knows no French cannot read the letters of the Francophone next door. If we face the plain fact that Early American Literature is written in English (without worrying that some American Studies commissar will call us Anglophiles for doing so), we may lose our tenuous grasp on Americanness, at least momentarily, but we will find the sacrifice richly repaid in the long run. For by shifting our attention from the imagined nationality of these writings to their indisputable language, we may find ourselves, for the first time, in possession of the ground of historical kinship and continuity that national literary history was designed to provide but that American literary history, sucking its paws for want of an American language, has always had to make do without.

As the European historians of national literatures seem always to have understood, languages constitute the only adequate basis for literary history. In the first place, they are themselves historical in that they remain the same over time, permitting anyone competent in a certain language to read anything ever written in that language, at whatever time, in whatever style; and they also change, enabling us to distinguish among texts written at different times as well as to measure the temporal distance between past texts and those written in our own time. As things that change, languages make history necessary, for change is what history was invented to explain. As things that endure, they make history possible, for unless differences can be seen as changes in some unchanging entity, the record of those differences will be a chronology, not a history. Indeed, although it is not necessary to think so, linguistic change may well have provided both the original motive and the model for the ideas of history that emerged during the Enlightenment and that we now take so much for granted.

If languages meet the essential criteria of history, they are also essential to literature. Whatever else literature may be, it is first of all a selection and arrangement of words in some language. Every text that has ever been called literature arose out of its language, is received in the context of its language, and remains dependent for its intelligibility on the survival of that language. Nor should the particular language employed by any work of literature be confused with the idea of language in general. The fact that we can read some languages and not others should tell us that even if there is a universal language, as linguistic philosophers like Roman Jakobson have sometimes supposed, we do not know it; and it is only their hermetic monolinguism that permits certain critics to think they are talking about "language" when they are in fact only talking loosely about their own. The language from which a literature is made and in which it is received is a specific language, a "tongue."

As the common ground of history and literature, languages offer the only basis I know for a history of literature that can be historical and literary at once. Without such a shared ground, what is called literary history must be either a history of something else—some such reified concept as a nation, an idea, or a genre—supposedly reflected in literature or else a chronology of literary events whose only connection is some recurring theme or form or style. In Michael Riffaterre's words, "[T]he stuff literary history works with (and on)—themes, motives, narratives, descriptions—is first and foremost language. Literary history has validity, therefore, only if it is a history of words" ("Formal Approach" 110).

The changes that give a language its history occur by way of a dialogue between that tongue and its users. The performative state of a language at any time conditions every utterance that employs it. As Ernst Cassirer once said, "No poet can create an entirely new language. He has to adopt the words and he has to respect the fundamental rules of his language" (226). But every utterance also conditions its language to some extent, the more so when one of its users asks the language to say things it has not been required to say before, thus expanding its lexicon, changing the meaning of existing words—perhaps even the way words mean—and inventing new syntactical forms in which words can be arranged. These innovations enter the general performative repertoire of the language just to the extent that they become available through publication, mechanical or oral, and serve the aims and interests of its users.

As participants in this process of linguistic change, all writings have historical value. Because the linguistic circumstances of a particular time are the primary conditioning factor in the production of all texts written at that time, J. G. A. Pocock and Quentin Skinner maintain, every text is intimately related to its historical moment. The linguistic situation becomes the most important context for the historical interpretation of a text, while any text can tell us something about the performative state of the language—its users' "world," as Benjamin Whorf would say—at the time of writing.

From the point of view of linguistic change, however, some writings may be said to have more historical significance than others. While most writings merely reflect the performative situations from which they sprang, adding nothing new to the language, and while some invent novelties that, for one reason or another, do not pass into general use, a few introduce changes that, for equally various reasons, become part of the common verbal currency. "The Italian language, the English language, the German language," Cassirer says, "were not the same at the death of Dante, of Shakespeare, of Goethe, as they had been at the day of their birth." Although necessarily conditioned by their languages, such writings give those languages "not only a new turn but a new life" (227, 226), contributing significantly to the linguistic circumstances in which they themselves will be received by later users. And when such writings are read later, amidst circumstances that they themselves helped to

Pocock's paradigm

create, they necessarily produce in the reader a sort of historical short circuit, a shock of recognition, an impression of presentness that seems to deny their age. This appearance of timelessness, created by history, is what we call literature. It is that peculiar "response of the reader to a text" which Riffaterre identifies as "the causality pertinent to the explanation of literature" ("Formal Approach" 99).

What I am proposing here is an idea of literary history based on the model of evolution: an array of purely ad hoc changes— *mutations*, if you will—in a coherent, temporally continuous system that assume a pattern of relation and value when they are viewed, as they must be, from a point within that system. From our point of view within the biological system, the mutations of the past that have the greatest significance are those which appear to have created us and our environment. From our present point of view within the linguistic system we call English, the most significant verbal performances of the past, the ones we call literature, are those which appear to have created, and hence to participate in, the language that constitutes our world.

René Wellek outlines the desiderata for a literary history of this sort in "The Concept of Evolution in Literary History." "What is needed," Wellek says, "is a modern concept of time, modeled not on the metric chronology of the calendar and physical science, but on an interpretation of the causal order in experience and memory" (51). And in his efforts to devise a scheme that would not make literary history dependent upon the history of something unliterary, he comes very close to identifying language as its historical ground. Such a scheme, Wellek says in "Literary History," would "look for the essence of a work of art in a system of signs and implicit norms existing as social facts in a collective ideology, just as, for instance, the system of language exists" (117–18).

F. W. Bateson and Josephine Miles, whom Wellek identifies in the former essay as the only surviving evolutionary historians of literature, draw somewhat closer to the linguistic model by making English the historical ground on which its literature stands. Because they regard literature merely as a reflection of linguistic change rather than one cause of it as well, however, their definition of literature remains ahistorical, and the history of English becomes, as Wellek notes, just another framework of unliterary chronology for the arrangement of "timeless" literary works ("Literary History" 107). If language is not just to offer an analogue of literary history, as it does for Wellek, it must be specified. In order to be something more than the historical "background" of literature, as it is for Bateson and Miles, linguistic change must be recognized as a result as well as the cause of textual performances. Only then can a specific language become the common ground of literature and history, where the texts we call literature contribute significantly to the linguistic changes that, in turn, lead us to call those texts literature.

It must be admitted that the evolutionary scheme I have proposed emits an odor of presentism and historical intentionality strong enough to send revisionist historians screaming for the exits. Acutely aware of the baneful effects of such pseudo-evolutionary schemes as nationalism upon the study of past writings, these revisionists have often located the evil in narrative, in the very idea of a continuity between past and present, and have sought to escape that evil by deconstructing the present point of view in order to let the past speak in its own unfamiliar, different voice. In the introduction to their collection of revisionist essays on colonial American history, Jack Greene and J. R. Pole describe "the historian's world of the past" as "a world in which subjects [are] judged to be significant less for what they might reveal about subsequent events than for what they [tell] about the specific world of which they are a part." Only by eschewing the narrative method that forges a diachronic link between past and present can historiography "recreate past societies in their own integrity, and, in so far as possible, without distortions of teleology" (7).

As the revisionists themselves concede, however, the present is finally inescapable. Because it consists in our linguistic equipment, which we cannot forget, the present unavoidably conditions our reading of any past text, making its statements mean things that they could not possibly have meant when they were written. So long as we go on reading texts amidst circumstances different from those in which the texts were written, a diachronic link will remain intact, implicit in our ability to read—and in our fate to misread—words set down long ago, in other worlds.

But even if we could escape the present, we would, as literary historians, have no wish to do so, since it is the present that lends both historical and literary studies their subject. "Only an interest in the life of the present," Benedetto Croce insists, "can move one to investigate past fact" (12). The very existence of the past lies in our perception of its differences from the present; without such perceived differences, there would be no past, no history. Like all differences, furthermore, those between past and present depend on a perceived identity. Chaucer's poetry and Robert Mezey's are different because they are both English poetry. Chaucer's poetry and Adam's off-ox are different only insofar as they are both things. Since differences and identity are inseparable halves of a single binary system, the historian cannot choose between them. Even historians who insist upon the differences, rather than upon the similarities, between past and present depend upon an idea of identity both for the identification of differences and for their explanation. In other words, historiography implies narrative: the story of successive accidental changes in some essentially unchanging thing. Having argued cogently and at length against historians who misread theistic texts of the eighteenth century in order to align them with the humanist present, Richard DeProspo sets out a new historical theory that, by underscoring the radical difference of such documents, "will make their theism interesting and meaningful" (*Theism* 55), evidently to the present.

The present point of view is no less essential to literature, insofar as that word designates not a property inherent in certain texts from the past but a present impression of their linguistic presentness and a resulting present decision, as John Ellis puts it (50), to use them in literary ways: read them for pleasure, teach them in literature courses, include them in literary anthologies, write about them for literary journals, and the like. Since, except in histories of taste, *literature* is an altogether present thing, no literary scholar should seek to obscure or nullify the present point of view in order to concentrate exclusively on the circumstances of textual production, for fear of depriving the word of its value and equating it indifferently with *writing*. Neither, to be sure, should the perception of present-ness in a text be allowed to discredit the effort to discover the factors that conditioned its production, for that is a perfectly proper aspect of literary study. For a literary scholar, however, such investigations aim primarily to explain the peculiar factors in the past that pro-duced a text we presently call literature.

Nor does our present point of view, as its adversaries often claim, necessarily subject the past to its imperial will, ignoring alien matters wherever it cannot make them seem familiar. As any num-ber of failed efforts to rescue some "neglected" title demonstrate, certain texts simply cannot be made to speak our idiom. To occupy the providentially governed world of *Uncle Tom's Cabin,* we must leave our own; and though such imaginative departures have unde-niable historical value, they leave literature behind, except as a syn-onym for fiction. This idea that the present point of view dominates the past stems largely from our habit of equating the past with a set of texts chosen for their literariness, their apparent modernity. So vividly does *The Scarlet Letter* seem to reflect our own image that only through dogged efforts of the scholarly will and the historical imagination can we recover the pre-Freudian source and meaning of Hawthorne's words. These hard-won glimpses of strangeness, however, are no truer, no more a datum of experience, than our im-pressions of linguistic familiarity, which are no less in need of expla-nation.

Still other attacks upon critical presentism have been launched on behalf of such political and sociological interests as gender, race, and class. Having discovered that the present has tended to be largely male, white, and economically privileged, the partisans of America's social victims have denied the authority of the present itself and sought to shift the locus of textual value from the point of textual reception, where literary judgments are made, to the circum-stances of production, where such things as the sex, color, and social standing of authors come most readily into play.

Here again, the mistake lies in regarding present and past as matters of choice, with the latter the clear preference. Although the present is inescapable and essential to the idea of literature, it is by no means necessarily uniform. As a linguistic situation, it comprises as many different positions as there are varieties of modern English. Each of these equally present linguistic points of view, theoretically, projects its own past and defines its own literature. To the extent that several of them occupy the same institutional space, they will compete among themselves for recognition, financing, and power. But when the fight heats up and the contestants begin to insult each other, we must remember that literature is not the exclusive property of any one of them. If each could define the linguistic point of view that conditions its literary judgments and defend its judgments on that ground, we might stop hearing such ill-considered notions as the radicals' claim that the word *literature* is merely an instrument of oppression wielded by sexist, racist nabobs to frighten the powerless, and the reactionaries' counterclaim that literature is self-evident and undebatable.

As for any suspicions of teleology that may be raised by this evolutionary model of literary history, they are easily dispelled. The evolutionary model recommends itself precisely because it does not imply such historical purposiveness. In language as in biology, evolution simply refers to accidental changes in elements of the system that, depending on their adaptability to changing circumstances, will either die out or survive to become part of those circumstances and, hence, factors conditioning later points of view on the evolutionary process itself. Valuing the linguistic presentness apparent in a past text—that timeliness we call timelessness—no more supposes that the writer had the present in mind or that the text participates unconsciously in some eternally ordained scheme of history than biology supposes that the dinosaurs formed part of a divine plan for the building of Los Angeles. Could we view linguistic change from a point outside it, the pattern would probably prove random, without a plan. Viewed, as they must be, from some point within the system, however, past changes assume degrees of significance according to their perceived historical relations to the linguistic point from which they are viewed. Although every text has, theoretically, equal value as a source of information about its own time, some will seem more significant to the present than others—more literary— by virtue of their perceived linguistic familiarity.

Teleology has no logical standing in an evolutionary scheme that avoids the popular mistake of removing the present from the system of change and considering it final or otherwise unconditioned. As the product of past changes and the circumstance of further changes, the present itself is always changing, creating new pasts, discovering new literatures. When the rhetoric of progress set the tune of literary history, the past divided itself into literary expressions of optimism or moral improvement and critically negligible expressions of skepticism or fatality. When literary history joined the war of the artists and intellectuals against the official culture, taking up the modernist rhetoric of alienation and dissent, it discovered a literary past in writings that its predecessors had either disparaged or ignored. And now that literary historians have adopted the highly technical idioms of linguistic philosophy and the social sciences as an expression of despair over the arrangement of contemporary affairs, the important past has come to reside in texts linguistically different from the present, resolutely unliterary, in the apparent hope that their example will reform the present so as to make them literary.

The relations between past and present that give rise to the ideas of both history and literature are essential to literary history. Without this diachronic dimension, Tzvetan Todorov has said, the genre becomes merely a sociology or a psychology of literature ("Literary History" 145). With it, literary history necessarily becomes a narrative and hence subject to the various charges that have been brought against it: presentism, teleology, a dependency on either nonliterary history or the reification of such textual features as themes, forms, and motifs for its continuity. The blame, however, lies not with narrative but with the narrative protagonists literary historians have chosen: nonliterary entities like nations or Puritanism, on the one hand, and historically discontinuous literary entities like the novel or Romanticism or father-figures on the other. When literary history takes a language as the ground of relations both between history and literature and between past and present, narrative survives, but the problems mistakenly ascribed to it disappear. On this evolving ground, literary history becomes a narrative of significant, enduring changes induced in a language by texts whose consonance with the reader's idiom leads to their being called literature.

From our point of view as producers and products of modern English (whatever differences of gender, race, class, or nationality may subdivide us), the single most important event in the history of the language, rivaled only by the Norman Conquest, has to be its discovery of the New World, which began with the earliest English references to that event, around 1510, and, after nearly five hundred years of steadily increasing activity, is still going on. Call this evolution what we will—progress, decline, cosmic jest, or anarch blunder— we discern in its beginnings the headwaters of the linguistic current in which we swim and have our intellectual being. It is the European conquest of America, Tzvetan Todorov maintains (referring not just to Americans but to all inhabitants of the modern world), "that heralds and establishes our present identity" (*Conquest* 5).

For medieval English, as for every other Old World tongue involved in the discovery, the altogether unanticipated appearance of a land of unknown size, shape, and meaning in the midst of the Ocean Sea taxed the language in a way and to a degree unprecedented in its history. Not only did it have to take account of something new in the world but it had to reconceive the fundamental idea of the world itself—its geographical form and symbolic meaning, the role of human activity in the determination of these things, and hence the very nature and function of language.

The ultimate scope of the discovery can be glimpsed in the words of Germán Arciniegas: "When it dawned on Vespucci that another continent existed—a continent apart from the three already known—and when he proposed that it be named 'the New World' . . . his words were an understatement. What would be new thenceforward was not merely the expanse of land he announced . . . but the whole world. Europe would soon be new, the Occident would be new, and new also would be the compass of man's imagination" (5). But nowhere is the essentially linguistic nature of the task set by the discovery or the thoroughgoing changes it would require more succinctly stated than in Columbus's journal entry for November 27, 1492, where he remembers telling his companions that "in order to make unto the sovereigns an account of all they were seeing, a thousand tongues would not suffice to express it, nor his hand to write it, for it appeared that it was enchanted" (Todorov, *Conquest* 24). To rescue these new things from the realm of enchantment and make them intelligible at home—indeed, to perceive them at all—every Old World language involved in the discovery would have to change. For, as Paul Armstrong says (his technical discourse modulating into an eerily precise echo of Columbus's words): "Semantic facility with generating and comprehending new sentences is closely related to epistemological competence in extending prior knowledge to assimilate something surprising, unprecedented, and for that reason perhaps bewildering" (31).

The writings we call Early American Literature enact and document one aspect of this linguistic discovery, standing as they do at the crucial point where the geographical history of English, previously confined to a corner of Europe, first crosses the eastern shoreline of the New World with the planting of English colonies from Newfoundland to Guiana. In our eyes, this point of contact between English and America marks the beginning of a long process of geographical expansion, demographic redistribution, and linguistic change that has created the present English-speaking world—and hence the kinship we feel with any text that appears to have participated in that process. The virtual obsession of American literary historians with the Puritans and their putative influence on later generations must arise not from any sympathy with their baroque theology or their unpleasant behavior but from their invention of words like *independence* to describe the proper allegiance of a congregation to Christ, rather than to the bishops, and *primitive* to denote the original purity from which the church had strayed and to which it must return. Although the coinages of English reformers (Barfield 59, 150), these words are American in that they translate ideas that Calvin had conceived, in part, from letters by Durand de Villegagnon regarding a Calvinist colony in Brazil. They are our words because in conveying the idea of a political separation authorized by "nature and nature's God," they laid the foundation for the Declaration of Independence and, through its example, for virtually all subsequent wars of national liberation (Arciniegas, 110–12, chap. 6).

From their own point of view, of course, the colonists stood not early in our history but at the farthest stretch of their own, anticipating a future, constructed from Old World memory and desire, that resembles very little if at all what in fact transpired, and certainly did not include the likes of us. Mary Rowlandson's surprise at seeing her narrative supplant the orations of Cicero in the university curriculum could be exceeded only by the shock John Smith might have felt upon learning that the "backe sea" he paddled up the James River to find actually lay three thousand miles farther west. The places where these people lived and wrote dotted the westernmost edge of a linguistic realm that extended north into the Maritime Provinces of present-day Canada and south through the Caribbean, Darien, and Surinam to the Amazon; and whose eastern limit, except for scattered commercial outposts in Muscovy, Asia, and Africa, was the English Channel. Perched on this frontier between the known and the imagined, the colonists of British America struggled to make their language, which had been formed in a very different world, apprehend the new one that was unfolding before them. And wherever the writings of these linguistic experimenters were read, they created new ideas of the possible, of the real, gradually breaking the verbal equivalent of what Seneca had called "the sea's bonds," eroding the conceptual foundations of the Old, pre-American world, and replacing these with the linguistic structures of the new.

The proliferation of such writings during the period of colonial development in British America and their publication throughout the English-speaking world made the seventeenth century a period of unprecedented linguistic upheaval, raising language itself to general consciousness as an object of practical and theoretical study. Linguistic treatises of every sort, Murray Cohen reminds us, came on the book market: prescriptive grammars, spellers, usage manuals, the first English dictionaries—all aimed at imposing some order on an exploding language. Voyage narratives themselves, Peter Cornelius has shown, routinely included observations about the languages spoken in the lands visited, especially about the possible relation of those languages to the original *lingua Adamica* from which all modern tongues had departed at the Tower of Babel. And from such confrontations of Scripture and experience grew those linguistic theories we identify with the Enlightenment: the idea of a natural language whose elements and structure conform exactly to those of the natural world; the valorization of "primitive," untutored speech, including regional dialects and the English vernacular; the debate between the progressive, elitist view of language as a learned skill that separates humans from the brutes and the democratic idea of language as a natural gift that makes all humans essentially one; the codification of a scientific discourse grounded in empirical observation rather than in received ideas and aimed at the conquest of nature rather than at its sacramental interpretation; the distinction between ancient and modern languages and the association of the former with original, unchanging authority, the latter with a changing present called "newes" and "the novel."

Through all of this vigorous activity, historians of English agree, there runs a steady current of verbal secularization, a shift in the semantic bearing of words like *dissent, disagree,* and *obscene* from metaphysical ideas to the sensory world and the experiencing mind. Attributable in large part to the present human discovery of a place altogether unaccounted for in Scripture or in ancient philosophy, this semantic revolution generated a whole new rhetoric of self-fashioning and soul-making in which words like *discovery* and *experiment* would acquire radically new meanings, and words like *curiosity* and *ambition* would lose their pejorative connotations to become forms of virtue. All in all, it is not too much to say that the linguistic circumstances from which the writings we call Early American Literature arose and to which those writings contributed greatly are a prime source of the language in which our own ideas of politics, science, economy, psychology, and human morality are framed. As the title of Edward Phillips's dictionary of 1658 so aptly phrased it, the discovery of America brought into being a "New World of English Words."

Phillips's title bears a message that cannot be overemphasized: the linguistic discovery changed the whole world of English words;

it did not divide the language into two separate streams, one American, the other British. The efforts of writers on the frontier to make the language say "America" flowed back to the stylistic capital, London, in the form of letters, reports, dispatches, and, before long, printed books. These writings taught readers back home in England new ways of conceiving the world and their place in it and prompted untraveled but especially alert writers like Shakespeare and Bacon to pursue the hinted drift of these documents farther than any colonist ever did. Owing to the transatlantic exchange of written materials, this "Americanization" of English proceeded more or less uniformly throughout the literate regions of the Anglophone world all during the period of colonization, accelerating steadily as the number of English speakers in America and the volume of their publications increased. In the centuries since the word *America* first appeared in English and since the first Englishman set foot in the New World, the presence of America in the language and that of the language in America have never stopped growing pari passu. By the time of the Revolution, Philadelphia had become the second largest city in the English-speaking world, and America had become, as Martin Kallich suggests, perhaps the single most common topic of British poetry. By the end of the nineteenth century, the demographic center of the English-speaking world had removed from London to the eastern seaboard of the United States, carrying the stylistic capital of the language along with it. Today, that center of linguistic fashion appears to reside in the vicinity of Los Angeles, and "American English," as Randolph Quirk says, "has come to have the fashionable prestige in Britain . . . that British English [once] had in the United States" (26).

By "British" and "American," of course, Quirk means not two different languages, like English and French, but two regional varieties of a single, uniform grammar. Although a great deal has been made of such differences ever since English began to be spoken in America, no argument for separateness has ever quite managed to overcome the experienced fact of identity. Whereas the evidences of national linguistic difference tend to comprise such incidental matters as spelling, pronunciation, and nomenclature, the areas of experienced uniformity are essential, permitting Americans and Britons to grasp without difficulty each other's subtlest written forms: their poetry and their humor.

So patent is this basic uniformity that all arguments for a separate American strain of English, like those for a separate American literature in English, appear to arise from a political need to assert differences in the face of obvious identities. David Simpson's 1986 book *The Politics of American English* illustrates the point quite nicely. After carefully unearthing the political motive behind the earliest theories of American English, Simpson then adjudges these separatist efforts to have succeeded in producing a unique national idiom that distinguishes the writings of the American Renaissance. Like all such nationalistic attempts to neutralize the embarrassments of language, however, this one forgets that the dream of America's linguistic independence was itself an international property. In the eyes of Rufus Griswold, indeed, it was an altogether English delusion. "Some critics in England," he complained, "expect us who write the same language . . . to differ more from themselves than they differ from the Greeks and Romans, or from any of the moderns. This would be harmless, but that many persons in this country, whose thinking is done abroad, are constantly echoing it, and wasting their little productive energy in efforts to comply with the demand" (*Prose* 50).

The point here is that English, like any language, has two dimensions, temporal duration and spatial extension, both of which are crucial to any consideration of its history. "Chronology and geography," Richard Hakluyt insisted, "are the right eye and the left eye of all history" (*Voyages* 1.19). What John Smith said of history in general—that, divorced from geography, it "wandreth as a vagrant without certain habitation" (2.625)—is especially true of those European languages that owe their modern development in large part to their growing presence in the New World and the reciprocally expanding presence of the New World in them. Although the spoken dialects of English may vary widely among geographical regions—so widely, in some cases, as to be mutually unintelligible—these dialects vary no less within each nation than they do from one country to another. Meanwhile, the written language, far from dividing into distinct national styles, has evolved with increasing uniformity over the past four centuries, thanks to the growing international commerce in printed materials. The usages of rural Arkansas or urban Newcastle remain geographically isolated as long as they are only spoken, but once such local variations find their way into print, they can influence the written language wherever English is read.

Although we have been led to suppose that too much attention to the language in which colonial texts are written would further compromise their already tenuous Americanness and, hence, have been persuaded to locate that property in an unhistorical, unliterary idea of national history, we may now see that it is only by dismissing the imagined nationality of our subject texts and cleaving to the fact of their language that we can even begin to understand their historical and literary Americanness. When we think of Early American Literature as imaginative writings of a certain quality composed by sometime residents of the future United States, we are left necessarily with the least literary, least American body of writing in the annals of American literary history. But the moment we think of these writings as constituting a crucial phase in the Americanization of English, Early American Literature takes on an entirely new meaning. *Early* stops meaning "less" and comes to indicate an especially important moment in the development of modern English, the point where the language takes up in earnest the task of, literally, coming to terms with America. The word *America* stops referring to a nation not yet in existence when colonial writings were produced, and therefore incapable of conditioning their production, and comes instead to describe any selection and arrangement of English words attributable to the writer's efforts to take hold of "America." And *literature* stops denoting the forms of writing given that name in the seventeenth century or, worse, in the nineteenth and recovers its functional meaning: writing that, by virtue of its role in the evolution of the reader's linguistic world, appears to transcend its own historical moment and speak directly to the present.

Defined as writing that, in its efforts to make room in the language for the New World, helped to create the stylistic circumstances in which that writing is now received, Early American Literature is a very different subject from the one bequeathed to us by the national literary historians. Instead of beginning with the settlement of Jamestown, it starts, as far as English is concerned, with the earliest recorded appearance of the word *America* in the language and includes some of the most historically and literarily important English writings of the Renaissance and the Enlightenment, from the English translation of More's *Utopia* to *Robinson Crusoe* and beyond. Instead of stopping at the imaginary borders of what would one day be the United States, the subject now includes writings from any part of the globe where the language confronted the New World—Shakespeare's London, Aphra Behn's Surinam, Sir Francis Drake's California, Captain Cook's Hawaii, Janet Schaw's Jamaica, Frances Brooke's Montreal. And instead of having to make do with such stylistically insignificant texts as Anne Bradstreet's "Contemplations" simply because they were written in verse in New England, Early Americanists can now look for their subject materials wherever the literary presence of English writings can be attributed to the stylistic innovations arising from the historical presence of America among their circumstances of production.

2

John Smith's True Relation and the Idea of American Literature

Does the fact (if it is one) that John Smith's *True Relation of Virginia* (1608) is, in Everett Emerson's words, "the first English book written in America" make it "the first American book" (*Captain* 45)? What have its language and its place of composition to do with the Americanness of the book itself? Is English more American than, say, Spanish, a language in which many books were written in America long before Smith's? Does something remarkable happen to English when it is written in America, something that does not happen to other languages or does not happen to English anywhere else? If so, aren't all books written in English in America equally, as well as similarly, American; and shouldn't we be able to detect in them this common Americanness? Or does America affect English in more than one way, producing a wide variety of American writings in that language? In that case, how do we reconstruct from these differing effects a single cause that will permit us to call them all American? Is something further required, perhaps, to make a book written in English in America truly American—a particular subject, theme, attitude, style, or form? But if language and place of composition are not sufficient conditions of a book's Americanness, why are they even necessary? Aren't these American subjects and the rest available to writers in any language, no matter where they live? Can't an English poet imitate Whitman at least as well as Bryant imitated Wordsworth?

Leaving these hard questions up in the air for the moment, we may ask whether Smith's *True Relation* is "unquestionably the earliest book in American literature," as Moses Coit Tyler claimed (1.21) and as its placement at the beginning of countless histories and anthologies of American literature seems to confirm. What qualifies it as literature? Smith certainly did not intend it to be literary, if by that we mean fictional or metaphoric or artful or something of the sort. On the contrary, he seems to have been trying his hardest to sound plain-spoken and businesslike, so that his readers back in England would take his word for the sometimes incredible and largely unwelcome things he had to tell them. Nor was he employing a recognized literary genre. Although European readers often doubted the reports of New World explorers and regarded them as a source of entertainment, the form known as the "brief true relation" claimed for itself a purely utilitarian purpose, the transmission of objective information from America to Europe without any intermeddling—or, in Whitman's word, any "composition" (717)—on the writer's part. Modern studies of Smith's writings routinely discover in them such qualities as "vividness," "immediacy," and "sensitivity to nature," suggesting that their literariness lies in the quality of his prose. But is Smith really such a "good writer" that critics cannot help but admire his style? If so, why are his literary virtues not more widely recognized? Why does the *True Relation* almost never count as literature unless that ostensibly universal category is first modified by the adjective *American*?

For the fact is that Americanists are almost the only readers who appreciate Smith's literary virtues, leading us to infer that the literariness of the *True Relation* is somehow bound up with its Americanness. What that connection is, however, is never made clear. We are told that Smith "repeatedly and memorably deals with later major themes of American literature" (Lemay, "Captain" 33). But that does not say that he deals with these themes in a literary way. It doesn't even state the case very accurately, inasmuch as Smith could not possibly deal with something that did not yet exist. The case is, rather, that James Fenimore Cooper's novels deal in a literary way with themes that can also be found in the *True Relation*. But even if it could be shown that this thematic resemblance is not simply coincidental, the demonstration would not automatically make the *True Relation* itself literature, any more than Shakespeare's histories automatically make literature of Holinshed's *Chronicles*. As for the literary properties that Smith's writings are said to possess in their own right—their "vigor," "individuality," "suspense," and all the rest: if these are seldom claimed to be worthy of critical admiration all by themselves, neither are they shown to be features of a typically or uniquely American sort. On the contrary, the literary traits that Americanists manage to discover in the *True Relation* are normally treated as at best incidental to its Americanness—its chronological priority in the production of "American" books—and at worst smudges on the textual window through which the American past might otherwise be more clearly seen.

What makes the *True Relation* American—its place in American history—is not evidently literary; and what makes it literature—its agreeable style—is not necessarily American. To call Smith's report a work of American literature, therefore, is to say a good deal less than the phrase appears to imply. *American* in this case does not define the literary properties of the text; it merely denotes some circumstances of its production. *Literature*, on the other hand, seems to say something about the text itself, the way it is written. Since the literary qualities normally ascribed to the *True Relation* are neither self-evident nor widely recognized, however, the word refers more evidently to the circumstances in which the text is received—the inclination of certain (by no means all) Americanists to treat it literarily, remarking upon its manner as well as its matter and reading it in a literary, as well as a historical, context.

Very tenuously related to each other in any case, these two sets of circumstances—historical production and critical reception—are in this particular case almost completely disjunct. Not only do they lie nearly four hundred years apart in time, but, since Smith was not writing literature in 1608 and those who call his report literature now do not ascribe its literary features directly to Smith's historical situation, American production and literary reception lie as far apart logically as they do chronologically. How, then, does the adjective *American* get dislodged from its historical situation in the seventeenth century and attached to the present critical situation to produce something called American literature that begins with the *True Relation*?

In order to call the *True Relation* American literature and actually mean what the phrase implies—writing whose literariness is American—we would have to do three things. First, we would have to persuade ourselves that Smith's writing—and not just its writer, or its place of composition, or its subject—is in some sense American. Since literature, by whatever definition, is a subset of writing, *American* cannot be made to describe a sort of literature until it is seen to define a sort of writing. Furthermore, since Smith wrote in English, *American*, in the case of the *True Relation*, must describe a sort of English writing. Second, we would have to offer some justification for calling this writing *literature*—something more persuasive than a patriotic desire to locate the seedbed of *The Pioneers* and *Walden* on American soil. For unless the *True Relation* can be shown to be literature in the same general sense that, say, *Hamlet* is, the word will do no more for its nominee than would the word *bread* applied to a stone. And third, we would have to show that the Americanness of the writing has some direct bearing on its claims to the title of literature, that its literariness truly warrants the modification implied by the adjective *American*. Then, and only then, could we say that the *True Relation* is a piece of American literature, and not just a piece of English writing composed in a place now part of the United States and decorated with bits of what Philip Gura has called "lovely Elizabethan language" ("John Who?" 265).

Can we say that the selection, use, and arrangement of words that make up the text of the *True Relation* constitute an American way of writing? What property of that text would justify such a statement? We know that it could not be something at once universal and unique—a property shared by all the writings Americans have ever produced and present nowhere else. Americans have written in so many different languages, styles, and forms, about so many different subjects, from so many different points of view that, even if we had time to read and collate all the writings Americans have ever produced, our research would be unlikely to discover something at once common to them all, peculiar to them alone, and at all significant. Nor could we say that the American features of the *True Relation* are the ones it shares with some particular subset of writings by Americans—writings of a certain quality, or in certain genres, or on certain subjects. Unless we already know what American writing is, we cannot possibly know what subset of writings by Americans will best exemplify it. Our only choice, therefore, is to restrict our inquiry to the *True Relation* itself, looking not for resemblances to other writings that we assume to be American simply because Americans wrote them but for properties of its own, features of style and structure that appear to embody in a form of words the American circumstances of its production and may therefore be justifiably called American.

In order to determine where, if anywhere, America conditioned the selection, use, and arrangement of words in the *True Relation*, we must first decide how it could have done so. Although the factors that condition or determine all such lexical, semantic, and syntactic choices are potentially numberless, they may be grouped, for the sake of convenience, into four general categories: the writer, the medium (including the language, the genre, and the physical form in which the text is transmitted), the subject of the text, and the intended audience. These factors, of course, do not work independently. A particular subject can condition the choice of genre, as can the writer's intention to reach a certain audience. Genres, in turn, condition the treatment of subjects and the definition of the audience. The possible combinations are manifold. Nevertheless, these four categories will include all circumstances of production for any text and so may identify the portals through which the America of 1608 might have made its way into the *True Relation* to assume a form of words.

Difficult as a rule, the problems of identifying and analyzing the circumstances that bear on the production of the *True Relation* are doubly complicated. In the form in which it comes down to us, the text appears to be the work of two different writers, writing in different situations, employing different genres, prose styles, and instruments of textual transmission to reach different audiences for different reasons. The facts of the matter, so far as we know, are

briefly these: in the spring of 1608, when he had been in Jamestown
for about thirteen months, Smith wrote a confidential letter to a
"worshipfull friend" (*Works* 1.27) in London, recounting the fortunes of the colony to date, with particular emphasis on his own
contributions to its survival. Not long after this letter arrived in
England, it passed into the hands of a third person, now thought to be
a certain John Healey (5), who edited it, apparently to enhance its
value as a promotional pamphlet, and then had it printed for distribution among the London Council of the Virginia Company and for
sale to potential colonists and investors, as well as to general readers
on the lookout for news from the New World. The resulting text is
not so much a piece of writing by Smith in Jamestown as a reading of
his letter by Healey in London, with enough quotation from the
original to give us a sense of its character, but also with enough
excisions of what the editor calls matters "fit to be private" (24), as
well as enough apparent additions of material deemed fit to be public, to prevent our ever knowing exactly what Smith's letter con-
tained.

In spite of these textual difficulties, it is possible to identify, at
least tentatively, the various circumstances in which the *True Relation* was produced and to discover where and in what form America
may have figured in each of them. Smith wrote his letter in America,
in the very midst of the things it relates. Healey prepared his edition
of the letter in London, outside America itself and yet in the midst of
a community whose economy, social structure, politics, and image
of itself had already begun—thanks to earlier reports like Smith's
and earlier publications like Healey's—to reflect the growing presence of America on the horizon of European awareness and desire.
Smith had gone to America, as Sir Francis Drake and Sir John
Hawkins had, with the idea of improving his rank in English society
by proving himself, through feats of honor, a true chevalier, worthy
to command men and to own property. He wrote his letter not so
much to report conditions in the colony as to assert his right to
govern it, resting his claim partly on the record of his own accomplishments but even more on the writing of the report itself, which
at once presumes and creates the authority he seeks. In Smith's

project of self-fashioning, America figures not exactly as a "land of opportunity" (Lemay, *American Dream* chap. 9), if by that we mean a place to become someone new, but rather as a natural place, outside history and artificial society, where one can become in the eyes of the world what one already is in the eyes of God.

If America for Smith is a scene of self-realization, for Healey it is an outpost of empire: a potential source of wealth in its own right and a way station en route to the even greater wealth of Asia. His publication of Smith's letter aims to recruit colonists for this overseas enterprise and to encourage persons of wealth to invest in it. With enough support of both sorts, the imperial scheme may prosper and so make speculators like Healey dukes in the commercial nobility of a new, "American" England. Here, America may be truly called a land of opportunity, a source of power by which persons of lowly birth can dismantle the feudal hierarchy and replace it with an aristocracy of wealth.

No less than the situations and intentions of the two writers do their respective genres expose their words to American influence. Smith's letter takes the form of a brief true relation, the eyewitness narrative devised by New World explorers to capture the unprecedented experience of discovering things hitherto unimagined and to persuade readers at home, who had not seen these things, to accept them on the authority of a single, unverifiable, often unknown witness, however much they might contradict the accumulated wisdom of the past. Having been invented by persons with ambitions very close to his, this form suited perfectly Smith's apparent intention to acquire authority in England by going to America, by discovering there things unknown to Aristotle, and, not least, by writing a sort of document normally assigned to persons of authority.

Healey, on the other hand, writes a promotional pamphlet, another genre invented to meet the peculiar conditions of American discovery but quite different from the brief true relation in its primary concern to create a community of readers rather than an individual writer. Whereas the events reported in Smith's narrative conduce mainly to the discovery—literally, the "invention"—of John Smith as a person of consequence, the same events, packaged in

a promotional pamphlet, become an inventory of colonial properties, offered to readers large-minded and bold enough to reach out
and take them.

The language from which the *True Relation* was produced—and
into which it was reinserted every time it was read—was, in 1608, in
the midst of the most rapid and thoroughgoing changes in its entire
history, owing to its application to a world fundamentally different
from the one in which it was born. Medieval English was structured
according to an idea of the world as a complete and completely
known design, an unchanging stage erected by divine fiat at the
moment of creation for the drama of Christian redemption, whose
plot lay revealed in Scripture. Fashioned to that purpose, English
was necessarily ill-equipped to deal with the world created by the
discovery of America, a world that grew larger with every attempt to
map it and thus seemed to owe its shape and meaning as much to
human action as to divine decree.

At the same time, English was peculiarly adaptable to this new
world, partly by virtue of its readiness to swell its lexicon with
borrowed words but principally because of its inferior rank in the
hierarchy of European languages. Unlike Latin, the learned tongue
of timeless universals whose ideological center lay in the medieval
and classical past, English was an untutored language of secular
news, centered firmly in the changing present. As a thing of lowly
status, it enjoyed a latitude of improvisation, experiment, and
change denied to the studied languages, with their highly codified
grammars. Not that early modern English had no rules; rather, in
spite of repeated attempts to impose rules upon it, the language,
then as now, resisted confinement within a priori forms—tending,
like the emerging New World itself, to create its own rules out of its
own experimental actions.

Like an evolving species, seventeenth-century English changed
by producing mutant forms, which existed side by side and com-
peted with each other for cultural dominance. From this expanding
verbal store, Smith and Healey drew two very different registers:
Smith, the so-called plain style, whose lexicon of native, concrete
words and whose uncomplicated syntax depict the world as an object of individual experience and its writer as a person of indepen-

dent judgment unclouded by received opinion; Healey, the ornate
style, whose Latinate diction and elaborate syntax portray the world
as a system of shared ideas and the writer as someone thoroughly
instructed in those codes. The plain style is closely associated with
the exploration of America, in that the accumulation of useful data
regarding this unwritten place demanded a reportorial style more
attentive to observed matters than to rhetorical manners, just as the
success of any colony depended on the empirical, practical habits of
mind that this style expressed. By this measure, Healey's ornate,
courtly style might seem to bespeak a world without America, except that he uses it, in his framing remarks, to mediate between the
bluff, inelegant, upstart America of Smith's narrative and the classi-
cally furnished, richly veined, subservient America of England's imperial desire.

The instruments employed by Smith and Healey for the transmission of their respective texts—manuscript letter and printed
book—and their different audiences—a personal acquaintance and
the reading public—provide additional openings for America among
the factors that conditioned the words we find in the *True Relation*.
To Smith, writing secretly in his quarters and addressing someone
apparently in a position to assist his ambitions, America presented
itself as a series of adventures demonstrating his innate capacity for
leadership. Accordingly, his letter embeds its information about
Jamestown in a narrative of his own sequential observations and
actions, capitalizing on his position as the only available source of
knowledge about portions of this unmapped region so as to turn the
facts of geography, climate, botany, zoology, and anthropology into
correlative objects of the writer-explorer's emerging character. Typically, the letter recounts the principal events of the voyage in chronological order, from the time of European departure to the moment
of composition, sticking closely to those things Smith has witnessed
firsthand and choosing its subjects, apparently, as much for what
they contribute to his stature as for what they add to the reader's
knowledge about America. At least, these effects are not always easy
to distinguish. Even when the narrative pauses in its temporal
march, as it often does, to describe some arresting scene or to offer
advice, these episodes appear as islands in the stream of Smith's

unfolding experience and hence as exemplary acts of careful observation and sage judgment, as well as reports of things observed or
judged. Under the combined pressures of public obligation and personal desire, geography and chronology, once regarded as mutually
independent properties of human history, combine to form a new
kind of historiography: a story of a new world and a new man emerging together through individual action—history as autobiography.

   To Healey, on the other hand, Smith's letter evidently seemed a
potentially valuable addition to the growing library of printed America, the already existing volumes of which doubtless guided the
editor's transformation of the writer's cursive self-discovery into a
printed object of general knowledge. Although printing had, by
Healey's time, outgrown some of the social opprobrium attached to
it in the previous century, the medium still bore—much as televi-
sion does for us—an association with social ambition, religious dissent, and political opportunism, thus characterizing as unworthy by
definition anyone who depended upon it for the acquisition of fame
and power. To publish one's confessions was to confess oneself a
nobody. As Thomas Fuller said of an autobiographical writer in
1662, "It soundeth much to the diminution of his deeds, that he
alone is the herald to publish and proclaim them" (1.276).

   At the same time, the public press offered an instrument of
power and a medium for the distribution of power unequaled in
human memory, and those who disdained to employ it—like those
whose antique scruples forbade investments in mining—soon found
their inherited powers usurped by bounders with a great deal to gain
and nothing to lose. For the hereditary aristocrat and the ambitious
upstart alike, therefore, the trick was to publish without seeming to.
One's private writings found their way, unaccountably, into the
hands of an unidentified middleman, who, perceiving the public
value of these disinterested missives, had them printed—at first
anonymously, so as to impute to their author no unseemly desire to
become known, but eventually under his correct name, thus embarrassing him with some unwelcome but extremely useful publicity.

   Of all the projects—political, social, commercial, or religious—
requiring the assistance of the printing press at this time, none de-

pended upon that mechanism more than did the colonization of America. In John Parker's happy figure, England built its empire on books: translations of narratives and geographies by the Continental explorers of the sixteenth century; reports by the early English privateers, Northwest navigators, and colonial dreamers who implanted in the soil of the New World and in the mind of the Old the seedling idea of a British America; and, most significantly, gatherings, by Richard Hakluyt and his successors, of all these fugitive relations into a bibliographic model of concerted national enterprise and a revelation of England's historic destiny. The printing press created a network through which the noble patrons, commercial underwriters, and practical executors of England's colonial undertaking shared their acquired knowledge and accumulating vision of America with each other and with the literate populace, cutting across the social divisions of court, city, and country to form an expanding new subculture of Englishmen whose mental geography, swelled by printed words, extended beyond the British Isles to the ever-expanding Atlantic frontier (Wright, *Middle-class* chap. 14; Stillwell, 61–77). Given the power of social currency held by the press, it is difficult to suppose that a writer as ambitious as Smith would not have hoped to see his report find its way into print and have composed it with that larger audience at least at the back of his mind. In any case, he does not seem to have been disappointed when, upon returning to London, late in 1609, he learned that his letter had been printed and that he had become what every effective explorer had to be—a published writer.

Arriving at last at the subject of the *True Relation,* we can see that this is only one of several apertures through which America could have found its way into the text. Nor does this one offer America a more direct access to the text than any of the others. On the contrary, the treatment of America in the text is conditioned in part by all those other factors, as well as by the history and status of America as a subject. By no means is that treatment governed solely, or even principally, by some unitary set of geographical or historical facts to which we can attach the name America. For the vast majority of English-speaking people in 1608, America existed entirely as a special set of words, which had arisen with the first English news of the New World, in 1509, and had been evolving for a century, conditioning each new utterance on the subject and being conditioned by each of these in turn. As one of the earliest English documents about America written by someone who had actually been there, Smith's report marks a particularly important episode in this discursive evolution. Nonetheless, it remains only one such episode and must be considered in light of the America of its own time, from which it arose and to whose subsequent development it contributed so significantly.

Although it is nearly impossible for us not to locate Smith's Jamestown in the America we know, we should at least try to remember that the words of the *True Relation* arise from and refer to an America that resembles ours in very few respects. To Anglophones of Smith's day, the word *America* designated a landmass of undetermined size and shape, stretching longitudinally from somewhere in the northern frigid zone to the Straits of Magellan and extending westward anywhere from many hundreds of miles, as in parts of New Spain, to almost no distance at all, as at the Isthmus of Darien. Whether North America more closely resembled the former or the latter was a matter of endless debate, one that would not be settled finally until Lewis and Clark trekked across the continent, two centuries later. For the present, the question elicited responses couched in figures of desire, rather than of knowledge, with some theorists projecting very brief journeys up Virginia's rivers to the South Sea, while others imagined a land of vast extent, depending upon whether they saw England's destiny as lying in the Asian sector of the known world or in a new and as yet undiscovered western empire. The latter of these two theories had begun to acquire some measure of authority by 1608, owing, on the one hand, to the repeated failures of Sir Martin Frobisher and Sir Humphrey Gilbert to discover a northwest passage and, on the other, to such grandiose, if equally unrealized, imperial schemes as those propounded by Sir Walter Raleigh. This long process of semantic change had only begun, however, and for most of Smith's contemporaries the word *America* still denoted "an island environed round about with Sea," rather than "a continent of huge and unknown greatness," about which the little that is known "is nothing to that which remaineth to be discovered" (Hakluyt, *Voyages* 5.94, 6.193).

Smith's ambitions inclined him quite naturally toward this emerging but unauthorized and still largely unwelcome idea of America as a vast New World, an unbounded land of human possibility where a man of true virtue might throw off the artificial constraints of a society in decline and prove his natural nobility through heroic action. The status and power of Smith's immediate superiors, in contrast, arose from, and depended upon the maintenance of, the Old World order, with its attendant image of America as a formless wilderness lying outside the providential circle of known lands and athwart Europe's path to Asian riches. To them, North America was a narrow barrier to be penetrated as quickly as possible and relieved of gold and pearls in the meantime, an inhuman, godless domain where survival demanded the preservation of divinely instituted social forms.

The reported contest between Smith and his superiors for control of the Jamestown colony encapsulates the three-hundred-year history of the debate between these two visions of America, with Smith's rise from disgrace to preferment presaging the eventual displacement, in the nineteenth century, of the Old World picture by the New. Certain general resemblances between the America Smith imagined and the one we have inherited have inclined generations of Americans to regard him, rather than Gabriel Archer or Edward Wingfield, as a forefather, and his letter, rather than one of theirs, as the beginning of American literature. Hindsight, however, should blind no one to the fact that Smith's notion of America rested on no firmer evidence, was no less a projection of self-interest, than Archer's and Wingfield's; that despite its eventual adoption by the authors of American nationalism, his idea was no less a European invention than theirs; or, for that matter, that subsequent history has proved their version every bit as American as his. Above all, we must be aware that even in the *True Relation*, the expansive, revolutionary view that has been identified with Smith is by no means fully realized but only sporadically apparent, as if struggling toward consciousness in a mind unprepared by discursive habit to admit the experiential validation of its own desires.

To some extent, then, America can be said to have figured somewhere in all the circumstances surrounding the production of the *True Relation:* writer, medium, subject, and intended audience. Before we could call the text itself American, however, we would have to persuade ourselves that the writing reflects these still prior conditions, embodying them in its selection, arrangement, and deployment of English words. To see what such a demonstration might entail, we may look closely at two very different sections of the printed text: Healey's editorial apparatus and those remnants of Smith's original letter that appear to have survived Healey's redactions, noting as we proceed stylistic features that realize in a verbal form the various American circumstances of its production. To some extent, these observations must be speculative, for though the title page and the preface are clearly the editor's work, we cannot be certain which words in the narrative proper are Smith's. The most we can say is that even as printed, the letter pursues a course so contrary to Healey's expressed interests—providing information that he finds either irrelevant or incomprehensible and withholding information that he considers essential—that while he may have deleted portions of it, he can hardly be supposed to have written it.

Without the manuscript of Smith's letter to compare with the printed version of 1608, we cannot be certain whether in preparing it for the press the editor erased all lineaments of its original addressee or whether Smith intended a more general audience from the outset. In any case, the title page of the 1608 edition implies an audience quite different from that interested gentleman to whom Smith is supposed to have written. Here the document to follow is identified, first, as a true relation: a genre familiar to book buyers as a source of information about a strange new world, one altogether different from their own and yet, somehow, part of it at the same time. What the document will relate, the title continues, are "occurrences and accidents . . . as hath hapned"—which is to say, completed historical transactions, including some that, whether lucky or unlucky, were unexpected, not "provided for" in the prior design of the expedition or in the providential world-picture from which that design was drawn. More particularly, the occurences and accidents reported herein are those "of noate"; but "of noate" to whom—the reporter, his "worshipfull friend," the Virginia Company, or the curious public—and according to what criterion of notability the title does not specify. Will the document accede to and reinforce an existing idea of importance? Or will it, perhaps, seek to replace established ideas with a brand-new standard of its own?

These noteworthy events are then said to have happened in Virginia, a name already familiar to readers of the day as a synonym for British America as a whole, rather than in Jamestown, a name chosen by Smith and his companions after they landed in Virginia but, perhaps for purposes of "national security," never mentioned in the text. In the title, Jamestown appears only as "that Collony which is now resident in the South part of Virginia," a specification that locates the notable occurences of the report simultaneously in a familiarly strange place and, by means of the word "now," in that peculiar precinct of history called "newes." What "hath hapned" there is still happening as the reader peruses these words and, in sharp contrast to events portrayed in ancient histories or in romances, has consequently not yet achieved a final form in which it may be intellectually and morally comprehended.

Like the setting of these reported events, their time is at once present and far distant. It begins not on a date in the reader's calendar but with the first planting, the opening event of the narrative itself, as if the events were taking place in a new order of time peculiar to themselves and available to the reader only through this narrative. The report is then said to cover all the time from this distant new beginning "till the last return from thence," a phrase which both indicates that these are the words of an editor in England, not of the writer in America, and repeats the suggestion that the new history initiated by the first planting is still being made, in the continuing present, by living persons in another world.

The living person responsible for this particular piece of "newes" is variously identified in the four printed states of the title page successively attached to this edition. The original version said that the document was "written by a gentleman of the said Collony," thus grounding the authority for the report in the social rank of its author but, at the same time, restricting that rank to the Collony, as if a different, perhaps inferior aristocracy ruled there. The second state identified the writer as "Th. Watson Gent., one of the said Collony," indicating a person known to be a gentleman here in England as well as there in Virginia. The third state named "Captain Smith, Coronell of the said Collony," removing the title of gentleman altogether once the actual writer had been discovered. And to complete this gradual displacement of hereditary rank by an emerging individual identity, the final state excised the initial *Cor* and terminal *ll* from *Coronell* to produce "Captain Smith, one of the said Collony," whose authority seems to arise entirely from his presence there and whose existence in the reader's world—like that of the "said Collony"—is owing almost entirely to the narrative to come. Only in describing that narrative as Smith's letter "to a worshipfull friend of his in England" does the title suggest that Smith has an existence and a status in the reader's world other than those created by the text. Smith is known to someone whom the untraveled reader might also know. But even here, the failure to name that English gentleman stretches the extratextual connection between Smith and the reader almost to the vanishing point, preparing that reader to enter an altogether new—one might even say a novel—world, where setting, action, and character are made entirely of words.

Copies of the *True Relation* that bore some version of the title page naming Smith as the author also included a preface "To the Courteous Reader," in which the editor apologizes at exquisite length for the earlier misattributions of the document, explains the error, and points out certain virtues and shortcomings of the text as printed. Casting the reader in the role of a large-minded, unprejudiced aristocrat whose very "willingnesse to reade and heare this following discourse, doth explaine to the world" an enthusiasm for the colonial enterprise—which is to say, in the role of the letter's original addressee—the editor then portrays himself as a supplicant to aristocratic patronage, thus simultaneously acknowledging and obscuring the transfer of colonial support and authority from the aristocracy to the commercial and professional classes. In order to prove himself worthy of the courteous reader's condescension,

Healey then launches an extended, ornate conceit in which he becomes an actor who, having anticipated his cue, first retires in embarrassment to avoid "the hatefull hisse of the captious multitude" but then, counting on the "curteous kindnesse of the best" patrons and disdaining "the worst," returns apologetically to the stage and "receives a generall applauditie of the whole assemblie." Thus enrolled in a fictive conversation between witty courtiers, the purchaser of this book is now prepared to hear how Thomas Watson came to be identified as its author.

The manuscript, Healey explains, came to him "by chance . . . at the second or third hand," lacking the writer's name but bearing the recommendation of several "well willers of the action," in whose company Healey has already enlisted the reader and now includes himself. Sensible of the letter's value to all such courteous and benevolent persons, he had it printed, only to discover, first, that someone—a pressman perhaps—had unaccountably ascribed it to Thomas Watson and, then, "that the saide discourse was [in fact] written by Captaine Smith." This worthy the editor now introduces as "one of the Counsell there in Virginia," restoring for "The Courteous Reader" some of the status Smith lost, bit by bit, as succeeding states of the title page shifted the writer's authority gradually from his rank in English society to his presence in America. Having discovered "the Author," the editor resumes his theatrical conceit and delivers Smith over to the "wise" audience with the request that if the performance seems "worthy an applauditie," the praise go directly to him, "whose paines," Healey says, "in my judgement deserveth commendations."

Only in a few minor respects, Healey insists, can the printed text be considered imperfect. First, "the names of Countries, Townes, and People" may be incorrectly transcribed, they being "somewhat strange unto us," who know these things only by hearsay. Second, the printed text omits certain portions of the original manuscript, which, he says, "being as I thought fit to be private . . . I would not adventure to make . . . publicke." Finally, and most important, Captain Smith has proved strangely dilatory in relaying information of the very sort that "well willers of the action" most require: "the situation of the Country, the nature of the clime, number of our people there resident, the manner of their government, and living, the commodities to be produced, and," above all, "the end and effect it may come too . . . "—a list of omissions apt to make the courteous reader wonder what sort of information Smith does in fact provide.

No matter, says Healey; everyone who has been there agrees that "the Country is excellent and pleasant, the clime temperate and healthfull, the ground fertill and good, the commodities . . . many, for our people." The bad times are all past, the hard work is all done, and "those that shall succeède, may at ease labour for their profit, in the most sweete, coole, and temperate shade," simultaneously improving themselves, rescuing savages from "the unknown paths of Paganisme," and contributing to "the everlasting renowne of our Nation" and "the Weale publicke in generall." With these assurances—made necessary, it appears, by Smith's failure to provide anything to the purpose—the editor bids his audience "Farewell," relinquishing the stage to the author, who will now presumably address the "Courteous Reader" on his own behalf.

The transatlantic bridge between writer and reader is not quite complete, however. Before Smith is permitted to make his own courteous, if somewhat perfunctory, obeisance—"Kinde Sir, commendations remembred etc."—the reader hears the title of the piece recited once more, but with a notable emendation (1:27). This time, it ends with the phrase "till the last returne," omitting the words "from thence" and thus removing the reader, abruptly, from the European world of courtesy created by the preface, across the Ocean Sea to the American scene of writing, where history is made and not just acted out. With this single stroke, the editor's efforts to locate Smith in England are all undone. By the time Smith's narrative has come to the end of its opening paragraph, Healey's courteous readers will find themselves anchored in the strangely named "Bay of *Chissiapiake*" and beset by hostile Indians.

Turning to the narrative proper, we may view it synoptically as moving back and forth between two principal subjects: troubles at the fort and adventures among the Indians upriver. The first four pages of the narrative (27–33) introduce these two themes, relating, in turn, the departure from England, the transatlantic crossing, the arrival at Jamestown, the securing of the fort, and the first explorations of the river—a period of six months, from late December 1606 to late June 1607. What may be called part 2 (33–35), then, develops the subject of troubles at the fort during the summer of 1608. Part 3 turns to the second subject: trading expeditions up the Chickahominy during the fall (35–43) and Smith's captivity and release by Powhatan in December (43–61). Part 4 (61–63) returns to the fort and the intramural squabbles of January and February 1608. Part 5 (63–79) recounts Smith's second visit to Powhatan with Captain Newport in early March. And part 6 (79–97) recapitulates the opening pages by interspersing difficulties at the fort with trading expeditions in the backcountry, from March until June 2, 1608, when Smith signed his letter and put it on board the *Phoenix*, bound for England.

Whether or not the paragraph that concludes the 1608 edition forms part of this pattern has long been a matter of debate. Some readers have found its reassuring generalities incompatible with the foregoing particulars of civil disorder, hardship, and death; others have seen no reason, without some external evidence, to conclude that Smith did not write it. Whatever the historical fact may be, that fact vanished with Smith's manuscript, leaving only the reader's impression that this peroration resembles Healey's preface far more closely than it does anything Smith has said up to this point. The paragraph immediately preceding recounts Smith's disposition of an impertinent savage: "But for his scoffing and abusing us, I gave him twentie lashes with a Rope and . . . bidding him shoote if he durst . . . let him goe" (95). The closing paragraph, in contrast, immediately leaps to a loftier, altogether more sanguine view of the colonists' situation: "we now remaining [are] in good health, well contented, free from mutinies, in love one with another, and as we hope in a continuall peace with the Indians" (97). Then, too, the speaker in this passage has the interests of the adventurers, the "Nation," "our gracious Soveraigne," and "almightie God" far more in mind than does the narrator of the preceding pages, whose primary concern appears to be his own advancement, and whose implied audience seems to demand fewer reassurances of Smith's selfless motives than does the reader addressed here and in the printed frontmatter. Most telling of all, however, is the fact that the frame completed by this paragraph seems to be the one established by the title page and the preface, not the one created by Smith's own salutation, "kinde sir" (27), which forecasts a complementary close, on the order of "Your obedient servant," and a signature.

But even if we take these protestations of public-mindedness to be Smith's own words, we must also notice that the foregoing narrative devotes considerably more attention to his own exploits than to communal affairs at the fort. Although the goings-on in Jamestown that Smith reports absorb approximately ten of the thirteen months covered by his letter, they take up only eight of the thirty-six printed pages of the 1608 edition, whereas his several expeditions into Indian territory occupy less than three of those thirteen months but twenty-eight pages of the printed text. Since Smith is a subordinate at the fort and the leader of the parties sent to explore the interior, this apportionment of space has the general effect of making Smith loom larger in his narrative than he apparently did in the day-to-day running of the colony. No less remarkable is the increasing attention Smith gives to affairs at the fort as the narrative proceeds and he assumes greater responsibility for the decisions of the Council. The second half of the narrative devotes nearly twice as many pages to what happened in Jamestown as to trading sorties among the Indians, largely, it appears, because Smith has acquired, as a result of his earlier dealings with the Indians, a measure of power at the fort equal to that which he earlier enjoyed only when commanding a small party of foragers in the back country.

The reader's impression that Smith's narrative has more to do with his own rise from disgrace and subordination to consequence and command than with the conduct and condition of the colony as a whole is strengthened by the deployment of personal pronouns in the text. Generally speaking, the first-person plural predominates at the fort, the singular on the river; "we" gradually gives way to "I" as the narrative progresses, until "I" comes to preside, in the closing pages, over events in the settlement as well. Throughout parts 1 and 2 (27–35), the pronoun "we" performs the principal actions: crossing the ocean, setting up camp, making the first survey of the river securing the fort, and suffering the hardships of the first six months

in the colony. Faint glimmerings of the impending pronominal shift
do appear in the narrator's reference to himself as the receptacle and
medium of all this information—"I doe not remember" (31)—and in
his use of the reflexive "my selfe," first, in recounting the initial
exploration of the James River (29) and, then, in connection with his
ostracism by the Council for having, apparently, overstepped his
authority during the voyage from England (33). Even so, the singular
pronoun remains largely submerged in the collective throughout
these early pages. The party that explores the river comprises "Captain Newport and my selfe with divers others" (29). And if Smith's
disgrace separates him grammatically from the "others," sickness
reunites them: "My selfe having also tasted of the extremitie
thereof" (33).

The narrator emerges in the text as a distinct entity for the first
time with Smith's election to the office of cape merchant and his
receipt of the Council's commission to trade with the Indians for
corn (35). Once this persona appears, it begins to distinguish itself
from the other colonists, especially from those who refuse to work
and from Newport, who squanders the truck brought from England
for barter with the Indians. As the trading party moves upstream, "I"
takes command of the text, relinquishing center stage only when "I
returned towards our Forte" (37). There, "we" reassumes control
until the next expedition begins, and "I" takes over again. This
second voyage up the Chickahominy is "my journey," although the
barge and pinnace remain "ours" (39). On the next trip, however, the
former vessel becomes "my barge" (41), and here again "I" predominates until the party arrives back at "our fort" (43).

By the time the narrative has arrived at the famous fourth voyage into Powhatan's kingdoms, the singular pronoun has acquired
enough presence to embody an idea of discovery, a desire to expand
human knowledge of these unknown territories, in opposition to the
Council's idea of the country as a mere source of provender for the
fort. Realizing itself upon this ontological ground, the narrative "I"
becomes an object of dispute between "malicious tunges" who im-
pugn Smith's motives and "some of the company as desirous as
myself" to push farther upstream. At the same time, this emergent
persona becomes an object of interest to itself, reporting its own

interior reflections—"This occasioned me to suppose . . . " (43)—
and defending its motives against "the malicious judges of my actions at home" (45). What spurs this subjectivity are Smith's decisions to leave all but two members of his party behind with the barge
and to abandon these two and push on alone with his Indian guide—
decisions that lead to his capture. The narrative has already begun to
report certain actions, like the removal of a log impeding the progress of the barge (43), for no apparent reason except that "I" performed them. From here on, until Smith's return to the fort after his
release, what the title page has called "things of noate" will be determined less by what a reader might want to know than by the simple
fact that Smith himself saw them.

Solidified by the lengthy account of Smith's sojourn with Powhatan, the identity of the narrator remains noticeably intact
throughout the passages following his return to Jamestown, where
"they . . . welcommed me" (61). Although the fort is still "ours" and
colonial business is again conducted by a communal "we" (61–63),
that community is both set apart from "myselfe" by its increasingly
apparent tendency to go to pieces whenever Smith is away on the
river, and internally divided into two factions: one hostile to Smith,
led by Archer and called "they," the other loyal to Smith and called,
simply, "me."

These rhetorical efforts to maintain his hard-won identity in
the midst of his fellow colonists take a somewhat different form
when Smith returns to Powhatan's camp with Newport. Now "I,"
the person who has been here before and knows the country, contends with "we," the entire English delegation sent by the Council
to negotiate with Powhatan, distinguishing himself by making
snide remarks about Newport's excessive credulity (71–73) and by
emphasizing the few occasions when "I" manages to detach itself
from the company—referred to as "they"—and meet with Powhatan alone (63). From here on, "I" stands firmly in the center of the
narrative. Back at the settlement for the last time, "I" deals deci-
sively with some mutinous Englishmen and summarily dispatches a
few thieving Indians, thus proving Smith no less important to the
internal order of the fort than to its sustenance from without, as well
as discrediting by implication "their" decision to make farmers of

"my" professionally trained band of explorers (83–87) and nailing the last plank in that laboriously constructed identity which began this narrative as an indistinguishable part of a collective "we" but can now confidently sign itself "John Smith."

As the first person arises chronologically in narrative time, it also expands geographically in expository space by way of digressions from the straight line of narrated action into lateral descriptions of the countryside. According to the conventions of the brief true relation, brevity is a condition set by the reader, a busy man in Europe who wants a factual report on the progress of his American enterprise in the shortest possible form. In the case of the Jamestown colony, this undertaking involved the establishment and provision of a fort, the search for a passage to the South Sea, and some prospecting for gold and pearls along the way. Any divergence from this plan, either in the conduct of the colony or in a report of that conduct, would constitute a digression, an act of self-indulgence on the writer's part, calling attention to his own resourcefulness and bravery, supplanting the interests of the reader with his own ambitions, and generally taking up the reader's valuable time. As the preface to the *True Relation* makes clear, the Virginia Company wants information about the fort that is to serve as the base camp for the expedition to the South Sea, about the organization and provisioning of the people who will mount that expedition, and about those "commodities" that will cover its costs and reward its underwriters. What Smith gives them instead are increasingly detailed descriptions of lands lying alongside the direct watercourse to the South Sea, territories of little or no interest to the adventurers and mentioned here, it seems, only because Smith discovered them.

In the opening pages of the narrative, where the collective "we" performs all the action, Smith takes virtually no interest in topography. He says nothing about the situation of the fort except that it is "a very fit place for the erecting of a great citie" (29)—surely the last thing the adventurers want to hear, although, perhaps, a matter of interest to Smith's "worshipfull friend," who may have dreamed of founding a duchy for himself in America. The account of the early explorations inland conforms somewhat more closely to instructions from the Company, concentrating on narrated progress up "the great river" and restricting description to the stream itself—its width, depth, and navigability. The first notable digression from this narrative course describes an Indian town that "I visited" (37). Although more detailed than it needs to be, this passage still adheres to the colonial plan inasmuch as that village provides an exceptionally generous supply of food for the fort. At the same time, this remarkable provision redounds directly to Smith's credit, since "I" discovered the town and procured the corn through skillful negotiation with the Indians.

The more individuality Smith gains from such accomplishments, the more his desire wraps itself in an idea of heroic discovery for its own sake, rather than for vulgar trade (43). The object of this desire, furthermore, is not the "backe Sea," the accessibility of which Smith begins to doubt and the discovery of which would in any case merely enhance the status of Captain Newport, to whom, as the principal agent of the Virginia Company, "all discoveries did belong and to no other" (85). The desired object, rather, is that "vast and wilde wilderness" (45) that opens outward on both sides of the river as Smith travels inland, making him forget his orders and wander away from the stream of his narrative into the expanding landscape of his discovered identity.

Insofar as Smith's rhetorical self emerges temporally in the course of his narrative progress upriver and expands spatially by way of descriptive digressions into the flanking regions discovered there, that self owes its identity largely to the Indians whose lands these are. The first person surfaces initially in the account of Smith's success in establishing trade with the Indians, including his promotion to cape merchant in recognition of that success and his superiority to Newport in this business. The first two major digressions from the straight narrative line that leads, in the minds of the Jamestown and London councils alike, directly to the "backe Sea" describe two Indian towns that Smith has discovered—the earlier of which owes its space in the text to its potential importance as a source of corn for the fort, whereas the latter comes to seem so much a landscape of the narrator's unfolding self that the text seems on the verge of calling it "Smithtown." The narrative "I" triumphs when

Smith leaves his companions and is captured by Powhatan, who treats his captive commoner as an equal, a representative of Europe.

The next major digression, far and away the longest in the narrative, has to do with Indian ceremonies, beliefs, and customs—subjects of no apparent interest to the Virginia Company but of obviously very great personal significance to the only European who has ever witnessed these exotic practices. Back at the fort, after Smith's release, "I" stands apart from "us" when Powhatan sends "me" gifts for "my selfe" and for Newport, to whom the narrator gives the Indian title "my father." Nor will Powhatan's emissaries go near the fort until "I" goes out to meet them, for they know only "me" and Newport, whom "I" introduced to them. Unlike Smith's English publisher, the Indians call him by his name (61), thus awarding him the status of their own kings, the only Indians who have names in the letter. And, having earlier made him cape merchant at the fort, they now make him a "Werowance" in their own world. However one looks at it, the authoritative identity constructed by Smith's narrative is an Indian gift, and, as the letter explains, it "is a generall custome, that what they give, not to take againe" (69).

Although the Indians are a principal source of Smith's increasing authority, in the colony and in his report alike, they are off-limits as far as the Jamestown charter is concerned. At best, they are pagans to be rescued from error for the greater glory of God, or guides to riches and the South Sea for the greater glory of England; at worst, they are potential impediments to these designs who must therefore not be "offended"; in any case, they are something to be avoided rather than cultivated. As a result, Smith's commerce with the Indians amounts to a transgression of godly, civilized forms, a departure that he must both undertake and justify if he is to raise his standing in the colony. Conceiving of itself as a European outpost, the colony means to maintain its transatlantic lifeline, receiving supplies from England until it can produce enough food to sustain itself. Instead of "going for England," however, Smith insists that they "goe toward *Powhatan*" (37) for supplies, a policy dictated by the colonists' sloth, by the uncertainties of shipping, and by Smith's own desire to make himself indispensable. For the establishment of an American supply line, Newport, the admiral of the European sea routes, proves useless and must defer to Smith, the cape merchant, who learns the Indians' language, customs, values—even their ways of thinking—and employs this exotic knowledge to save the fort from starvation and himself from inconsequence.

Having tapped this source of power to his considerable advantage, Smith soon develops a thirst for more, a desire to explore the Indian country that "the necessitie . . . to take in provision" (43) has opened up. But while the needs of the colony may justify trade, discovery seems to have no justification except Smith's intractable will—that is, until he ascribes his motives for pushing farther up the Chickahominy to imputations of cowardice by his detractors at the fort and to demands for action from the investors at home: "as well for his own discharge as for the publicke good" (45). What is more, in crossing the line between British and Native America, he does not leave divine providence behind, as Europeans tend to suppose. The colonists brought God across the Ocean Sea in the form of an intention to convert the Indians. In trading with them, Smith finds that their hearts are no less subject than any Christian's to providential influence (37), for God helps him strike advantageous bargains with the savages, even though "some bad spirrits [at the fort] not content with Gods providence" (41) still place this savage commerce outside the pale. Any fears that Smith himself may entertain regarding the moral condition of a people who "acknowledge no resurrection" (59) evaporate in the heat of his growing confidence that he is the principal agent of divine providence in this enterprise and that God attends him wherever he goes. Although everyone is sick during the first spring, he recovers "by God's assistance" (33); and when, returning from captivity, he finds himself deposed from the Council and charged with the deaths of Robinson and Emry, "it pleased God" (61) to preserve him amidst his Christian foes no less than from his pagan captors. To learn "the publike good" and God's intentions, it seems, Smith need only consult his own inclinations.

In spite of these attempts at self-justification, the depth of Smith's narrative penetration into Indian territory during his captivity and the breadth of his expository digressions upon Indian ways might well seem to his readers, as they sometimes do to the narrator himself, a severe departure from the Company's designs for the colony. With Smith's separation from his companions and his capture by Powhatan, his letter ceases to report the colony's progress toward realizing the adventurers' plans and becomes an effort to know another world—one largely irrelevant, if not perfectly inimical, to those plans and altogether unlike the lawless, brutish desert of the colonial imagination. Instead of executing him, as "I expected," his captors show him "what kindnes they could," first delivering him to their king, who expresses a wonderful curiosity about European science and theology, and then leading him "in exceeding good order" to their village, where he is comfortably lodged and fed "more venison then ten men could devour." In all this time, "I wanted not what they could devise to content me: and still our longer acquaintance increased our better affection" (49)—an ever-widening circle of sympathy that comes to include vast stretches of fruitful land inhabited by a disciplined and loving people.

Of these inhabitants, far and away the most impressive is the emperor Powhatan, whose retinue, costume, and "Majestical countenance," Smith says, "drave me into admiration to see such state in a naked Salvage" (53). In exchange for further information about the aims and methods of the English, Powhatan reveals to Smith the extent of his inland kingdoms, which Smith contrives to imagine as embracing both the South Sea of his colonial duties and "the great and spacious Dominions" of his own desires. This momentary equipoise of the communal and individual selves, made possible by Smith's having assumed the identity of "the English" in his dealings with Powhatan, is then upset by the emperor's offer of a piece of his kingdom as a new site for the colony: "hee desired mee to foresake Paspahegh and to live with him upon his River." That Smith understands "mee" to mean the whole colony is clear enough in his next sentence: "hee promised to give me . . . what I wanted to feede us, Hatchets and Copper wee should make him, and none should disturbe us" (57). Nevertheless, the arrangement implied here—with Smith dispensing Powhatan's largesse and collecting tribute from the English—is hardly one that the Council would approve, since it erases the line of authority that now runs from the colony through Admiral Newport to King James and establishes a new chain of command leading up through Cape Merchant Smith to the emperor Powhatan.

Abhorrent as it may be to Smith's superiors at Jamestown, the vision of a feudal barony in this "Desert . . . exceeding fertil" (53) takes possession of his letter, which moves immediately from Powhatan's offer of land to a description of the rivers in this region and then to the detailed treatise on Indian customs. Since the adventurers have no use for these exotica, and since Smith offers them merely as things that "I observed" (21), the passage seems less a report to someone else than the writer's own contemplation of his newly acquired circumstances. At the very least, the motives for this disgression remain obscure. Does Smith wish to bring these barbarous practices to light, rescue them, as it were, "from the unknowne paths of Paganisme"? Or does the passage lead the other way, into that fascinating, seemingly benign, yet ultimately inscrutable darkness that is the source of Smith's new possessions and power? The text itself seems uncertain of its tendency, for the meditation upon savage ways breaks off abruptly and the narrative resumes to speed Smith "home" to the fort. Being nonreturnable, however, his Indian gifts follow him back to the settlement, where he is first court-martialed for having exposed his party to capture, then rescued by Newport and elevated to the Council, and then showered with presents from Powhatan, who released Smith in exchange for his promise to recommend the removal of the fort to "the countrie [the] King had given me" (23), and who now wants this pledge redeemed.

Although Smith is obviously in no position to deliver the colony into Indian hands, his association with Powhatan has proved too valuable to be simply forsworn. "By a mischaunce" (23), a fire has destroyed the fort, leaving the English entirely dependent for survival upon the Indians, who refuse to deal with anyone except Smith himself and those Englishmen to whom he has introduced them. Intent upon securing his ascendency, he enlists Captain Newport in a new trading party and sets out to renegotiate his alliance with Powhatan. On this voyage, however, the Indians seem far less benignly generous than when they entertained Smith alone. Whether Newport's credulity brings out their natural deviousness, or Smith's reluctance to share his source of power with his rival leads him to paint them a shade darker than the naive Newport can see, their gifts now seem a smiling mask upon a savage grimace, an invitation less to self-enhancement than to disaster. The king of Paspahegh proves "a politick salvage" whose cunning inclines Smith to "suspect some mischief." Although Powhatan himself still displays "such a Majestie as I cannot expresse, nor yet have often seene, either in Pagan or Christian" (65), a welcoming speech by three of his "Nobles" prompts Smith immediately to doubt "if there be any such amongst Salvages" (65). As for the emperor's protestations of goodwill, "Experience had well taught me to beleeve his friendship, till convenient opportunity suffred him to betray us" (69).

The problem is that the Indian's treachery is no more reliable than their benevolence. When one of Powhatan's men endures terrible hardships to assist Smith, he must admit that "this kindnes I found, when I litle expected lesse then a mischiefe" (73). At one moment, the emperor's representations to Newport evoke a knowing sneer: "This faire tale had almost made Captaine Nuport undertake, by this meanes to discover the South Sea which will not be without trecherie, if wee ground our intent upon his constancie" (75). But at the next moment, even the "politicke salvage" Opechancanough can partially disarm Smith, who is astonished when "with a naturale kind affection, hee seemed to rejoyce to see me" (77).

The Indian, it appears, cannot be known from without, comprehended in the structure of European ideas—translated, in short, into English. Smith has words for treachery and for kindness, but none for that infernal intermixture of benevolence and malice in the Indian character, that power at once to smite and to save which seems to lie across the language barrier between himself and Powhatan, beckoning him to self-fulfillment by way of self-annihilation. If he could cross that line with some assurance of returning, freighted with Indian gifts, to the world from which he departed and find himself not transformed into a painted savage but, rather, fully realized in his rightful estate as a natural nobleman, then his transgression would be justified. As he knows, however, Indian gifts are fatal, and since he has come to this strange new world to raise his standing in the old familiar one, not to trade his European prospects for a savage kingdom, he must stay this side of the line, taking from Powhatan what will serve his own purposes without letting himself be drawn so far into the dark that white eyes, accustomed to the daylight, can no longer see him. His rude welcome at the fort, following his lone sojourn with Powhatan, shows clearly how little tolerance the colonial establishment has for insubordination and how easily even the appearance of transgression can discredit his motives in a civilized court of law. And there is reason to suppose that the skeptical attitudes assumed in the report of Smith's second visit to Powhatan are meant primarily to dispel any suspicion that he has "gone native." At the same time, he has known the authority that goes with the title of werowance, and he can ill afford to distance himself utterly from the source of that power.

What his letter must do, then, is maintain a delicate balance between the language of his readers and that barbarous tongue which constitutes his peculiar authority, his reason for writing, and his claim upon the reader's attention. If he says only what his readers already know, his report will do nothing to alter the colonial arrangements that determine his status. And if he says only things that his readers do not know, they will not understand, let alone believe him. Indian words bespeak his special knowledge, gained from firsthand experience, and are therefore essential to the authoritative self that the letter would fashion. But, in order to retain their credibility, these unfamiliar words must be seen to expand the English lexicon rather than to supplant it, enlarging the linguistic domain to include the place that Smith has made for himself, rather than positing an utterly new world that English cannot touch.

Far and away the greatest number of Indian words in the letter are names of places and people. Since these things already have names when the English arrive, no suspicion attaches, necessarily, to Smith's use of those names, even though he does employ them more often than a European reader, having no map on which they appear and no prior acquaintance with them, might find helpful. On the other hand, renaming is an important aspect of political conquest and religious reclamation alike, and his penchant for giving the "Countries, townes, and People" of this other world names that are, as the editor's preface observes, "somewhat strange unto us"

(23) might well strike even the most sympathetic reader as a trifle unaccommodating if not utterly indifferent to the national and evangelical purposes of colonization. This idiosyncratic usage is re-markable in those passages where he seems consciously to avoid the names Jamestown and James River, referring to these places instead as "our fort" and "our river" or "the river we dwell upon" (53), and especially so when, recounting Powhatan's offer of an inland site for the colony, he adopts the Indians' lexical point of view and calls Jamestown "Paspahegh" (57).

Although the tendency to use Indian vocabulary increases as the narrative moves from the coastal regions held by the colony into those interior regions that Smith thinks of as belonging to him, the letter never loses sight altogether of its primary aim: to win the reader's assent for the author's plainly self-serving construction of America and his own virtues. Accordingly, the letter is at some pains to make this other world as available to the reader as it can without relinquishing possession of that world altogether. In order to fit the Indians into some system that a European reader might understand, it describes the party that captures Smith as being commanded by "sargeants" (47) and a "Captain" (49). It calls Opechancanough, Kek-ataugh, and the rest "Kings" and calls Powhatan "Emperor," using their Indian names, in the European manner, to denote both the person and the territory he rules. This usage, however, proves a source of considerable confusion insofar as the name of a chief seems to apply primarily to his people, who move from place to place, and to a place only when his tribe happens to be there.

What is needed, it seems, is a less extreme order of translation, one that will not sacrifice experienced fact to communicability. To this end, the letter adopts Powhatan's kinship terminology for the relations between superiors and subordinates, English as well as Indian, calling Newport "my father" and one of the admiral's under-lings his "childe" (55). The problem with this method is that in employing the words Smith used when speaking to Powhatan, the letter seems to address Powhatan rather than the English reader, who hardly needs to have Smith's official relation to Newport trans-lated into familial terms in order to understand it. Indeed, the letter itself sometimes seems unsure of its intentions in this regard. At one point, Smith refers to Newport as "my father: whom I intituled the Meworames, which they call King of all the waters" (57), leaving the reader to wonder to whom the words "my father" in this passage are addressed if Meworames is the title Smith used in speaking to Powhatan.

This discursive middle ground, or no-man's-land, between the contending ranks of English and Indian words offers ample room for linguistic maneuver but no clear checkpoints to demarcate a line of transgression. In reporting Smith's first audience with Powhatan, the letter contents itself with paraphrasing the emperor's half of the conversation: "Hee asked mee the cause of our comming" (53). The next time Smith converses with the emperor, however, during the expedition with Newport, the letter slides from paraphrase into direct quotation, thus moving a step closer toward an acknowledgment of the Indian's independent status, his irreducible otherness (as well as correcting, incidentally, Benjamin Franklin's belief that Bunyan was the first English writer to mix narration and dialogue). The words given to Powhatan here—"Your kinde visitation doth much content mee, but where is your father whom I much desire to see, is hee not with you" (65)—are, of course, not really his, since he speaks no English. They are, rather, an attempt to render Smith's sense of Powhatan's culturally transcendent "Majestie" by combining the eloquence of a courtier with the sort of noble simplicity that was even then recommending itself to King James's translators of the Bible. Still, in allowing Powhatan to speak for himself, the letter grants him a "Majestie" equal to James's—or even superior, insofar as Powhatan, not James, dictates the name of "our fort"—thus repaying in kind the noble rank that Powhatan has conferred on Smith by treating him as an equal, giving him land, and dubbing him werowance.

The authority that Smith seeks to establish by means of this letter clearly depends upon his capacities as a translator no less than on his skills as a trader and an explorer. In order to make himself indispensable to the colonial enterprise, he must first redefine it as a discovery and occupation of Indian territories rather than as a search for gold and pearls en route to the South Sea. He must then demonstrate his own superior qualifications for the role of mediator between "the naturals," as the Jamestown charter calls the Indians, and the English—or "culturals," as we may say. How well Smith actually understood the Indians is both uncertain and beside the point. The letter represents him as perfectly capable of grasping every nuance of Powhatan's most complicated and detailed explanations, despite occasional suggestions that their conversation in fact relies heavily on "signes" (67). Paradoxically, however, the surest evidence of complete bilingualism is an inability to translate, a way of expressing how far apart two languages lie in the mind of anyone who knows both equally well. When the letter observes that Powhatan sits in state "covered with a great Covering of Rahaughcums" (53) or that Opechanconough serves Smith "sixe great platters of fine bread, and Pansarowmana" (77), it is simultaneously displaying Smith's familiarity with the Indian tongue, suggesting that English in its present state cannot fully comprehend that other world, and proposing a new, polyglot English better equipped to realize the new Anglo-Indian America of Smith's discovery. It is also, of course, giving hostages to Smith's enemies, actual and potential, by making his self-proclaimed knowledge and power seem the result of a pact with the heathens.

The figure that emerges from these delicate equilibrations and endless rhetorical adjustments is that of a man attempting to create a space for himself on the frontier between two warring empires, the British America of King James and the Indian America of Powhatan, both of which would subjugate him to their own impersonal designs, each of which gives him the power to resist the will of the other. That there are two empires, both equally powerful and equally limited, rather than one, as Europeans suppose, complete in itself and hedged about with darkness, Smith has learned by traveling alone beyond the boundary of his given world into the despised, forbidden territory of the "naturals." "Trucking with these Kings" (77) has given him an ironic, relativistic view of kings in general, including his own, just as the resemblance between some Indian women reciting their heathen spells and "an old woman her Pater noster" (59) invites a skeptical view of all religious practices, his own among them. Nevertheless, these are the worlds from which he must fashion a new one for himself. In either, he is a subject; outside of both, he is nothing, neither werowance nor cape merchant. Only by moving back and forth between them, representing "our great King" (57) to Powhatan and "the great king" (53) Powhatan to the English—both those at the fort and his readers at home—can he acquire power, lands, rank, authority, and consequence: a name. Although the imported forms of European polity restrict his movements, he cannot simply throw them over, for they both lend him status in Powhatan's court and point the direction of his European ascendancy. He must, therefore, suppress all redskin tendencies at the fort—whether these take the form of mutinies against constituted authority, defections to the Indian camp, undue trust in Powhatan's goodwill, leniency toward Indian thievery, or excessive payment for Indian corn—no less resolutely than he forestalls the paleface inclination of certain disgruntled colonists to abandon the fort and return to England. Irrelevant to his own purposes as gold mines, pearls, and the South Sea may be, he must sustain the adventurers' hopes for quick wealth and the admiral's anticipations of fame even as he endlessly defers their realization, for these Old World dreams authorize the explorations that discover the New World and the new John Smith.

To the extent that the *True Relation* appears to embody its peculiar American circumstances in a form of words, the writing itself may be called American, even if it should turn out to resemble no other text ever written by an American. That textual Americanness does not in itself allow us to call the *True Relation* literature, however. Although the word "literature," in ordinary usage, implies a certain sort of writing, the only thing at once common and unique to the many different sorts of writings that have been so designated is that they have all been called literature at some time or other and treated accordingly. Literariness, in other words, depends not on how texts are written—their authorship, form, style, subject, or intentions—but on how they are read, how they are used. A poet can write poetry on poetic subjects in poetic language for a poetry anthology addressed to readers of poetry and still not succeed in writing literature if no one decides to treat the product that way—if, for example, the only people who read it are historians seeking information about the writer's life and times. On the other hand, a soldier like John Smith can write a personal letter in the plainest possible language about the most circumstantial matters and end up writing literature if, centuries later, certain readers decide, for reasons of their own, to locate that document at the headwaters of American literary history.

What is more, as the critical history of the *True Relation* shows, a text can lie buried in the historical archives for generations after its initial appearance; then suddenly find itself, for some reason, the object of widespread literary attention and remain so for decades; then vanish from the literary scene for a while; and then return to literary consideration on an entirely different basis. Although literary treatments routinely imply that literariness is an inherent property of texts and that fluctuating critical fortunes merely demonstrate the critical blindness of prior eras, the case appears to be that the literariness of any text depends entirely upon the disposition of actual readers to grant it literary status and treat it accordingly.

By removing literariness from the text, the "use" definition of literature explains our persistent failure to identify the property that inheres in all literary texts. Removing literariness to the circumstances of reception, however, simply relocates the problem without solving it. If no text is itself literary, why, at any one time, do some texts get singled out for literary treatment and not others? And, why do certain texts belong to literature at one time but not at others? Are these choices purely arbitrary? Or do all acts of literary reception, no matter how various their objects, rest upon some common literary principle? Of all the documents written in or about British America between 1509 and the American Revolution, how did Smith's *True Relation* come to be called literature, while countless other writings in the same form, by similarly situated persons, and about virtually identical subjects, have slept unnoticed in the proceedings of historical societies?

As we observed earlier, various reasons have been offered for this puzzling choice. The *True Relation* is the first book written in the first permanent Anglo-American settlement. It employs an agreeable style, at once vigorous and sensitive. It introduces themes that recur in later American literature. None of these explanations seems to answer the question, however. Chronological priority in the pre-history of the United States hardly qualifies as a literary virtue. The stylistic felicities of the *True Relation* are not self-evidently superior to those displayed in, say, George Sandys's translation of Ovid, a work seemingly lost to literature. As for the supposed recurrence of Smith's themes in the writings of Cooper and Thoreau, even if that were a fact, it would not make the *True Relation* literature—any more than Virginia's admission to statehood makes Smith a United States citizen.

These attempts at explaining why the *True Relation* wears the mantle of literature seem to offer post-factum justifications for a judgment already made on quite different grounds, rather than to recapitulate the actual reasoning that led to the judgment. In this respect, they do not differ markedly from the reasons commonly given for the survival of literary masterpieces. Critics have called *Hamlet* "beautiful" or "true," without disclosing their sources of information concerning absolute beauty and truth. They have called it "timeless," forgetting the timeliness of their own judgments as well as those earlier times when the play was considered old-fashioned. They have called it "influential" or "prophetic," suppressing the knowledge that literary history is a two-way street, where each new present identifies its own traditions and precursors. To be sure, literary discussions routinely justify their choice of texts by enumerating the particular virtues of the texts chosen. But insofar as similar virtues can be found in any number of "neglected" texts, while in discussions of canonical texts the literariness of the object is usually taken for granted, literary recognition seems to precede and motivate, rather than to follow and depend upon, critical analysis. Like the historical, stylistic, and thematic arguments on behalf of the *True Relation*, the criticism of *Hamlet* seeks to discover why that text is already recognized as literature and to concur in that prior judgment. Depending as it does on this recognition of literariness, criticism can express it but can neither create it nor nullify it.

Readers are inclined to call a piece of writing "literature," I submit, precisely to the extent that it seems to these readers to speak directly to them, in their own language, about their own world. Because the readers of any period—no less than those of different periods—live in more or less different worlds, they discover themselves in different texts. Unanimity of literary taste varies in direct proportion to the homogeneity—social, economic, political, racial, sexual—of the critical community, the group of individuals making decisions about what is literature and what is not. Different communities choose different literatures and employ different methods of literary treatment, according to their various constitutions. So-called general readers choose their literature mainly from new titles and canonize their choices by buying them and reading them with pleasure. Academic readers tend to choose older texts and to signal these choices by teaching and writing about them. As long as different groups do not compete for control in the same market or constituency, they coexist quite amicably, keeping their mutual contempt more or less to themselves. When two or more of these critical communities seek to occupy the same social or institutional ground, however, each tries to make its own literary definition, canon, and methods prevail over the others. Nevertheless, all of these different literatures are chosen on the same principle: their apparent conformity with, participation in, even responsibility for, the world in which their respective advocates see themselves as living.

Like every other text invested with the mantle of literature, the *True Relation* has invited this peculiar treatment by the still unexplained capacity of its words to describe worlds altogether different from the one out of which they arose and to which they originally referred, worlds that John Smith could not even have imagined. The *True Relation* entered the literary salon on the arm of American literary historians of the late nineteenth and early twentieth centuries, who perceived in its bluff artlessness a distinct foreshadowing of their own democratic, expansive, anti-European republic of self-reliant, self-made men. As my analysis of the *True Relation* in its own historical context is meant to show, however, this received text bears only the slightest resemblance to the one Smith wrote. Far from being an incipient democrat advancing an idea of natural, New World equality against the artificial distinctions of Old World society, he seems to have been a feudal reactionary, one of many seventeenth-century Europeans who deplored the commercialization of the aristocracy and saw in the New World a theater for heroic action where true knighthood could recover its rightful accolades from the upstart rich. While this vision of America as the locus of a lost golden age required the unrecognized chevalier to dispute the authority of his undeserving superiors, his assertions that God is on his side cannot be equated with Emersonian self-reliance, especially insofar as the nobility demonstrated in America required the recognition of a European monarch. And although this land of regressive opportunity had to be larger and more fertile than the one that was to further enrich the usurper aristocracy on its way to the ultimate wealth of the Indies, Smith has no idea how big the continent actually would become. His America, vast though it seems, still lies within easy reach of the never-forgotten South Sea.

If the *True Relation* that Moses Coit Tyler called literature is not the one that John Smith wrote, neither, I think, is Tyler's a text in which today's readers can recognize themselves. At least, I have trouble imagining an educated reader of the present day who automatically identifies personal desire with the divine will, or believes that history enacts an eternal design discoverable through individual experience, or imagines that this providential scheme displays itself more vividly in natural America than in historically cluttered Europe—who entertains, in fact, any of the notions that Tyler's readers held concerning themselves and saw reflected in the *True Relation*. This secular theology ceased to inform serious historical inquiry some time ago, removing from the canon all those texts whose literariness was bound too tightly to its sinking metaphysics to survive. If the *True Relation* cannot speak as directly and cogently to the contemporary ear as it did to progressive American literary historians from Tyler to Robert Spiller, it will vanish from the ranks of literature to become an antiquarian document once again, as it was in the eighteenth century. And if that happens, no amount of historical research into the circumstances of its production or critical palaver about its sinewy style will succeed in rescuing it.

The fact is, of course, that, far from showing signs of impending literary demise, the *True Relation* and Smith's writings in general are receiving more literary attention these days than at any time since formalist criticism unseated historical scholarship from the chair of English studies, three or four decades ago. As in all such cases, the critical methods employed and the justifications given for employing them vary considerably from study to study. The primary motive, however, seems to be in every instance the same: a recognition on the reader's part of something immediately familiar in Smith's words. Pressed to say where, in the unfamiliar diction, unbuttoned syntax, and untethered pronouns of the *True Relation*, today's readers might find intimation of their own world, I would call attention, above all, to those features of the text which seem to ground reality—the physical world, individual identity, social organization, and history alike—in human action rather than in a set of eternal forms. Whatever Smith himself may have assumed regarding the ontological status of the New World, his narrative depicts the Virginian interior as coming into being with his discovery of it, as extending only to the limits of his awareness of it at any moment, and as existing seriatim, in the form of successive perceptions—of words on a page—rather than all at once, in the timeless form of a map.

Similarly, although Smith himself seems to have believed that his heroic character preceded its unveiling in the New World, his narrative depicts that self as originating in, and expanding with, the act of geographical discovery. Hence it is tied more closely to the places discovered, which are the cause and adequate symbol of its becoming, than to some prior source and ultimate destination in a heavenly home. And while Smith doubtless shared the prevailing opinion that European society reflected divine intentions rather than a historical evolution, the disquisitions on Indian culture in his narrative establish a temporal point from which European civilization could begin to see itself as a historical development—whether as a rise from barbarism or as a decline from natural nobility.

This verbal construction of a world instinct with time—complete at every moment yet endlessly changing—is in fact so familiar to the modern reader that its constituent elements are apt to pass unnoticed. The tendency of Smith's words to refer simultaneously to their announced objects and to their speaking subject, both of which unfold in concert with the unfolding of the text; the arrangement of materials, both recollected and reflective, in the order of their occurrence, rather than according to some established scheme of knowledge; and the location of significance in the shifting relations among things, as seen from a moving point within them, rather than in their fixed relations to a known beginning and ending, as seen from a stationary point above them—these are the protocols of modern rhetoric. No mind informed by the language of Henry James, Gertrude Stein, and Wallace Stevens will find anything untoward in Smith's tacit identification of history with the career of a single, eventful life or in the propensity of his words to become actions in their own right, rather than merely a report of completed nonverbal actions. The efforts of the *True Relation* to reconcile the conflicting demands of personal experience and public expectation; its apparent inclination to go on and on, stopping only when circumstances dictate instead of coming to some foreordained conclusion; its active participation in the history that it recounts—all these qualities contribute to the reader's sense that the world portrayed here belongs as much to the twentieth century as to the seventeenth, creating that impression of timelessness which expresses itself in the varieties of literary treatment we persist in giving this strangely inveterate text.

It need hardly be said that the text just described is not one that Smith himself would recognize, let alone acknowledge to be the one he wrote. We have, in other words, two very different *True Relation*s, the American one that Smith produced in 1608 and the literary one that modern readers receive now. In order to call the literary one American, then, we must establish a connection between the two. And since they are separated both by some four hundred years and by our different reasons for calling the one American and the other literary, the connection that would enable us to think of the *True Relation* as a piece of American literature must be at once historical and logical.

Establishing a historical connection between the written text and the read one depends on our seeing them as different aspects of a single, temporally continuous entity. We know that this entity cannot be "the text itself." Since the identity of the text is our problem, it can hardly provide our solution. Neither will "America" satisfy the demand for historical continuity, as Americanists have routinely supposed, for Smith's America and ours are only nominally the same place. Nor will "literature" answer the historical requirement. Smith was not writing literature; the *True Relation* has not always been literature; the literary qualities it presents to contemporary readers bear little or no resemblance to those it held for earlier readers—all of which is to say, once again, that "literature" is merely a name given to different texts at different times, depending upon the circumstances of reception, not an actual thing that exists continuously over time, giving rise to the particular texts in which readers find it.

The only thing common to both the produced and received texts—the American *True Relation* and the literary one—is the language, the specific grammar, in which the *True Relation* was written and is now read. This grammar must be the same for both texts, must have endured in the same essential form throughout the period between production and reception; otherwise, we would not be able to read—or, rather, misread—the text at all. This language must also have changed during that time, to account for the substantial differences between what Smith's words meant to him and what they mean to us. Since English is the language in question here, that grammatically enduring, stylistically changing tongue constitutes the historical common ground on which the American *True Relation* and the literary one are chronologically related. Indeed, to say that English has changed over the centuries since 1608 without ceasing to be English is to satisfy the fundamental definition of history: changes occurring over time in some enduring entity.

Necessary though it is to our quest for an idea of American literature that will embrace both the *True Relation* Smith wrote and the one modern readers receive, this historical relation based on language still does not justify our calling the literary one American. Before "American" can modify "literature," we must discover within the chronological relation a logical one. The Americanness of the produced text, in other words, must be shown to have some bearing upon the literariness of the received text—to be responsible, in some sense, for the inclination of modern readers to treat the American text in literary ways. Without this logical connection, all we have is an American piece of writing that contemporary readers tend, for reasons not necessarily related to its Americanness, to regard as literature.

We can begin to see a possible basis for this logical connection if we first remind ourselves of the complex interrelationships between writing and linguistic change. Every piece of writing is conditioned by the performative state of its language at the moment of production. At the same time, every piece of writing—like every other form of utterance—also conditions its language to some extent—inventing new words, altering the meaning of familiar words, expanding the current phraseology. While all such changes are no doubt equally important to the development of the language, they assume an order of relative importance when viewed, as they must be, from some point within that presumably random process. Each point of view imposes on the historical evidence its own scale of significance. Whatever the reader's linguistic situation, certain texts from the past will appear to have contributed significantly to that situation—to have laid the lexical, semantic, and syntactic ground for their own reception. These are the writings, I suppose, that readers feel inclined to call literature and to treat in literary ways—appreciating their apparent "timelessness" and trying to discover its mysterious causes. As Wallace Stevens observed, the people we call poets are not those who write verse but those who give us the words from which we construct our world (*Necessary Angel* 30–31). And like all true equations, this one is reversible: it is the words of our world—not particular forms or subjects—that enable us to recognize our poets, our "authors."

Approaching the problem of American literature from this direction, we find ourselves in a position to see why a text like the *True Relation*, which reflects and defines the American circumstances of its production with particular vividness, might strike a consciously modern reader as literary. When the professional student of English looks back over the history of the language, as one necessarily does, from the linguistic coign of vantage provided by the inventors of the modern style, the most significant changes in English since 1500—

the date from which linguistic historians normally trace the "rise of modern English"—appear to result from two reciprocal developments: the continuously growing presence of America in the language from the moment when that word first appeared in English, and the increasing presence of the language in America from the moment when the first English speaker set foot in the New World.

Insofar as this evolving dialogue between English and America seems to describe the historical line that connects our present performative situation to, say, Chaucer's, any text that can be shown to have engaged actively in that dialogue, thus moving the language closer to our modern, "Americanized" English, will be both American and literary by definition—American in that its selection, use, and arrangement of words simultaneously reflect and deepen the impact of America upon the language; and literary in that it will appear to contemporary readers to participate in the creation of their own modern world. What makes the *True Relation* American—its stylistic acknowledgement that the discovery of the New World both permitted and required a new idea of the world as a whole and of the function of language in the world—also makes it literature— a recognizable linguistic episode in the development of modern reality. Conversely, the literariness of the *True Relation*—its perceived allusions to the world inhabited by the modern reader—is inextricable from its Americanness—its efforts to adapt an Old World style to the altogether new, modern world that was born with the discovery of America.

3

Paradise Lost: Milton's American Poem

When Rufus Griswold pronounced Milton "more emphatically American than any author who has lived in the United States" (qtd. Spencer 174), he doubtless meant to inflame as much as to enlighten his audience. Whether or not the jeremiad informed the American self in the seventeenth century, that genre certainly set the tune, in the nineteenth, for journalistic lamentations over the persistent failure of American writers to produce a native literature; and Griswold, like an exasperated schoolmaster, may simply have been searching for the most insulting possible model to hold up before the class—as if to say, "Why, even Milton is more American than you Americans are."

More likely, Griswold was echoing the *Westminster Review*, where Ebeneazer Syme had already found Milton "the most American author that has ever lived" (Ruland 394). If so, Griswold may merely have been calling Milton progressive, according to the common practice, both in England and in the United States, of labeling progressive sentiments American and traditionalism British, irrespective of the actual country where these tendencies manifested themselves. Just as Europeans had once attributed syphilis to any nation but their own, progressive Americans tended to regard conventionality—whether social, political, or literary—as British, and English conservatives routinely branded all forms of unwelcome innovation American. By adopting this nationalistic shorthand,

Griswold would have been aligning himself with that critical faction for whom "American literature" meant a new and distinctive way of writing, as opposed to those who reserved the term for the masterpieces of future American Dantes and Chaucers.

Whatever he may have intended in calling Milton an American writer, Griswold surely did not mean his remark to set his readers' heads a-shaking, the way it does ours. To contemporary Americanists, the notion that Milton's writing is American merely removes Griswold from serious consideration, bespeaking his ignorance—not greatly to be wondered at, since he wasn't a professor—of what American literature really is. How could Milton's writing possibly be American, we say, when he himself was not? To be sure, American authorship is not a sufficient condition of literary Americanness; the vast majority of writings by Americans never appear in any course, anthology, history, or study of American literature. Nonetheless, authorial citizenship is always a necessary condition for admission to the national canon—whether of traditionally revered or of unjustly neglected writings—even though we may neither fully understand the logic by which nationality gets transferred from author to text in some but not all writings by Americans nor quite grasp the "Americanness"—whether uniform or diverse—that all these "American" texts purportedly share. Merely to think of Milton's work as American, we feel, is to erase the whole catalog of distinctions between American and British writings that the institution of American literature has labored so mightily to compile and upon which its very existence as an academic institution depends.

And yet, Milton seems fated to tease the literary lobe of what has been called the American mind, in both its creative and its critical functions, with a persistence that is quite remarkable. If Griswold and Syme are the only critics who ever went so far as to call God's Englishman an American, they are by no means the only ones to have registered in print a sense of Milton's brooding presence on the national literary horizon—a phantom peripherally visible when the critical eye attends to some more central feature of the native landscape but invisible to the direct gaze. Cooper listed Milton among the English writers whom every American should consider "his countrymen" (1.100). James Russell Lowell said that American democracy had realized the dreams of "the puritan and republican Milton" (122). George Sensabaugh's *Milton in Early America* (1964) testifies again and again to the peculiar attractions exerted by Milton upon the mind of both seventeenth-century colonist and twentieth-century professor alike. The modern critical industry responsible for the production of Milton editions, scholarship, and interpretation is, in the main, an American enterprise—and, as such, a cause for some bemusement among British scholars. When Melville set out to embody in Captain Ahab what seemed to him a dominant strain in the American character, he turned instinctively to Milton for one of his models; and there is no reason to suppose that Melville's Miltonism has played no part in the virtual identification of American literature with *Moby-Dick*, as reflected in the simultaneous rediscovery of that novel and institutionalization of the field in the 1920s.

Nor does this American fascination—not to say obsession—with Milton show signs of abating. No issue of *American Literary Scholarship* fails to list some new discovery of Miltonic traces, however faint, somewhere in the national canon. Indeed, so many articles of this sort have been produced over the years that, were they ever assembled in one place, they might well create the impression that Milton composed the "Library of America" all by himself. The workings of his invisible hand can be detected as well in the dominant image of American literary history as a string of textual beads, of varying shapes and colors, arranged upon a Puritan wire. Milton— or at least Wordsworth's vision of him as an imposing spirit—must lie somewhere behind this otherwise inexplicable historical myth: it predates by many years the discovery of Edward Taylor's poems, and the idea of Puritanism as a source of poetic inspiration can hardly have arisen from anyone's reading of Anne Bradstreet or Michael Wigglesworth. However that may be, Milton continues to hover over American cultural history like a tutelary spirit, rescuing the wilderness from Chaos and lending it an intelligible form that it cannot give itself. Proof enough, if proof be needed, can be found in Keith Stavely's *Puritan Legacies* (1988), published by an American university press and prized by the Modern Language Association of America for construing the first three centuries of New England cultural history as a re-enaction of the conflicts dramatized in *Paradise Lost.*

Remarkable in itself, Milton's enduring presence in America becomes even more so when set against the apparent nonexistence of America in Milton. The contrast is enough to wring the heart, like a tale of unrequited infatuation. While Americanists seem able to find Milton wherever they look, the Miltonists, most of whom are themselves Americans, seem strangely incurious regarding Milton's own attitudes toward America. To the inexpert eye, the standard checklists of Milton criticism published in this century discover almost nothing concerned directly with the poet's interest in the New World. This impression may be inaccurate; a proper Miltonist, knowing what lies beneath these titles, might be able to recognize several items bearing on the topic. Even so, their relative scarcity, compared to the numberless discussions of, say, Milton's classical and scriptural sources, only confirms the suspicion that, at least in the view of his American devotees, America occupied no significant place in Milton's mental geography.

If the Miltonists' indifference to America fairly reflects Milton's own, the fact is more remarkable still. America was, after all, very much in the news of his day—was in fact the source of the genre called "newes." When he wrote *Paradise Lost,* Europeans had been in the New World for nearly two hundred years, the English, off and on, for over a century. His birth coincided with the planting of the first permanent English colony in America. He was a schoolboy and a budding Puritan in the year of the Plymouth landing, a prodigiously learned man at the time of the great migration to Massachusetts Bay. All during these years, reports from the New World and writings about it poured from the English press, changing readers' minds about the shape of the world and of human history and about their own place in these unfolding schemes. As a man who read everything, Milton can hardly have been unconcerned with these intellectual upheavals, especially given the presence of several prominent colonial adventurers among his colleagues in the Cromwellian government and of large numbers of his coreligionists in the emigrant population. It is never safe to assume that Milton did not know or care about something that was there to be known; it would seem downright foolhardy to entertain such an assumption regarding an event as literally earthshaking as the collision between the Old World and the New was proving itself to be, every day of his life. We can no more imagine a Milton unaware of, or indifferent to, these upheavals than we can remove ourselves from the world they have produced.

Nevertheless, the evidence—or, rather, the lack of it—appears to lend credibility to this otherwise incredible notion that Milton thought very little about what the discovery and settlement of the New World were doing to his old one. The concordances, encyclopedias, and geographical dictionaries that modern scholarship has compiled to aid the navigator upon Miltonic seas contain few if any references to America, leading one to conclude that the subject touched the poet's consciousness very seldom and then with only a glancing blow. Even those Miltonists whose chosen topics of research would seem to place especial value on data of this sort end up finding very little to their purpose. Coming to Milton from two books on the influence of the New World voyagers upon Elizabethan literature, Robert R. Cawley was obviously on the alert for similar New World echoes when he did the research for *Milton and the Literature of Travel* (1951). The notable absence of the word "influence" in Cawley's title, however, betrays a certain disappointment. Although Cawley manages to establish Milton's familiarity with Peter Heylyn's *Cosmographia* (1652), Raleigh's *Discoverie of . . . Guiana* (1596), and the collections of Samuel Purchas (1613, 1625), he turns up very few direct references to America in the poetry itself. He does notice that, having relied largely on classical and biblical sources for the geographical ideas expressed in his earlier writings, Milton turned to modern authorities like Heylyn during the composition of *Paradise Lost,* only to return to the Ancients throughout the remainder of his career. Cawley can even say that *Paradise Lost* "contains, for a work basically classical and Biblical, an extraordinary amount of geographical material of the new kind" (141). The fact remains, however, that America itself figures quite insignificantly in the modern geography of the poem—astonishingly so, given the importance of New World discovery and exploration in the genesis of these new theories.

Only once, so far as I have been able to discover, has an explicit case been made for an American presence in Milton's poetry. In a paper read before the 1981 International Milton Conference, Jackie DiSalvo lists the probable sources of Milton's knowledge about British America and then identifies in *Paradise Lost*—especially in the account of Satan's voyage, the description of Eden, and the morphology of Adam's fall—poetic redactions of the colonists' reported experiences at sea, in the American wilderness, and with its native inhabitants. A seemingly routine exercise in the "new historicism," DiSalvo's essay is in fact quite remarkable, first for its uniqueness among Milton studies and second for the very curious response it got at the conference. If her propositions are as plausible and her evidence as visible as she makes them seem, why have the American ingredients of *Paradise Lost* gone unnoticed by generations of American Miltonists, ever on the lookout for something new to say about this much-studied poem? And if her argument is in fact original, revealing a whole new allusive aspect of the poem, why did her respondent, Jon S. Lawry, greet her paper with a flurry of quibbles and irrelevancies whose purpose seems less to confront the argument than to wish it away?

DiSalvo, Lawry says, has noted most of the American references in the poem, and further research along this line would add nothing significant. At the same time, she has failed to include among Milton's possible sources of information about the New World reports from Quaker Pennsylvania—although Lawry himself offers no evidence that Milton knew these documents. In any case, Milton, as a typologist, "would have found very little interest in the specific time and place of the New World" (34). If one is determined to find American allusions in Milton, the portraits of Satan and the wilderness in *Paradise Regained* are much closer to "the image Milton would have had of the New World" (35); but, really, the important connections between Milton and America lie not in its influence on him but in his influence upon it, particularly upon the Christian humanism of Harvard College, Cotton Mather, and the Transcendentalists.

Together, DiSalvo's originality and Lawry's response suggest not so much an utter want of American elements in *Paradise Lost* as a powerful disinclination among American Miltonists to look for such elements or to acknowledge them when someone points them out. To be sure, DiSalvo's ability to uncover allusions hitherto unseen is owing in part to her critical method, which, by regarding the historical thing signified as well as the poetic signifier as a text, reveals metaphoric connections that remain hidden to traditional historicisms. Even so, criticism usually manages to discover whatever it seeks, and the fact that America had not previously been found in *Paradise Lost* at least suggests a lack of critical desire to find it. It is also true that the American ingredients that DiSalvo identifies in the poem have been so thoroughly metabolized by Milton's antique theology as to make very little apparent difference to our conception of its overall structure and argument. Although they add to the poem, they do not seem to condition significantly its historical or cosmological vision. To say that, however, is quite different from attempting, as Lawry does, to deny DiSalvo's findings any value whatsoever, as if in pointing out Milton's apparent interest in America she had discovered in the poet something perfectly shameful, like a secret affection for the romances of Mademoiselle de Scudéry.

This tendency of Americans to forget themselves when looking into Milton is particularly noticeable in Margerie Hope Nicholson's *The Breaking of the Circle* (1960). A model of both historical learning and critical self-awareness, her book is concerned directly with Milton's ambivalence toward the discoveries of the new science, as reflected in Adam's curiosity and Raphael's cautions regarding the existence of other inhabited worlds (8.1–178). Despite her mastery of Milton's sources, however, Nicholson never suggests that these other worlds may well have been associated in Milton's mind with America, even though current speculations about human life in space received their primary motivation, their only evidence, and much of their language from reports of the discovery of inhabited lands in the Western Hemisphere. Nor, despite her acute consciousness of her own modern perspective on the poem, does she observe that the same connection might occur quite naturally to American readers, who, accustomed to thinking about space exploration as a replay of New World conquest, can hardly help perceiving their own history foreshadowed in Adam's unchecked imaginings. While it must be said in Nicholson's defense that book 8 of *Paradise Lost* never names America and that Raphael denies Adam's other worlds any value as an object of human aspirations, her uncharacteristic failure to detect in this passage a connection at once historical, critical, and directly germane to her topic looks less like an oversight than a repression—a disinclination, like Lawry's, to see what is there to be seen.

All together, the findings of Cawley and DiSalvo, Lawry's pettifoggery, and Nicholson's uncharacteristic oversight suggest that America's inveterate regard for Milton, and for *Paradise Lost* above all his poems, arises from a feeling of particular involvement in that poem and a wish to be excluded from it at the same time. For reasons that *Paradise Lost* itself will not fully explain, American Miltonists prefer it to anything else in the oeuvre, devoting more pages of criticism to it than to all the rest combined. Unless we take the evidentially unsupportable position that *Paradise Lost* is inherently superior to, say, *Paradise Regained*, we must locate the cause of this preference at least partly in the peculiar situation of Milton's modern American audience, who seem to see in the earlier epic something missing from the sequel, some desired reflection of themselves. What this image is and why its perception must be disguised both by Miltonists and by Americanists are questions worth considering.

To see where America figures in *Paradise Lost,* we must start back two hundred years before the discovery, with Dante's consignment of Ulysses to Hell in canto 26 of *Inferno,* for having presumed to sail outside the sanctified circle of the known world in search of a "new land" (127). According to the sacramental cartography of Dante's time, this exorbitant westward voyage would have taken Ulysses and his infatuated crew down the vertical member of the aqueous tau cross formed by the intersection, at Jerusalem, of the Tanais River, flowing from the north, or left; the Nile, extending south, or right; and the Mediterranean Sea, reaching downward from the Holy Sepulchre, the center of the human world and its point of contact with the divine, to the Pillars of Hercules, its westernmost conjunction with the encircling Ocean Sea. Like a T set inside an O, this cruciform body of waters divides the Island of Earth into Asia, Africa, and Europe—the realms of Noah's three sons—and connects the temporal circumference at three points to the eternal center, thus revealing to anyone who looks at it aright, from God's point of view, the divine justification of human history by the sacrifice of the Son. This is the stage constructed by God for the drama of human redemption. The only journey it permits or values is a pilgrimage from the historical periphery to the Holy Land at the center—which is to say, for Europeans, eastward or "up." Although Ulysses lived before the Christian revelation, the eternal law made itself known through his domestic affections and duties. By rejecting his "fondness for [his] son, . . . reverence / for [his] aged father, [and] Penelope's claim / to the joys of love" (89–91) in order to "experience the world beyond the sun" (109), therefore, he removes himself from the still center of the turning world to the ever-restless sea of a history without end—from Heaven to Hell.

Specifically, Ulysses is condemned for his evil counsel, his having abused the divine gift of eloquence to enlist his companions in his unholy quest for "manhood . . . out of the world of man" (111, 116), for "experience . . . beyond the world" (109, 122), and for mortal fame as a discoverer of lands never before seen by men (125). Himself driven by "the lust to experience the far-flung world" (92), Ulysses tells his crew, "You were not born to live like brutes, / but to press on toward manhood and recognition" (110–11), so to persuade them that their true selves are to be found not in obedience to the eternal laws bespoken by the domestic and social order but in human history, through individual ambition, defiance of authority, and desire for personal knowledge. It is, as Ulysses tells Dante, a "fool's flight" (117). Ambition violates the divinely ordained hierarchy of being. By making himself his own author, Ulysses makes himself his own end as well, while curiosity effectually denies the omniscient God by suggesting that unless men know a thing, it will not be known.

Accordingly, after Ulysses's ship has passed the Pillars of Hercules, which warn "all men back from further voyage" (102), and, after crossing the Line into the Southern Hemisphere, has raised on the horizon "a peak so tall" that he doubts "any man had seen the like" (124, 125), the crew no sooner cheers the discovery than a storm, commanded by "another" (129), breaks "from the new land" (127) and strikes the ship with three damaging blows and then a "fourth," which sinks Ulysses beneath the sea, removing him forever from the light (130–31). Whether or not the "other" who orders this final storm is other than the Trinity as well as Ulysses, it clearly presides over this fourth part of the world, the antipodes, and is provoked to fury by the explorer's desire to make history, rather than merely to enact a destiny written by God before time was.

Two hundred years after Dante, Amerigo Vespucci removed the New World from the *Inferno* to the *Purgatorio* in order to justify in his own case aspirations like those that had sunk Ulysses. "Very desirous of being the author who should identify the polar star of the other hemisphere," Vespucci unblushingly admits in a letter to Lorenzo de' Medici, "I lost many a night's sleep in contemplation of the motion of the stars. . . . While I was at this work I recalled a passage of the poet Dante which occurs in the first chapter of the 'purgatorio,' in which he invents a fiction of a flight into the heavens in our celestial hemisphere and his finding himself in the other hemisphere. Endeavoring to describe the Antarctic pole, he says:

> [I turned then to my right and set my mind
> on the other pole, and there I saw four stars
> unseen by mortals since the first mankind.
>
> The heavens seemed to revel in their light.
> O Widowed Northern Hemisphere, bereft
> forever of the glory of that sight! (1.23–28)]

"It seems to me," Vespucci continues, "that the poet in these verses wishes to describe by the 'four stars' the pole of the other firmament, and I have no reason to doubt that what he says may be true; because I observed four stars in the figure of a cithern, which had little motion. If God grants me life and health, I hope to return at once to that hemisphere and not come back without identifying the pole" (Parry 177–78).

Dante makes his presence felt again, albeit implicitly, in Ves-

pucci's "fancy" that South America is the site of the Terrestial Paradise (187), which the *Commedia* locates atop the mountain seen by
Ulysses just before the storm ends his wanderings. Whether or not
Vespucci shared with Dante—as well as with Columbus (137)—the
belief that no one could ascend to that place except by God's permis-
sion, he never suggests that he is doing something forbidden. On the
contrary, he takes pride in disproving established authority, both
classical—as when he asserts "that by this voyage of mine the opinion of the majority of philosophers is confuted" (180)—and
scriptural—as when, having noted the variety of animals in Brazil,
he doubts that "so many species could . . . have entered Noah's ark"
(187). It is not the cautionary Dante but the adventurous Ulysses,
liberated from the moral universe of the *Commedia*, whose voice we
hear in Vespucci's remark: "Rationally, let it be said in a whisper,
experience is certainly worth more than theory" (180).

It is Ulysses, once again, who speaks throughout the pages of
Richard Hakluyt's *Voyages:* condemning "the fault and foolish
slouth of many in our nation, choosing rather to live indirectly . . .
then [sic] to adventure as becommeth men" (6:23); attributing to
God himself both the motivation for Columbus's voyages (47) and
the awakening of certain Englishmen "out of that drowsie dream,
wherein we have so long slumbered" (48); scolding those who "like
dormice have slumbered in ignorance" of the New World or who
resemble "cats that are loth for their prey to wet their feet" (71);
claiming authority on the basis of the writer's hardship, "which
some know by reading histories . . . , I by experience in my selfe"
(336); vaunting the unprecedented knowledge afforded by the discovery of that "fourth part of the world . . . unknowen unto our
ancestours" (232); celebrating that "paradise of the world" (163)
about which what is known "is nothing to that which remaineth to
be discovered" (193); and reiterating tirelessly the saw, "Nothing
venture, nothing have" (87).

That Ulysses' evil counsels of ambition, curiosity, and disdain
for constituted authority were becoming the parlance of virtue and
reason is apparent in the writings of Hakluyt's contemporary, Montaigne. In his address "To the Reader" Montaigne takes as the ideal
of artless sincerity "those nations which are said to live still in the

sweet freedom of nature's first laws" (2), and in his essay "Of Canni-
bals" he repeatedly uses the discovery of America to qualify, if not to
discredit, the opinions of the Ancients and to supplant these with
the personal experiences of the New World voyager, a "simple, crude
fellow . . . fit to bear true witness . . . and wedded to no theory"
(151–52). Indeed, the *essai* itself, as Montaigne conceives that genre,
resembles the voyage to an unknown destination which simultaneously discovers and invents the true character of the author-
voyager, thus translating from America to the scene of writing Columbus's realization that "[t]he farther one goes, the more one
learns" (141).

This is not to say that Montaigne was an unqualified modernist
who regarded the forms of history, the self, and reality as arising
entirely from human action. Although the discovery of America
showed him that much remained unknown and that human character would change in the course of learning it, he appears to have
retained the medieval belief that all such historical developments
occur within a divinely instituted form of reality which, however
ineffable, precedes, governs, and lends ultimate meaning to all human action. The discovery of lands and peoples formerly unknown
did discredit "the testimony of antiquity" (151), forcing Europe,
"which had believed itself to be complete and in its final form," as
Lévi-Strauss says, to realize "that it was not alone . . . and that, in
order to achieve self-knowledge, it must first of all contemplate its
unrecognizable image in this mirror" (102). At the same time, the
naturalness that the New World populations seemed to share with
the Ancients persuaded Montaigne, among many others, that by
progressing westward, in the direction of human history, Europe
might arrive again at the pristine beginnings from which it had long
since departed. Instead of disproving the theory of history as a circu-
lar journey through time to its starting point, America might simply
enlarge the circumference of the human pilgrimage, adding to the
tripartite world a fourth part, of still unknown extent, and, by reori-
enting that circle from the vertical to the horizontal plane, locate its
beginning and ending on the surface of the globe rather than in
Augustine's heavenly "home" (89). Because this new geometry
placed America within the sanctified circle that had previously ex-

cluded the Western hemisphere, the New World voyagers eagerly adopted it in order to justify extravagances of the very sort that had done in Dante's Ulysses. "The revolution and course of Gods word," Martin Frobisher wrote in 1584, " . . . from the beginning hath moved from the East, towards & at last unto the West, where it is like to end" (Hakluyt, *Voyages* 6.4).

When, some eighty years further into England's colonial enterprise, Milton gave the sentiments of Vespucci, Montaigne, and Hakluyt's voyagers to Satan and put them back in Hell, he expressed quite plainly his opposition to this secular redaction of the divine plan for human history. *Paradise Lost* is thoroughly informed by Milton's doubt that the desires America had awakened and had come to symbolize, America would also satisfy. With characteristic prescience, he saw at a glance what it would take his successors nearly three centuries to realize: that the projection of individual desire westward through time and space would not justify that desire by bringing human history, in Emerson's words, "full circle" to its "rounding complete grace" (115) but would instead remove humankind irredeemably from all possibility of absolute justification into a history without beginnings or endings or final form.

Not even Walt Whitman, standing far enough along in that pilgrimage of desire to have seen "the rondure of the world at last accomplished" but nothing yet to "justify these restless explorations," could altogether abandon the belief that human history had some "inscrutable purpose, some hidden prophetic intention" that would redeem it from error and absurdity (414–15). How, then, could Milton, who had his own reasons for doubting the sanctity of human desires, either identify their dominant present object, America, with the divine scheme of redemption or simply forsake the ancient faith in ultimate purposes for a modern conception of value and meaning as mere historical contingencies endlessly subject to endless change? The discovery of America had inflamed the European spirit of ambition, curiosity, rebelliousness, and hunger for experience by lending these desires an apparent justification. For that reason, America had to be confronted. As a geographical and historical entity, a mere projection of desire, however, America could not possibly absolve all the human folly and error it occasioned. And for that reason, it had to be denied a place in the scheme of redemption.

Intended or not, the association in *Paradise Lost* between Satan's project and the American adventure is rhetorically unmistakable. The rumored creation he means to seek out is referred to repeatedly as "this new world" (1.650; 2.403; 4.34, 113; 10.257), the name coined by Vespucci and universally adopted to designate the discovered western lands. It is "another world" (2.347, 2.1004, 10.237)—one both additional to and different from that already known. And, like America in the European mind, it is the geographical locus of unfulfilled desire: a "happy isle" (2.410), "our last hope" (2.416), a "heav'n on earth" (4.208), where the unfortunate may "hope to change / Torment with ease" (4.892–93), "Heav'n's last best gift" (5.19), a place where "Hesperian fables" can at last come true (4.250–51).

Satan, the seeker after this undiscovered land, bears all the traits that readers of Hakluyt and Purchas had come to associate with New World voyagers. He is curious (2.838–39), restive under constraint, resolute (1.252–53), personally ambitious (2.7–8), imaginative (2.11), energetic (2.13), and a self-made man (4.859–61) who, like Columbus and John Smith, identifies his own advancement with the commonweal (2.481–82). From the beginning, he is associated with the wealth of the Indies (2.4–5), with the India merchants (2.636–42), with the Portuguese navigators of the African cape (4.159–65), and with Milton's acquaintance Galileo, who himself, Germán Arcineagas tells us (84), once sought to succeed Vespucci as pilot major of the Spanish fleets then plying the western ocean. Satan's voyage from the Hell in which God has imprisoned him to those more temperate regions (2.397) which he means to possess (2.840–41) is planned in Pandemonium, a council of colonial adventurers who have already been compared to mariners (2.285–90) and will comport themselves, after his departure, like the companions of John Smith on the Chesapeake, digging mines and exploring the rivers that feed their newfound lake (2.570 ff).

The voyage itself takes Satan through the Herculean Pillars of

Hell's gates, across the "illimitable ocean" of Chaos (2.892) on "sail-broad" wings (2.927), past a Sargasso that is "neither sea, / Nor good dry land" (2.939–40), to a prospect of Heaven and the immensely relieving discovery that "his sea should find a shore" (2.1011). Here, he surveys his landfall, experiencing the rapture of every New World explorer from Columbus at San Salvador to Keats's "stout Cortez . . . / Upon a peak in Darien" (34). And when, having corrupted the natives of this pristine land, made them slaves, and opened the door to colonization, he returns to Hell, he recounts his adventures in a perfect parody of those narratives framed by voyagers to elevate themselves from obscurity to consequence through carefully fashioned tales of their own resourcefulness and selfless bravery (10.460–503).

These American echoes in *Paradise Lost* imply an American presence among the voices that called the poem into being. Milton's stated intention to "assert Eternal Providence / And justify the ways of God to men" (1.26–27) indicates that these matters have come into question. Had no one ever doubted the existence of eternal providence or the justice of God's ways, Milton would hardly have felt called upon to assert the one and justify the other. Who these doubters are and which of God's ways they have deemed unjust, the poem does not say. The amplitude and elaborateness of Milton's rebuttal, however, suggest that these charges possessed both currency and force in the mid-seventeenth century, while the specific actions—diabolical and human, as well as divine—that preoccupy the narrative permit us to infer the arguments that occasioned it.

Since everything that happens in the poem arises initially from Lucifer's frustrated ambition and consequent rebelliousness, and ultimately from Satan's excitement of Eve's curiosity, ambition, intractability, and appetite for experience, it appears to be the proscription of these desires that has been called unreasonable and that Milton is most concerned to justify. Why, voices offstage seem to be asking—why should God prohibit a set of innate propensities that have recently demonstrated their virtue in the overthrow of tyrants, the conquest of superstition by science, the improvement of material life, the multiplication of human opportunities, and, not least, the discovery of a long-hidden world whose vast extent and bound-less wealth promise to requite every natural desire for dominion, station, and knowledge? Are the customary injunctions to unques-tioning obedience, deference, and resignation perhaps not divine commandments at all but merely human concoctions, laws enacted by self-appointed rulers to protect their own interests and then as-cribed to God in order to place their authority beyond dispute? Re-ports from the New World tell again and again of savage shamans cowing the credulous with pretended supernatural powers. May not the whole doctrine of inherited human frailty and of compensatory social hierarchies be impositions of just the same sort, Dark Age superstitions claiming divine sanction but insupportable in the face of experience and reason?

Such questions would have been provoking enough had Milton been a tropistic reactionary, quick to see heresy in any restive stir-rings among the subordinate classes. They required particular at-tention because they expressed his own radical Protestantism in a dangerously perverted form. America had produced no self-reliant voyager more scornful of entrenched authority, more confident of individual perfectibility through reason, or more thirsty for knowledge—in a word, more enlightened—than he. But if this faith in the ability of individuals to know the truth and to act upon it was to be validated and justified, the desire for self-government, personal fulfillment, and complete knowledge had to be detached from what-ever objects it might set itself and redirected toward eternal objects that, having been set by God, remain unaffected by the vagaries of human action and, hence, able to direct and justify it. Disinclined by temperament and training either to condemn desire altogether or to let it chart its own historical course, Milton aimed to reconcile the increasingly apparent conflict between human aspiration and subor-dination to divine law. To that end, the desire for station, knowledge, experience, and personal liberty had to be shown to play a crucial part in the divine history of human salvation revealed in Scripture.

Satan sees the world the way we do, like one who carries a candle in a cave. Only the present is visible. What lies ahead exists only in anticipation, in desire or dread. The path already traveled is only a memory. Shifting endlessly in time and space, the present view continually reshapes both what is expected and what is remembered and is itself conditioned by these continually metamorphosing images. This is the view of the explorer in terra incognita, an unmapped place of unknown size, form, and meaning that seems to precede discovery and yet to arise from it as well. Satan's knowledge of the newly created world consists entirely of fables and rumors, which his own experience corroborates or revises. Having removed himself from Heaven, the seat of knowledge, he does not know the origins, purpose, and end of the creation or the role he has been assigned to play in that history. To him, the world is coterminous with his desires, experiences, and memories, which he takes to be a sufficient source of truth.

Against this limited and time-bound view, this subjectivity that would assemble reality like a jigsaw puzzle from accumulating pieces of experience, Milton posits the unconditioned, comprehensive view of God, which takes in all creation and all time in an immediate, eternal instant. This is the view for which Milton begs the "Heav'nly Muse" (1.6) in the opening invocation. It is the vision that enables God to foresee Satan's success in corrupting the world and supplies the lessons that Raphael and Michael teach to Adam. It reveals a creation laid out as land looks on a map, with all its parts existing simultaneously in timeless space, forming a clear picture of God's immutable designs. From this absolute coign of vantage, time, too, appears all at once, with its beginning, its ending, and everything in between laid out like a chart. Just as the map of the cosmos discloses the harmonious totality of space that Satan sees only piecemeal and seriatim, the map of time displays the complete history in which he is unwittingly engaged: the story of his antagonism against the Son, his initial victory at the time of the Fall, his declining powers after the Incarnation, and his ultimate defeat at Armageddon.

To see the world and history this way, in its complete, eternal form, is to be free of all the limitations that come to Satan with his rebellion and to humankind with the Fall—those conditions Emerson calls "Illusion, Temperament, Succession, Surface, Surprise, Reality, Subjectiveness" and lumps together under the heading

"Experience" (272). Only in the knowledge and the willing acceptance of this divinely instituted form is freedom possible. As the sole source, the very being, of power, station, reason, and life itself, this form alone offers an escape from impotence, debasement, ignorance, and death. Those who mistake submission to the eternal form of truth for subjection by an arbitrary, unjust tyrant and seek freedom, as Lucifer does, through rebellion or, as Adam and Eve do, through disobedience soon find themselves not free, as Abdiel warns (6.181), but to themselves enthralled. In assuming control over their own actions, they exchange an all-seeing master for a blind one who, lacking God's eternal comprehension, can neither foresee the consequences of any act nor redeem an action whose consequences prove unbearable. Those who choose to create themselves, their own world, and their own history become the helpless victims of their own self-created fate.

The alternatives could not be clearer. On the one side, there is willing submission to God's absolute authority. Omnipresent, he is inescapable. Benevolent, his designs can be trusted. Omniscient, he relieves his creatures of the necessity of knowing more than their duty. To submit is to be content. On the other side is the desire to know more, to equal God by learning from experience what he knows by virtue of his unconditioned being. But these are "Vain hopes, vain aims, inordinate desires / Blown up with high conceits engend'ring pride" (4.808–9). Ambition betrays an ignorance of the order and purposes of creation. Curiosity denies the existence of the all-knowing God by implying that what humans do not know must remain unknown. Learning from experience is learning from error, and to err is to wander away from the truth—that Heavenly home from which all creation sprang and to which it is returning. "O pity and shame," Adam exclaims, "that they who to live well / Entered so fair, should turn aside to tread / Paths indirect" (11.630–32).

Milton has a word for this blind errancy: "adventure," the hunger for the forbidden unknown and for the imagined benefits its discovery will bring. Adam has been told to "Dream not of other worlds, what creatures there / Live, in what state, condition, or degree" (8.175–76) but to rest "contented" in what has been revealed to him. For, as Adam says, what is only imagined must be sought by "wandering thoughts," and since the fancy is apt "to rove / Un-checked," "of her roving is no end" (8.187–89). This is the lesson Adam has in mind when, discovering Eve's transgression, he calls her "advent'rous" (9.121). This term, which is synonymous with the words "inordinate" (unlawful), "exorbitant" (outside the sanctified circle), and "extravagant" (wandering), associates Eve's impious act with the building of the causeway from Hell to Earth, which Sin calls "Advent'rous work" (10.255), and with Satan's expedition, that "search / Of foreign worlds" he calls "my adventure hard" (10.441, 468).

Given all these associations of the word with impious action, we cannot help but remark its application to the poem itself, which the narrator introduces as his "advent'rous song" (1.13). Why would Milton have chosen to associate his composition, whose purpose is to justify God's punishment of excessive appetite, with the actions of Eve, Sin, and Satan, the main exemplars of that appetite and its baneful consequences, rather than with the cautionary, anti-adventurous spirit of God, the Son, Abdiel, Raphael, and Michael, who speak the lessons that the poem aims to teach? The answer appears to be that, far from condemning human desire out of hand or wishing it away, Milton acknowledges its power and seeks to redi-rect it from improper, human objects abroad in time and space to its proper, divine object in eternity. Although no less a human action than any transatlantic quest for empire, this poetic adventure as-pires upward, toward the eternal form that comprehends all time and space and owes nothing to the historical act of discovery. Instead of ranging afield, the poem will fly above the pagan epics to a place alongside Holy Writ. It aims to recover something lost in the course of human wandering, not to discover through further wandering something altogether new. And for his pilot, Milton calls upon a "Heav'nly Muse" (1.6), who can show him all creation and all his-tory laid out in their eternal design, the way God sees them, not upon the spirit of Columbus, who, earth-bound himself, merely dis-covered more fallen creatures in America (9.1116–17).

Even so, the emphasis, the spirit of the poem seems to lie more in its adventurous action than in its justifying moral form—especially when we compare it to Dante's *Commedia*. There, the form—of truth, of creation, and of history—completely surrounds the action, which it inspires and wholly governs. It is completely present at all times, supplying at every stage the absolute meaning of the narrative, which completely fills it. In *Paradise Lost*, on the contrary, information about the form of creation and history lies scattered about in the narrative, from which it must be extracted bit by bit and assembled if we would have a picture of the whole design. And when, with patient care and the help of practiced Miltonists, we finally comprehend the structure of creation and of the long struggle between the Son and Satan, we see that the action proper fills only a tiny portion of that form, the remainder being sketched in by means of summary and prophetic allusion. The form of the *Commedia* is predominantly spatial, an unchanging stage upon which the action occurs. That of *Paradise Lost* is mainly temporal, historical, arising gradually out of the action and depending upon that action for our knowledge of it. Above all, the form of space and time that Dante describes was, for him and his readers, literally true. Milton's Ptolemaic universe is, by his own admission, a convenient fiction— a supreme fiction, to be sure, but not something to be confused with observable reality more than a century after the death of Copernicus, in a world charted by Brahe, Kepler, Galileo, and, of course, Columbus.

It is this diminution in the structural and logical status of justifying, absolute form in *Paradise Lost* and its attendant emphasis upon the narrative action and the inordinate desires behind that action that give the poem, for all its outspoken animus against scientific curiosity, social ambition, political intransigence, and personal hunger for experience, its peculiar attraction, among theistic texts, for humanist, modern readers. The necessity of reminding generation after generation of American students that Satan is wrong, that his arguments are specious and his desires self-defeating, only shows that they see in him the advocate and example of everything they have learned to call virtue. Which of them wants to be considered unambitious, incurious, docile, content with their native circumstances? We can patiently reconstruct for them God's creation, with all its concentric orbs, retractable stairs, and golden chains; we can lay out the ordained scheme of history that begins with the begetting of the Son, climaxes in his incarnation, and concludes in his victory over Sin and Death; we can explain the compatability of divine fore-knowledge with free will, and they will write it all down on the final examination. But they will attribute their own existence to desires, like Satan's, to deny constituted authority; like Adam's, to learn about hidden matters; and, like Eve's, to discover the place of "nations yet unborn" (4.663). Quite rightly, too, for if everything had been as the divine law says it should have been, they would not be here to learn about their evil origins.

Considered in the light of its stated intentions, *Paradise Lost* is very much a product of its time and place. The poem aims to stem the rising tide of enlightened humanism, swollen by revolutionary developments in science and politics, and to reaffirm the absolute authority of divine providence by showing that the unsettled present, far from discrediting the scriptural world-picture, arises directly from the events recounted in Genesis and points directly to the apocalypse prophesied in Revelation. According to this theistic scheme, everything begins in God and ends there, outside historical time and material space. Apart from this eternal form, there is no justification for human history, no end to suffering, error, and death. If men mistake their divinely destined end for something achievable in time and space, through their own unaided actions, they condemn themselves to an endless quest for the endlessly receding objects of their own unstable desires. Paradise cannot be discovered on Earth, as Columbus and Vespucci had led Europe to suppose. It was destroyed in the Flood (11.829–38), and the Americans Columbus found were already "girt / With feathered cincture" (9.1116–17), like the fallen Adam and Eve.

The modern reader, however, receives this impassioned theodicy in a world created by precisely those aspirations that the poem so vividly dramatizes in order to discredit. Between us and Milton stretch three centuries of human effort to achieve in this world what he maintained could be found only in Heaven. The result of all this adventuring is largely what he predicted. We find ourselves in a history with no apparent origin or conclusion or justifying design, where "the end of our lives," as George Eliot's Maggie Tulliver laments, "will have nothing in it like the beginning" (209). This definitively modern condition Gertrude Stein equated with America, a "space of time" (*Writings* 258) whose story has no "beginnings or endings" (*Narration* 23). And so, it must seem to us, does *Paradise Lost*. In Milton's pointed exclusion of America from a redemptive scheme we have long since abandoned and in his morally derisive but poetically moving dramatization of American attitudes we read the story of our departure from the Old World, where history would end in a paradise regained, to this altogether New World, where, as Melville put it, stories "have no proper endings; but in imperfect, unanticipated, and disappointing sequels (as mutilated stumps) hurry to abrupt intermergings with the eternal tides of time and fate" (141).

America's fascination with a British poet seemingly oblivious to America appears to illustrate Robert Weisbuch's diagnosis of that cultural malaise he calls the "Atlantic double-cross": the tendency of American writers to fret over British influences in a way that British writers never reciprocate. While evidences of transatlantic influence can be found on both shores, Weisbuch contends, the British cases "all lack the refusing force," the symptoms of anxiety, we find in American writings (26). Like all such generalizations, this one fairly begs us to think of exceptions. The surprising thing in this case is how readily they spring to mind. Indeed, when British writing is examined in this light, it appears to be filled with refusals of American influence, extending all the way from Prospero's rejection of Caliban to F. W. Bateson's dismissal of Pound and Eliot as significant forces in the development of English poetry (6). In view of so much contrary evidence, Weisbuch's assertions of American difference seem less a description of national anxiety than an instance of it. Whether or not American writers have worried more about seeming British than the British have about becoming American, Weisbuch's apparent need to say so, coupled with the absence of any comparable study of American influences on British writing, does seem to bear out his basic contention—as well as to support the impression created by Milton criticism—that Americans think about England in a way that Britons do not think about America: as a potential threat to their national identity.

And yet, a case could be made that, at least since the Revolution, educated Englishmen have thought about almost nothing else but the impact of America, whether baneful or salubrious, upon British institutions, especially upon the English language, from which England's literature is made. The evidence for such a case is certainly no less abundant or conclusive than that which has been adduced again and again to distinguish American writings in English from their British counterparts. That this evidence of British resistance has never been assembled and interpreted suggests not so much its scarcity or inadequacy as its impertinence to the agenda of English and American studies in the United States. For reasons that only a complete history of our English departments could explain, Milton's literary value seems to depend on his perceived detachment from America, just as Melville's reputation seems to demand his separation from all things British. To suggest that Hawthorne's *The House of the Seven Gables* belongs to English literature in the same way that Rousseau's *Confessions* belongs to French literature, it is generally assumed, would simultaneously put the novel in unfavorable competition with *Bleak House* and call into question the very idea of an autocthonous American literature that gives Americanists their institutional identity and authority. To suggest, as Jackie DiSalvo has, that *Paradise Lost* is a more American poem than, say, Bradstreet's "Contemplations," it seems, would not only disgrace Milton but lower the cultural eminence from which specialists in "English literature," especially the American ones, condescend to America's literary pretensions.

This view of the matter suggests that English and American studies in this country are acting out an intradepartmental version of what Stephen Spender has called the "love-hate relations" between England and America proper. While the Americanists devote themselves exclusively to writings in English, maintaining that these are not English, the Miltonists concentrate upon *Paradise Lost,* the most American of his poems according to Cawley, never asking themselves what it is about this particular work that so appeals to them and slapping down anyone like DiSalvo who timidly suggests an answer. Led to the study of English literature in part by a deep distaste for modern, "Americanized" life, Americans find a spiritual ally in *Paradise Lost,* which, by simultaneously addressing and denying the history that has produced them, permits them, for as long as the spell lasts, to feel superior to themselves. While Americanists simultaneously see *Paradise Lost* wherever they look but deny the poem a place in the national literature for fear of destroying their subject, the Miltonists devote their ministrations not to *Paradise Regained,* wherein the original pre-American world is recovered on a new and timeless ground, but to the poem that ends with the departure of our first parents from the old world to face a new, unknown world that "lies all before them" (12.646) and includes us.

Only by removing *Paradise Lost* from the nationalistic satrapies of our English departments can we see that, despite Milton's citizenship, his poem is American in its circumstances of production, in its circumstances of reception, and in the historical development that connects these two points. What has raised *Paradise Lost* over all Milton's other writings in the American canon of English literature is not aesthetic superiority or any other identifiable feature of the text. It is, rather, the adaptability of that poem to the cultural requirements of Americans, its ability to reflect in the most flattering guise our own deeply conflicted feelings regarding the Old World that necessarily excludes us and the New World that has, by now, just about completed its five-hundred-year project of obliterating the Old. What makes *Paradise Lost* a poem for Americans is not its occasional allusions to such New World things as "Rich Mexico the seat of Montezume / And Cusco in Peru, the richer seat / Of Atabalipa, and yet unspoiled / Guiana, whose great city Geryon's sons / Call El Dorado" (11:407–11), nor even such metaphoric displacements of colonial reports as DiSalvo so astutely identifies. It is, rather, our own ineluctable sense that America is at once the historical occasion for the poem, making it both necessary and possible, and the thing that must be denied, expunged, if that history is to be redeemed. If America had not been discovered, *Paradise Lost* would not have been written, and we would not be here to read—or to misread—it. As Milton himself might have said, it is American as Hell.

4

Columbus: The Early American History of an English Word

When Emerson named *Columbus** among "the mind's ministers" (271), he cannot have been speaking of the Genoese navigator who explored the Ocean Sea for Spain at the end of the fifteenth century. In the first place, Emerson, like everyone else, then and since, knew very little about that long-dead person, and the little he did know was at best conjectural and in any case indistinguishable from posthumous legend. In the second place, the navigator himself could hardly have spoken on behalf of any nineteenth-century mind, since he died altogether unaware of the existence of the world that would inhabit, and be inhabited by, such a mind. In his own mind, the places he visited during his four transoceanic voyages all lay in Asia, not, as they did for Emerson, along the eastern edge of two linked continents filling the Western Hemisphere and filled with transplanted Europeans who looked upon someone named *Columbus* as their discoverer.

Rather than an actual person, Emerson's *Columbus* is just a word, a particular selection and arrangement of letters that was adopted long after the navigator's death. By Emerson's time, it had come to stand for a complex set of ideas, images, associations, opinions, and connotations—in short, for a host of other

*This word is italicized throughout this chapter to remind the reader (and the writer no less) of something otherwise easily forgotten—that *Columbus* is a name, not a person, and that its use in English writing, not its supposed bearer, is the subject under inspection.

words. Some of these had attended its earliest appearance, many had arisen in Emerson's own lifetime, all clung to the word in Emerson's own mind and could be expected to spring up in the minds of his audience at the sight or sound of the word, but none would have made any sense to the captain of the *Santa María*.

On Emerson's lips and in the ears of his audience, the word *Columbus* would have automatically implied the sentence "Columbus discovered America." Indeed, it is this predication that allows Emerson to call *Columbus* a minister of the contemporary mind and to be understood. So far as we know, however, Spain's first emissary to "las Indias" never called himself *Columbus* or heard himself called that. Nor did he ever hear the name *America*, which was not coined until a year after his death and would not denote either the geographical entity or the nation known to Emerson by that name for another three hundred years. As for the verb *discovered*, that would have meant nothing to a man who knew no English. But even if he had known the language as it was spoken in his day, *discover* would not have meant to him what it did to Emerson, for, according to the *Oxford English Dictionary*, the verb was not used to mean "obtain sight or knowledge of (something previously unknown) for the first time" (3.432) until 1555—in an English translation, as it happens, of an account of the life and voyages of one "*Christophorus Colonus* (other wise called *Columbus*)" (Arber 65).

Amidst the many uncertainties that surround the life of the man who set out for Asia in 1492, one thing is fairly clear: *Columbus* was not his name. If the few surviving records can be trusted, he was born Cristoforo Colombo in Genoa and was known, successively, as Colom, during his years in Lisbon; Colomo, after his removal to Spain; then Colón, when he adopted that name in order to claim direct descent from the Roman general Colonius (a.k.a. Cilonius) and kinship with the French admiral Guillaume de Casaneuve, whose nickname was Coullon and who, like the pretender himself, was called Colombo in Italy. In contemporary Latin writings, these vernacular names take a number of different forms, including Colombo, Colonus, and Colom, but never *Columbus*. As for what the man in question called himself, Cecil Jayne is not quite accurate when he says, "In all his voluminous writings he never once men-

tions his name" (1.xxxi), since the evidently autographic prologue to
the *Diario* of the first voyage calls him Xpoual Colon (18). It is true,
however, that every other surviving self-reference employs either
his jealously guarded title El Almirante or some form of the crypto-
gram Xpo FERENS, which he adopted in 1493 as a sort of trademark,
presumably to protect the titles and lands given him by the Spanish
monarchs, and which remains uncertainly deciphered to this day.

Where the word *Columbus* originated is a mystery. It appears
first in Sebastian Münster's *Cosmographiae universalis* (1550), his
Latin translation of his own German *Cosmographia: Beschreibung
aller Lender*, published six years earlier. Münster's source, however,
remains obscure. He, or one of the many contributors to his volume,
may have known that the navigator's spurious kinsman Coullon
was called *Columbus* in Latin. Even so, there is no evidence that the
pretender himself did or that he adopted that name in order to support his claim of kinship. As a result, the paper trail breaks off in the
middle of the sixteenth century, almost fifty years this side of the
navigator's death, leaving an unclosable gap between the man and
the name—a man never known by that name and the name of a man
never known except by name.

Columbus entered the English language for the first time in
1553, by way of Richard Eden's partial translation of Münster's *Cosmographiae*, entitled *A Treatyse of the newe India*. Before that, few
if any English speakers would have seen or heard the name. Some
may have known the navigator himself, or known of him during his
lifetime. His brother Bartolomé is supposed to have petitioned
Henry VII for support of a westward voyage to Asia, around 1489; and
as an old man, Sebastian Cabot remembered the excitement in
Henry's court "when newes were brought that don Christopher Colonus Genuese had discovered the coasts of India" (Hakluyt, *Voyages* 25.86). If Hakluyt's third-hand report of Cabot's words can be
trusted, however, these English courtiers did not call the discoverer
Columbus. What they did call him is anybody's guess. No record of
his brother's mission survives, and the only letter supposed to have
been written to him by an Englishman of that time is in Spanish and
never refers to the addressee by name (Quinn, *New American World
[NAW]* 1.98). The discovery itself had been mentioned some nine

times in English publications prior to 1553. But since these early English references to the newfound lands all attribute the discovery either to Amerigo Vespucci or to no one in particular, Eden's translation of Münster may be said to mark the first time that English readers ever heard the name *Columbus* or heard of the person who supposedly bore that name.

Although *Columbus* came originally from another language, since 1553 it has been, to all intents and purposes, an English word, one used ordinarily by English speakers to designate the discoverer and seldom by anyone else. Whenever a later English document employs some other name, that variant is almost always marked as "foreign." In referring to "*Colonus* (other wise called *Columbus*)" in his translation of Pietro Martire, Richard Eden indicates that he is transcribing the original text exactly and suggests that the name he had introduced two years earlier had already become the accepted English usage. When Richard Hakluyt shifts from *Christopher Columbus* to *Christopher Colon* (*Voyages* 6.233), he is including among his "English Voyages" Laudonnière's French *Treatise on Florida;* and when he repeats that linguistic hybrid in his dedicatory epistle of 1600, he follows it immediately with the words "alias Columbus" (1.47). Firmly established by the end of the sixteenth century, the identification of *Columbus* with English has long since been taken for granted, so readily that a current debunker can use the word to distinguish the hero of Anglo-American myth from the decidedly unheroic *Colón* of supposed fact (Sale 364).

Although just a word, Emerson's *Columbus* was nonetheless exactly what he said, one of "the mind's ministers": a powerful agent for Emerson's own ideas and an equally powerful commander of the thoughts of anyone who heard or saw the word. In this sense, *Columbus* ministers to our minds no less than it did to Emerson's. It does so, however, to quite different effect, owing to changes, since 1845, in the other words that *Columbus* calls to mind. A signifier of heroic individual accomplishment in Emerson's time, *Columbus* is apt to stand today for predatory colonialism and the subjugation of indigenous peoples. And even where the other words evoked by *Columbus* remain the same—*conquest,* for example—their meanings have changed—in this case, from "victory" to "victimization"—altering drastically the force of the word itself. To its twentieth-century users, as to Emerson, *Columbus* denotes the founder of the present; but whereas the Genoese who sailed for Ferdinand and Isabella stopped changing (so far as anyone knows) on the day he died, *Columbus* has changed continually over the centuries in order to remain the discoverer of a continually changing modern world.

This is all to say that *Columbus* has a history: though the word has remained intact throughout the centuries since 1553, its meanings have changed continually during that time. This history has nothing, necessarily, to do with the life of a person called *Columbus* or with the development of knowledge or of ideas about that supposed person. As a name used almost exclusively by English speakers, none of whom has ever known its supposed bearer except by name, to designate someone who never bore that name, *Columbus* is, strictly speaking, a person in name only. Instead of designating someone otherwise known to exist, *Columbus* originally preceded its referent, bringing the man so called into being by naming him. As a result, every subsequent use of the name refers not to a person but to prior uses, including the statements attached to them. A semanticist would say that *Columbus* has meaning but no referent. I would say, rather, that the word always has a referent but that in any instance this referent is one of its meanings and that, like the rest of its meanings, its referents differ markedly from case to case. Richard Eden's "Gentleman of Italie" (Arber 28) and Robert Johnson's humble petitioner scorned for his "poore apparell and simple lookes" (Quinn, *NAW* 5.237) are not different views of one person; they are different persons identically named.

Insofar as *Columbus* is an English word whose meanings, including its various referents, consist entirely in other English words, its history is also distinct from those of the Spanish Colón, the French Colomb, the German Kolumbus, the Italian Colombo, and the Portuguese Colom. It may be that these different histories coincide at certain points and even take a roughly similar direction. Nonetheless, each is divided from the others by the peculiar structure and history of its own language; and, since the referents of all of these names are wholly the constructions of other words in their respective languages, no two of them can be considered identical by virtue of a common referent. When something is made of words, words alone count. To change the words is to change the thing. To change the language is to change the thing substantially, altering the very atmosphere from which all words draw their meanings. While Richard Eden clearly regarded Münster's *Columbus* and his own as the same person, his translation of Münster's Latin text into English changed the meaning of the word by removing it from the complex network of verbal associations provided by the original tongue and surrounding it with a whole new set of associations peculiar to English. To cite only one example: in Münster's Latin, *Columbus* is just a name; in Eden's translation it is a Latin name and hence something universal rather than provincial, an object of learning rather than of vulgar knowledge, something worth the attention of the sort of people who (unlike Eden's readers) know Latin.

Implicit in the idea of *Columbus* as an English word whose meanings have changed over time is an invitation to recover its semantic history. Compared, say, to the history of a nation and its literature, the history of a single word seems quite manageable. In fact, the tasks involved are staggering. Anyone undertaking a history of *Columbus* would have to begin by compiling a list of every surviving document that contains the word—an English equivalent of Guglielmo Berchet's *Fonti Italiane per la Storia della Scoperta del Nuovo Mondo*, volume 2 of which transcribes all known passages having to do with Cristoforo Colombo in books and manuscripts by Italian writers up to 1550. Instead of fifty years, however, the historian of *Columbus* would have to cover five hundred, in order to fill the space of time between Eden's *Columbus* and those of the present. To describe this task is to despair of its completion. Ample enough before 1800, the documented uses of the word fairly explode in the nineteenth century. Indeed, *Columbus* probably appeared in print more times during the decade surrounding the quatrocentennial than it had in the previous 350 years together. After that, the recorded instances of the word are simply uncountable. The production of "re-visioned" *Columbus*es for the quincentennial alone must certainly equal, if not surpass, that of 1892.

But even if the historian of *Columbus* could identify every surviving instance of the word in print and in manuscript, these would constitute at best a fossil record of a much larger and more complex linguistic ecosystem comprising not only those writings that happen to have survived but many others since lost, as well as countless spoken utterances of the word, forever unrecapturable but nonetheless crucial to its semantic evolution and hence to any complete reconstruction of its history. The historian may be tempted to arrange these fossil documents chronologically and to regard each one as a link between its immediate predecessor and nearest successor, but the fact is that any surviving instance of the word may reflect influences for which no record exists: destroyed letters, vanished conversations, unwritten translations of foreign texts in the minds of bilingual readers. That there were many such readers is evident in the number of books about the discovery either written by Englishmen in other tongues or written abroad and published untranslated in London—beginning as early as 1516, with More's *Utopia*, and including such fugitive items as Alexander Pope's *Selecta poemata Italorum* (1740), which reprints Girolamo Fracostoro's "Syphilis sive Morbus Gallicus" (1530), an allegorical treatment of the discovery, with references to Colonus.

Because the archive is at best incomplete, the historian of *Columbus* must regard surviving instances of the word as episodes in its unrecoverable semantic development, fragments of a lost narrative separated from each other by unfillable lacunae. Nonetheless, a history of semantic changes in the word would have a good deal to recommend it. By taking as its subject a sensible entity that can be seen to have endured intact over a long period of time and also to have changed significantly during that time, the history of this word could serve as an implicit critique of histories whose subjects— "American literature," "the novel," and such—must be posited as existing apart from their supposed manifestations in successive texts in order for those texts to be seen as developments of the thing named, rather than merely as different things. To say that *Columbus* is always the same word, we need not posit for it either a single, unchanging referent or an ideal existence transcending its sporadic appearances, written and spoken. Since the referent of *Columbus* in any case is always one of its meanings, that cannot be the thing whose meanings change from case to case. As for the word itself, its regular reappearance in English writings after 1553 strongly suggests its existence in the lexicon of at least one English speaker at every moment throughout that time and its uninterrupted transmission, by hand and voice, from that day to this. Like languages as a whole, individual words endure not in some Platonic realm but in the minds—the linguistic competences—of their users, binding together, with an attenuated but unbroken linguistic chain, writers and readers far removed from each other in space and time. What remains the same in all instances of the word *Columbus* is the material word itself, the unvarying sequence of letters that enables us to recognize the word when we see it and to say without question that we are dealing with the same word.

If, in strictly observing these necessary conditions of continuity and change, a history of *Columbus* should suggest that the history of words is, finally, the only defensible sort of history; that the very idea of history arises largely from, and remains necessarily tied to, the perception of linguistic change; or that what we call the past exists primarily, if not entirely, in the form of surviving words, the project would amply justify the effort entailed in the writing and the reading of it. Somewhat closer to the main concerns of this book: a history of *Columbus* might well serve as a preliminary index of the many changes undergone by the English language as a whole as a result of its continuing "discovery of America," from 1509 to the present day. As the word *America* changed its meanings in the English lexicon with each new discovery, settlement, and political development in the place so called, the meanings of *Columbus* changed apace to keep America supplied with a discoverer suitably motivated and equipped for the task. The *Columbus* who "founde certayne Ilandes" (Arber 28) in 1553 would not serve as the discoverer of Spanish America, when the magnitude of those dominions came to light; or of British America, when England sought historical justification for its imperial designs in the New World; or of the United States, when the continental colonies left the British empire; or of that nation in any of its subsequent self-fashionings. *Columbus* may be said quite literally to have gone west and grown up with the country—the first of many to have become someone by going to

America—and the history of this semantic becoming has a good deal to tell us about the Englishing of America and the Americanization of English that, together, account for so much of the linguistic world in which we live and have our being.

By no means least, an attempt to rescue from present misreadings some past senses of a word still very much in use and to track the semantic course of that word through a major phase of its history—its discovery, Anglicization, and Americanization—can illustrate in small the general idea of Early American Literature as writings whose selection, arrangement, and use of words reflect the earliest incursions of America into their respective languages and which, for that reason, ask to be treated literarily in the several modern linguistic worlds that America has made. The *Columbus* that Emerson called one of "the mind's ministers" and that we call, variously, a missionary of progress, a scoundrel, and fortune's tot, was born not in Genoa in 1446 or thereabouts but in London in 1553 and did not acquire the traits of character for which we celebrate or revile him until the latter part of the eighteenth century. Documents from the intervening two centuries record significant moments in his initially retarded but finally accelerated coming of age as a minister of the modern mind.

The English Discovery, 1553

For the earliest readers of Richard Eden's *Treatyse of the newe India*, the word *Columbus* would have had no known referent nor much meaning in itself. These innocent readers could have recognized it as a proper name by virtue of its capitalization and italicization, its unfamiliar orthography, and its syntactical position as the subject of a sentence. They could also have inferred from the preceding word, *Cristophorus*, that *Columbus* was a person rather than a place. But until they read farther, they could not have told who this person was or what made him worth mentioning. Only from Eden's following words—"a gentleman of Italie, and borne in the citie of Genoa" (Arber 28)—could his readers have learned who it was that the name designated. In this single sentence, the word *Columbus* enters the language, is supplied with a referent, and acquires its first English definition. *Columbus* is the man of whom these things are said, and the person to whom these statements refer is named *Columbus*. In time, many other things would be said of *Columbus*, and the word would multiply its meanings and its referents many times over. But for the moment, *Columbus* consisted entirely in the words with which it is surrounded in Eden's text.

In another respect, the first readers of the *Treatyse* cannot be called innocent. Eden wrote for a small circle of intellectuals and literate merchants who certainly knew something about European activity at the other end of the ocean and would have brought that knowledge to bear on his sentences. Surviving documents indicate that the English themselves had been exploring the newfound lands since the 1480s; and although very little concerning these expeditions appeared in English publications before Eden translated the account of the Cabots' voyages by their friend Pietro Martire, in 1555, and Richard Hakluyt published the report of Robert Thorne to Henry VIII, in 1582 (Quinn, *NAW* 1.182), news of English involvement overseas must have passed by word of mouth among those who were drawn to Eden's book.

They may also have read any of the handful of English references to the discovery that appeared in print before 1553, including two English renditions of Sebastian Brant's *Narrenschiff* (1509; Quinn, *NAW* 1.98 and 128), an interlude entitled "Hyckescorner" (1510; Quinn, *NAW* 1.128–29), a distant redaction of Vespucci's *Mundus Novus* (1510; Arber xxvii–xxxvi), John Rastell's *New interlude . . . of the iiij [four] elements* (ca. 1517; Quinn, *NAW* 1.168–71), translations of Giovanni de Vigo's *Practica . . . copiosa* (1543) and of More's *Utopia* (1551), a brief item in Edward Hall's *The union of the . . . famelies of Lancaster & Yorke* (1550; Quinn, *NAW* 1.190), and Anthony Ascham's *A lytel treatyse of astronomy* (1552). If any of Eden's readers knew the very first of these, Henry Watson's translation of a French paraphrase of Sebastian Brant called *The shyppe of fooles* (1509), they had already heard of "one that knewe that the yles of Spayne was enhabytaunt wherefore he asked men of kynge Ferdynandus and wente & founde them" (Quinn, *NAW* 1.130). They may, then, have identified this unnamed explorer with Eden's *Columbus*, who, "longe conversaunt in the Kyng of Spaynes courte, . . . applyed hys mynde to searche unknowen partes of the worlde" (Arber 28).

Readers who knew languages other than English may also have seen one of the many editions of the *Epistola. . . de insulis Indie. . .*, a Latin translation of the letter from the first voyage of one Colom, which appeared throughout Europe after 1493. They may have read one of the available foreign accounts—that of Colonus by Pietro Martire (1516), that of Colùn by Oviedo (1547), and that of Colombo by Ramusio (1550). They may even have read Münster's *Cosmographiae* itself, although Eden's urge to translate it suggests otherwise. Indeed, the appearance of this and earlier English translations of books about the New World suggests that the subject had begun a descent from the higher reaches of learning to a linguistically narrower but socially much broader world, a growing society of ambitious nobodies whose only language was English.

Whatever prior understanding Eden's readers may have brought to that name, it is this character of the initially contemned but ultimately triumphant projector that Eden gives to *Columbus* by means of the other words, both translated and original, with which he surrounds it. Having "applyed hys mynde to searche unknowen partes of the worlde . . . and made humble peticion to the kinge, to ayde him in this his enterpryse, which doubtlesse shoulde redounde to [Ferdinand's] great honour, and no little commoditie to the hole countreye of Spayne," *Columbus* is "laughed . . . to scorne" by the monarchs, who conclude "that his ymaginacion [is] but vayne and phantasticall" (28). Nonetheless, *Columbus* persists in his suit for eight years, until Ferdinand, determined "to trie the witte of the man," gives him three ships. With these, *Columbus* crosses the ocean, "at the length [finds] certayne Ilandes, of the whiche two were very greate" (28), and ultimately returns to Spain, where he is "honorablye receyved of the Kynge and Quene, and greatly magnified with innumerable glorious tittles: willinge that he should no more thenceforth be called *Columbus*, but the Admirall of the great Ocean Sea" (29).

It is a most ambiguous story. By disputing the reigning view of the world, *Columbus* first discredits himself but finally discredits that view, thus earning himself "innumerable glorious tittles" and a "greatlye magnified" position in the very establishment whose authority to confer such rewards his discoveries have called into question. This ambiguity, however, is perfectly consistent with the lesson that Eden asks his "welbeloved Reader" to draw from his book. On the one hand, it contains "many straunge thinges, and in maner incredible." On the other hand, these things "shal not so much amase thy wittes, and gender in thee incrudelitie [sic], yf thou consider the saying of wyse Salomon, who affyrmeth that there is no new thing under the Sunne; and that the thing that hath been, cometh to passe again" (7). Although "in these our daies hath chaunced so great a secret to be found, as the like hath never been knowen or heard before" (9), every new discovery, however astonishing, is already provided for somewhere in the body of extant knowledge, above all in "moste holy scripture" (7). The only problem is that the provision does not become apparent until the new discovery sheds light back upon it, so that instead of illuminating the future and guiding present actions, the past gets its meaning from the present. Prophesy becomes such only in being fulfilled. Once we realize that the gold discovered in the tropics of the New World refigures the mines of King Solomon in "the south partes of the world" (8), then the present event discovers the past—finds it and unveils it— instead of departing from the past on a wholly uncharted course of its own. Far from contradicting what is already known and resting solely on individual witness, these apparently unprecedented discoveries are "proved most certayn by dayly [i.e., ordinary] experience and approved auctoritie" (7) working in perfect concert.

As Eden's story of *Columbus* shows, however, "dayly experience" modifies "approved auctoritie" in the process of verifying it: the world that covers him with "glorious tittles" is not the same world that "laughed him to scorne" when he sought a place in it. And the farther Eden looks into the fragile coalition of experience and learning in the production of knowledge, the more it breaks down. Not only are these recent discoveries altogether too big for the house of received wisdom; it is in the interest of Eden and his readers, no less than that of his *Columbus*, that they should be so. For it is the uniqueness of the discovery that makes the discoverer an authority, raising him above all those who considered "phantasticall" what his own experience has shown to be true. Accordingly, after assuring his readers that God is not mocked by the discoveries, Eden goes on to proclaim "dayly experience" more important than any "approved auctoritie" in the discovery of truth. As "the teacher and mestres of all sciences," experience has a way of upending the hierarchy of authority; for, lacking her aid, "many greate wittes have fallen into great errours," while "by her ayde, many base and common wittes have attayned to the knowledge and practyse of such wonderfull effectes, as could hardely be comprehended by the discourse of reason." Afoot with his empiricist, individualist, incipiently democratic argument, Eden approaches the Lockean position of attributing all ideas to sensation. Then, finding himself on the brink of apostasy, he draws back, citing the "approved auctoritie" of Aristotle for this anti-authoritarian idea and laboriously denying the extreme inferences that "rashe wittes" like Castiglione have drawn from it (9). Although the accumulated authority of the ages has been overthrown by the "fortunate successe" (29) of *Columbus*'s first voyage, the effect of his discoveries has been to extend that authority and to enlist him among its most renowned figures.

This uneasy partnership of ancient, collective learning and new, individual experience that Eden finds embodied in *Columbus* is further disturbed by Eden's peculiar view of the effects of the admiral's discoveries. In Münster, the suspect imaginings and dogged self-confidence of *Columbus* are vindicated merely by his having "founde certayne Ilandes"—an event which, however unexpected, does not greatly imperil the existing view of the world as a single, three-part landmass encircled by the Ocean Sea. Indeed, Münster's narrative of these events is entitled *De terris Asiae Majoris*. For Eden, however, *Columbus* initiated a series of voyages that have uncovered a "fourth parte of the earth" called "America, with the hole fyrme lande adherent thereunto" (8). The herald of an altogether new world, not just an explorer of the one already known, Eden's *Columbus* embodies the conflict between individual experience and established belief, and the triumph of the former over the latter, more than he does any cooperative relation, even the most troubled, between them. What is more, insofar as Eden's readers lived consciously in this new world and counted themselves among its developers, *Columbus* ceased to be an agent of Spanish power, as Münster had portrayed him, and became, in effect, their own progenitor. Not until 1682 would an English writer go so far as to call "the Famous Columbus" a "discontented Native of this Isle, born in England, but resident in Genoa" (quoted in Sale 336). Nonetheless, the early glimmerings of that patriotic fantasy are already evident in Eden's retroactive naturalization of this "Gentleman of Italie" by making him the patriarch of a burgeoning Anglo-American dynasty.

At the same time, Eden himself is not at all certain of *Columbus*'s historical significance, his precise relation to what preceded and what has followed his voyages. On the one hand, *Columbus* ranks first among the European explorers of the "newe India," by virtue of the detailed attention he receives in the *Treatyse*, as well as the assertion that *Vesputius*, his principal rival for space in the narrative and for priority in the discovery, learned the art of "sayling on the sea" from *Columbus* himself during the first voyage (37). On the other hand, Münster does not distinguish between the "newe India" explored by Portuguese mariners sailing "from Spayne . . . Eastward" (27) and the "newe India and Ilandes of the West Ocean Sea" (28) visited by *Columbus*, *Vesputius*, and *Magellanus*. Nor does he place much more importance on the voyages of *Columbus* than on those of the various other explorers he mentions. It is only Eden's faint distinction between "the landes of Asia the greater" and "the newe founde landes, and Ilandes" (42), at the close of his *Treatyse*, along with his prefatory allusion to "the fourth parte of the earth" called America, that sets these western voyages in a world altogether different from Münster's and thus singles out *Columbus* as its first founder.

But that is about as far as Eden goes toward separating *Columbus* from the past and placing him at the beginning of the present. Although America now exists, its history is as yet too short and too uncertainly consequential to require its own starting point. The break between the world before and the world after *Columbus* was clearly visible to Eden; his allegorical interpretation of *Columbus*'s first voyage as a departure from ancient learning to modern experience suggests as much. The implications of that departure for every "approved auctoritie," however, together with its as yet uncertain tendency and unforeseeable destination, send Eden back to the wisdom of Solomon, Augustine, and Albertus Magnus, just as the first voyage, in Münster's narrative, returns *Columbus* to the Spanish court, bedecked with old-world "tittles."

The upshot of Eden's conflicted allegiance to past learning and present news is that his *Columbus* remains suspended between two worlds, an old world created all at once by God and revealed in Scripture, and a new world "never knowen or heard before (what soever God meant to kepe this mistery hyd so long)" (9) and uncovered piecemeal by forward-looking individuals, impatient with the established order of things even as they long for preferment in that order. To describe the liminal situation of Eden's *Columbus* in these terms is to recognize how closely they suit Eden himself and the audience for whom he wrote. Like the *Columbus* of the *Treatyse*, these projectors, too, seek to become somebody in the world that has always excluded them, by attaching themselves intellectually, commercially, or physically to an altogether different world where personal accomplishment counts for more than birth, and "tittles" can be earned as well as inherited. Indeed, Eden's *Columbus* seems to have been constructed specifically to present his readers' ambitions in the most flattering light. Like them, *Columbus* is undeterred by ridicule and the threat of failure. Translated into English, he pits that "dayly" language against the complacent authority of the learned tongues and, in demonstrating its power to reveal long-hidden truths, affirms the virtues of English nationhood and patriotism. Although eager for his own advancement, he sees no conflict between his personal interests and those of the nation under whose flag he sails. Both are motivated by spiritual and material aims, seeking "the glorye of God and the commoditie of [the] country" (6). Any success enjoyed by the individual must "redownde to [the] great honour" of the king and "no little commoditie to all the hole countrye" (28).

But if Eden's *Columbus* embodies the situation and aspirations of the reader, he dramatizes the self-image of the writer no less. Eden, too, seeks the good of his nation and a name for himself by departing from the established domain of academic Latin to try the personally unfamiliar and generally unexplored reaches of English, a linguistic territory only recently opened up but rapidly expanding thanks to the spread of literacy, the development of printing, and, not least, the association of the vernacular with news *Of the new found lands* (xxxviii). Where *Columbus* dedicates his undertaking to Ferdinand, who provides for it, Eden dedicates his to the Duke of Northumberland, his protector as well as a "greate fortherer" of an earlier voyage by Sebastian Cabot (6).

Closer still, Eden is a sort of second self to *Columbus*, whose effect upon the world depends as much upon the publication of his discoveries as on those accomplishments themselves, just as "[t]he fame of Achilles was no lesse notable to his posteritie by Homers writing, then it was in hys lyfe tyme by hys owne marcial affayres." "Wherefore," Eden says, in words that would fit in the mouth of *Columbus*, "partelye moved [by] the good affeccion, which I have ever borne to the science of Cosmographie, which entreately of the descripcion of the worlde, whereof the newe found landes are no smal part, and much more by the good wyll, whych of duetie I beare to my native country and countreymen, whych have of late to their greate praise (whatsoever succede) attempted with new viages to serche the seas and newe found landes, I thought it worthy my travayle, to their better comfort, (as one not otherwise able to further theyr enterprise) to translate this boke out of latin into Englishe" (5).

The Invention of British America, 1555–1607

When the English first learned to say *Columbus*, the Spanish had already been in the New World for fifty years. By the time England planted its first permanent colony in Virginia, and Robert Johnson acknowledged *Columbus* "the first bewrayer of this new world" (Quinn, *NAW* 5.237), Spanish America was a century old, and figures called Colón and Colombo had become legendary in their respective tongues. During the sixteenth century, the discovery had been celebrated in a dozen Spanish, Italian, and Portuguese poems devoted to the subject, but seldom even mentioned in English verse. In the same year that Richard Eden told of *Columbus*'s having "founde certayne Ilandes," Francisco López de Gómara was calling the discovery of the Indies "the greatest event since the creation of the world (excluding the incarnation and death of Him who created it)" (quoted in J. H. Elliott 10); and though Thomas Nicholas translated this observation into English in 1578, no English writer would quite match it until Adam Smith, who, excepting not even the Incarnation, proclaimed "[t]he discovery of America, and that of the passage to the East Indies by the Cape of Good Hope, . . . the two greatest events recorded in the history of mankind" (2.141).

This tardy English response to the discovery is everywhere visible. The 1493 Latin translation of the letter announcing the first voyage of Colom was reprinted at least seventeen times by 1500, in cities throughout Europe, but not once in London. (No English translation of the letter would see print until after 1800.) When English readers first heard of the discovery from Alexander Barclay, France had already established itself as the leading producer of printed Americana, most of which either remained untranslated or found its way into English so slowly as to be already obsolete by the time it appeared. So small was the circle of Englishmen interested in America that information about it generally circulated in manuscript rather than in print; and when such materials were published, the market was soon exhausted, and they were not reissued. The publications that did appear, moreover, seem not so much responses to an existing interest in America as attempts, not very successful, to whip one up (Parker, chap. 6). England's participation in the production of books about America would increase dramatically after the founding of Jamestown (1607) and Plymouth (1620), but at least until the 1580s, when Drake circled the globe, Hakluyt published his *Diverse Voyages*, and Raleigh planted his doomed colony on Roanoke Island, the New World and who got there first were for most English speakers foreign topics when they were topics at all.

The reasons for this indifference lay partly at home, partly in America as that place appeared to English eyes. On the one hand, writings of the period display a hostility toward worldly travel and exploration that is rooted in Augustinian religiosity and could be labeled medieval if it had not in fact increased with every piece of news from the New World, fashioning a discourse of domesticity that would become a major strand of modern English. Edward Hellowes said it all in the preface to his translation of Antonio de Guevara (1578), when he noted "the opinion of certaine, which affirme that so unremovable bounds [of the sea] declareth Gods omnipotent ordinance, that every country so divided ought to content themselves to live, by the gifts of the same God and countrie" (folio Bb recto). Sixteenth-century publishers and book buyers showed a decided preference for old geographies, either surviving medieval texts like Mandeville's *Travels* or recovered classics like *The surveye of the world . . .* by Dionysius Periegetes, over contemporary publications, theoretical or practical. As late as 1585, the year that Henry Roberts complained of England's failure to celebrate heroes like Drake, publishers were still bringing out new translations of classical geographies, like that of Pomponius Mela's *De Situ Orbis* by Arthur Golding, as well as reissuing Pliny's *Natural History* and the works of Solinus Polyhistor, translated five years earlier. Even George Abbot's *Briefe description of the whole worlde* (1599), which mentions *Columbus* and the English expeditions in the New World, relies almost entirely on classical and biblical geography for its picture of the globe.

This ingrained disinclination on the part of all but a few "large minded" English adventurers to depart intellectually from the pre-American world was abetted by the uncertain size and importance of America itself. No one was apt to care much about the place or who had discovered it as long as it remained either a part of Asia or an obstacle in the sea road to Cathay, as it did throughout most of the sixteenth century. Although Eden had called America a fourth part of the world in 1553, he seems to waffle on this question in his 1555 translation of Pietro Martire when he says, regarding Mexico and Florida, "summe wryters connecte this lande to the firme lande of Asia: But the truth hereof is not yet knowen" (Arber 55). Like Münster's *Cosmographiae,* most of the geographies known to sixteenth-century English readers tended to include both eastward and westward travels and not to distinguish clearly between their destinations. As late as 1577, the word *Indians* was still being used, indiscriminately, to designate the indigenous peoples of Cathay, the Philippines, and America, simultaneously reflecting and promoting the literal confusion of these places in the English mind. So complete was this confusion, indeed, that Humphrey Gilbert had to devote large chunks of his 1576 *Discourse* to separating America from Asia in order to explain and justify his search for a northwest passage through the former to the latter. But even then, as a thing to be got through or around, America had no very great need for a discoverer or much lustre to shed back on one. Sir Dudley Digges spoke for all proponents of an obstructive but otherwise negligible America in 1612, when he adjudged it "nothing broad, however it be painted" (2).

Whatever it was, large or small, a part of Asia or a separate continent, America—at least its tropical regions, where the gold was—belonged to hated Spain; and while the Spanish might look to their adopted countryman Colón as the author of their present wealth and power, the English were apt to consider *Columbus* a foreign agent. Except for sporadic raids by privateers upon Spanish treasure ships, no English expedition had found anything more valuable than codfish in America—not even a passage through it to the riches beyond, let alone a site for a British Lima. And without some foothold in America, some reason to think of the place, the way Spain did, as part of their own history, the English felt little compulsion to think of it at all.

Like all conditions known to have been short-lived, however, England's initial unconcern for America displays to hindsight the symptoms of its eventual demise. Holinshed's *Chronicles* of 1578 include Cabot, Gilbert, Frobisher, Raleigh, and Ralph Lane among the nation's worthies, lending to English historiography an American dimension that would expand steadily in the *Annales* of William Camden (1625), in those of John Stow and Edmund Howes (1631), and in the several histories of Samuel Clarke (1650–71), and would eventuate in such Anglo-American chronicles as John Oldmixon's *British Empire in America* (1708) and William Douglass's *Summary . . . of the British Settlements in America* (1747–52). Among the earliest and most influential of all these expansionist tomes, of course, are the successive collections of Richard Hakluyt: his *Diverse voyages touching the discoverie of America* (1582), which lists *Columbus* alongside Mandeville and Benjamin

Tudelensis as one of "Certain Late Travaylers, Both By Sea and By Lande, Which Also For the Most Part Have Written of Their Owne Trauvayles and Voyages" (5); his *Principall navigations* of 1589, with the story of *Columbus*'s petition to Henry VII; and the greatly enlarged 1598 version, in which *Columbus* appears as a sort of Spanish Hakluyt, pricking forward his sluggish countrymen "unto their Westerne discoveries" (*Voyages* 1.20). Merely to skim this succession of imperial histories is to see at once recorded and stimulated the sporadic but relentless growth of America in the English consciousness as a prominent feature of its own interior landscape, a dwelling for the mind.

If the America that came first to English attention belonged to Spain, the America that manifests itself in English writings after the defeat of the Armada is a distinctly British entity, part of the new-found lands as a whole but quite separate from the Spanish Indies, Portuguese Brazil, New Holland, and New France. As the adopted name for those territories available, and hence vouchsafed, to British dominion, *America* assumed unwonted significance in the language, denoting an extension of England, a part of the world in which every English speaker lived linguistically. Who first discovered this America was a matter of some importance. Not only did its arrival on the conceptual scene want explaining, but England's rights to it needed some foundation, whether in scriptural revelation or in historical precedence.

Unfortunately, the name *America* had long been associated directly with those of *Vesputius* and *Columbus* in the English lexicon. In the very first English reference to *America* thus spelled, John Rastell explained that the newly found lands are so called because "Americus dyd furst them fynde" (Quinn, *NAW* 1.171). In 1553, Eden attributed the discovery to *Columbus*. Six years later William Cunningham lumped together *Columbus* and *Vesputius* as "the first authors" of a voyage "to Calicute" (67), confounding the East and West Indies in the process. George Gascoigne's "Prophetical Sonnet . . . upon Sir Humphrey Gilbert" (1576) calls *Columbus* the second Neptune, *Vesputius* the third (Quinn, *NAW* 3.7). *Columbus* stands alongside *Vesputius* and others in Geoffray Fenton's *Historie* (1579), translated from Guicciardini, as well as in Sir George

Peckham's *True reporte of the late discoveries* (1583). While these two explorers might serve to account for an America of uncertain size, location, and value, especially when Spain controlled it, they would not do for British America. As known Spanish agents, they had to be either naturalized or discredited.

Both of these stratagems can be seen at work in writings of the late sixteenth century, as England prepared to take possession of the America it had invented. Richard Eden had made *Columbus* the founder of an America available to Britons, but that was at a time when affection for things Spanish was royal policy at home and England had no official designs upon Spanish holdings abroad. Since then, Spain had become anathema: in Europe, the seat of the Inquisition, the capital of the Counter-Reformation, and the headquarters for Jesuit spies; and in America, the protagonist of the Black Legend. As a result, the Spanish *Columbus*, although "a Gentleman of Italie" (Arber 28), had his working papers lifted and turned over to the Florentine Vesputius, the Venetian Cabots, and the Welsh Prince Madoc. If Vesputius did not precede *Columbus* in the chronology of New World discovery, he did so in the order of English writings on the subject; and the adoption of his given name for British America lent him an Englishness that *Columbus* could not match. The Cabots had come to notice through Richard Eden's translation of Pietro Martire, who had known them personally. Although themselves no more English, or less Spanish, than *Columbus* or Vesputius, they had the inestimable advantage of having lived for a time in England and sailed, occasionally, under English colors. It was, however, the legendary Prince Madoc, rescued from obscurity by John Dee in 1578 and thrust to the fore by Humphrey Lhoyd and Richard Hakluyt in 1584, who gave *Columbus* the most competition for the title of discoverer (Quinn, *NAW* 1.67, 3.107). Supposed to have reached America from Wales around 1170, the Welshman made *Columbus* seem not only a foreigner but a Johnny-come-lately.

Whatever success may have attended these efforts to topple *Columbus* from his perch, they succceed most in proving the name too firmly established to be ignored. Eden's translation of Pietro Martire's "fyrst Decade," in 1555, had added substantially to the shadowy *Columbus* he had introduced two years earlier, and the name figures somehow in nearly all English writings about America published in the two decades prior to the founding of Jamestown. Whether *Columbus* is defended against his detractors, as in George Abbot's *Briefe description of the whole worlde* (fol. D7); cited as an authority for statements about the New World, as in Sir George Peckham's *A true reporte of the late discoveries* (Quinn, *NAW* 3.41) or blamed for the transmission of syphilis to Europe, as in John Frampton's *Joyful newes out of the newe founde worlde* (1577), the name appears wherever *America* does, as if the two were inseparable in the English vocabulary.

To say that *Columbus* sprang to everyone's lips because the name had become familiar is to utter a tautology. Still, nothing succeeds like success, and the familiarity of *Columbus* is evident in the regular use of the name as a recognizable example. To illustrate the penchant for mutiny among colonists, Richard Hakluyt's *A Notable historie . . .* (1587) cites "the troubles which lately happened unto Christopher Columbus, after his first discovery" (Quinn, *NAW* 2.239), without further explaining the allusion. The first English poem to mention *Columbus*, Robert Seall's *Commendation of the adventurus viage of the wurthy captain M. Thomas Stutley . . . towards the land called Terra Florida* (1563), makes *Columbus* an example of enterprising vision, intially ridiculed by the experts but ultimately confirmed by experience. When a word has acquired this sort of semantic utility, all the learned shoutings in the world won't drive it from the language.

Firmly ensconsed in the lexicon and closely identified with the America that England was coming to regard as its own, *Columbus* had to be made a Briton, if only in effect or in posse. When Madoc leads off, *Columbus* remains somewhere in the historical lineup, usually in the number-two position, between the legendary Welshman and the documented Cabots. Richard Hakluyt, who introduced Madoc to English readers, also released the story of Bartolomé's early petition on his brother's behalf to Henry VII, thus providing *Columbus* with an English connection and initiating the theme of the "lost chance," the opportunity England missed, whether by misfortune or folly, to reach America ahead of Spain. Recited initially as a warning

[handwritten margin note: Genealogy]

against further inaction, in the years to come this tale was repeated so often, with so many embellishments, that *Columbus* seemed to have intended to serve England rather than Spain—even to have actually done so, at least in spirit. As Edward Fairefax put it in his translation of Tasso (1600), *Columbus* was not really a Spaniard, but a "knight of Genes" (380). For its part, according to the *Discourse . . . of Sir Humphrey Gilbert* (written 1566), Spain had disowned *Columbus*, regarding him as a foreigner, envying his accomplishments, and maligning his name with the fable of the Biscayan pilot. Having failed to throw *Columbus* overboard, the English were busily finding him a berth in the ship bound for Virginia.

The Settlement of British America, 1607–1776

The arrival of that English vessel in America, with *Columbus* securely aboard, seems to have redoubled the efforts of writers to make the discoverer an honorary Englishman. When British America consisted mainly of dreams interrupted by episodes of piracy, there may have been general agreement with Andre Thevet's judgment that "[t]his land by good right is called America, taking name of him who first found it out" (fol. 42 verso), although Thevet's insistent tone suggests that the matter was even then not beyond dispute. In either case, the opposition found its tongue soon after the landing at Plymouth, when Peter Heylyn recommended that America be renamed "Columbana, Sebastiana, or Cabotia" (400), for one of its "English" discoverers. The 1625 edition of Samuel Purchas's *Hakluytus Posthumous* refers pointedly to "[t]he Columbian (so fitlier named, then American) World" (2.19). In 1634, Thomas Herbert pressed the English claim still farther, proposing the names "Modocya, Brittania, Colonia, or Columbina" (223); and forty years later, John Josselyn was still upset about the naming of the New World after "Americus Vespucius the Florentine," when those naturalized Britons "Columbus and Cabota deserved rather the honour of being Godfathers to it" (148). After 1775, the name *Columbia* would serve to divorce America from Britain. At this wooing stage, it was coined to hallow their dubious connection.

For Britain's title to American territory was anything but clear, even in British eyes. With the planting of permanent colonies in Virginia and New England, the question of who had got there first, once largely academic (which is to say, unimportant), became a matter of immediate concern to colonial projectors who wished to spare England further charges of brigandage or at least to avoid open conflict with the Spanish. In a poem of 1607, Michael Drayton concedes the priority of *Columbus*, who might nonetheless have sailed for England had King Henry not let slip the opportunity offered him by Bartolomé (1.498). The dedicatory poem signed "T.T." that opens John Smith's *Generall Historie* (1624) puts *Columbus* first in a line of English discoverers: the Cabots, Frobisher, Humphrey, Amadis, Raleigh, Grenville, Drake, Gosnold, and Pring (1). William Strachey divides the New World along national lines in order to make *Columbus* the discoverer of Spanish America, the Cabots discoverers of those territories "from Florida nor-ward, to the behoofe of England" (13). John Smith himself attacks the problem geographically rather than politically, crediting *Columbus* with the discovery of "certaine Iles" in 1492 but of the continent only in 1498, a year after the Cabots (1). And virtually all of these strategies are offered seriatim in Thomas Gage's *The English-American* (1648), beginning with the dedicatory verse by Thomas Chaloner, whose *Columbus* discovered a New World for "us," then proceeding to Gage's lament for King Henry's lost chance, and concluding with an outright dismissal of the question. As for who it was that made the "First-discovery," Gage sniffs, "to me it seems as little reason, that the sailing of a Spanish ship upon the coast of India, should entitle the King of Spain to that Countrey, as if the sailing of an Indian or English ship upon the coast of Spain should entitle either the Indians or the English unto the dominion thereof" (A5).

But however an apologist for English colonization might resolve the problem, *Columbus* was, in Strachey's words, "ever-famous" (13) for having found America first, and so had to be confronted by anyone concerned to justify England's claim to territories in the New World. What is more, the fame of *Columbus* rested on the most solid of grounds. Other voyagers may have crossed the ocean before him. Even so, they left no written report of their discoveries for later explorers to follow and still later historians to use as evidence. As a result, these prior discoveries were literally inconsequential—without consequence in the chain of human events—which is to say, not historical. The supposed discoveries of "Arthur, Malgo, and Brandon," of "Madock and Hanno, a Prince of Carthage," John Smith concludes, "no History can show." The accomplishments of *Columbus*, on the other hand, "we finde by Records" (1).

The idea of authority broached here is worth remarking, for it signals a fundamental shift in the ground of authority for human action during the preceding century and locates *Columbus* at the pivot of that change. The man who wrote to Ferdinand and Isabella from Hispaniola in 1500 rested the authority for his actions squarely on divine revelation: "God made me the messenger of the new heaven and the new earth, of which He spoke in the Apocalypse by St. John, after having spoken of it by the mouth of Isaiah; and He showed me the spot where to find it" (148). John Smith's *Columbus*, on the other hand, has authority by virtue of his early place in a sequence of human actions. For the man who signed his letter *El Almirante*, the meaning and importance of his actions preceded them; his history was already written. The actions of Smith's *Columbus* derive their value and significance from their unforeseen consequences, just now coming to light. Far from complete, the history that confers authority upon *Columbus* is still being written, in the present, by explorer-authors like Smith, who are steadily enlarging the consequences, and hence the significance, of the discovery.

The growing acceptance of America as an English habitation, as well as a place in mind, is accompanied by a sharp increase in the number of appearances by *Columbus* in print. Between the planting of Jamestown and the mid-seventeenth century, the name shows up over twice as often as in the preceding fifty years. To feed the growing appetite for information about America, publishers brought out more original writings on the subject and more translations of foreign works in twenty-five years than had appeared in the previous one hundred, while editors like Samuel Purchas revived earlier translations that had been allowed to go out of print for want of readers. Before 1607, *Columbus* had appeared in only three English poems. By the time Milton's Adam heard the name from the archangel (9.1116–17), it had appeared in two poems by Michael Drayton (1607, 1612) and one each by Baptist Goodall (1630), Thomas Nashe (1633), John Gough (1640), Thomas Chaloner (1648), and John Dryden (1663).

As a result of this exposure, *Columbus* became increasingly useful as a familiar reference-point for arguments on various subjects. Drayton's dedicatory poem for a book on the cultivation of silkworms by Nicholas Geffe (1607) cites the accomplishments of *Columbus* to show

> From small beginning how brave noble things
> Have gathered vigor and themselves have rear'd
> To be the strength and maintenance of Kings
> That at the first but frivolous appeared. (1.498)

In Robert Johnson's *Nova Britannia* (1609), the initial failure of Portugal and Spain to heed *Columbus* illustrates the mistake of judging visionaries by their "poore apparell and simple lookes" (Quinn, *NAW* 5.237). For Bacon in the *Novum Organum* (1620), *Columbus* exemplifies the proper procedures of argument: he set forth the "reasons for his conviction" and then made them "good by experience" (*Works* 4.91). In David Person's *Varieties* (1635), the name stands for "practicall-curiosity" (book 4, section 11). Remarking, in *The Advancement of Learning* (1640), the tendency of schoolmen to doubt the possibility of some action until it has been accomplished and then to wonder that it had not been done sooner, Bacon observes, "And the same happened to *Columbus* in the western navigation" (39). And when John Booker accused John Taylor, the water-poet, of stealing an idea from him, Taylor compared his rival to Vespusius, who used the maps of *Columbus* and then bragged about finding more than his predecessor had (5).

Above all, *Columbus* became a virtual synonym for *discovery*. The prologue to John Gough's tragicomedy *The Strange Discovery* (1640) takes care to correct the audience's natural supposition that the play will deal with

Christopher Columbus, and his brother,
Whose navigable paines did first discover
America. . . . (qtd. Cawley, *Voyagers* 323)

The verse dedication that Thomas Chaloner wrote for Gage's *English-American* compares the "new discoverie" of the New World in this book to that made by *Columbus*. And *Men Before Adam* (1656), an anonymous translation of Isaac de La Peyrére's *Praeadamitae* (1655), equates the author's discoveries with those of *Columbus* and prays that this scholarly discoverer may escape the obloquy that was heaped upon his nautical forebear (19–20).

Noticeable in these allusions is a change in the meaning of the word *discovery* itself, apparently as a result of its connection with *Columbus* and *America*. In 1555, Richard Eden used the verb *discover* to denote a single, completed act of disclosure. "In this fyrst navigation, [*Columbus*] discovered vi [six] Ilandes" (Arber 66), and if more should be later found, those would constitute new discoveries. Once these successive discoveries were lumped together under the name *America*, however, this single entity grew larger with each new discovery, and that noun came to mean not an instantaneous unveiling of a whole but an extended process of knowing something that seemed to grow larger with each attempt to uncover it. In the words of Thomas Heriot, the little yet known about this place "is nothing to that which remaineth to be discovered" (Hakluyt, *Voyages* 6.193). Rather than something done once and for all in 1492, the discovery of America by *Columbus* had merely begun an uninterrupted process that was still going on. *Columbus*, accordingly, became "the first discoverer" for much of the sixteenth century, then simply "the discoverer," once again, as the word came to convey its progressive sense unaided. Originally an isolated piece of news, then the first event in the history of America, *discovery* came to describe American history as a whole, and modern history came to be equated with continous discovery.

The increasing attention paid to *Columbus* during the seventeenth century reflects a growing awareness among English readers and writers not just of the New World but of changes in the whole world as a result of the discovery. After countless centuries of ignorance and two more of indifference, opined the writer of *The Present State of Jamaica* in 1683, "the World at last is come to the knowledge of this new World almost wholly" (117). Along with this widespread knowledge there grew up a general sense that life since the discovery was fundamentally different from what it had been. Presumably there for the taking, if only imaginatively, America offered unprecedented opportunities for individual action and collective enterprise—a space at once geographical and psychic for the realization of personal ambition, for dreams of self-determination, for the satisfaction of curiosity and the gratification of desire. What had been at first "another World" (108), distant and different from the one always known, came, as a result of "the new Searches and Plantations" since *Columbus* (117), to seem *this* world, a place altogether different from the one previously known. And with each phase of this gradual but thoroughgoing mental reorientation, the present, long regarded as a continuation of the past, understandable in terms of received knowledge, came to seem a radical departure from the past, something to be understood on its own terms, according to principles arising from, and continously revised by, present experience.

So great were the apparent differences between the world before and after the discovery that, to many observers, history seemed to have begun anew, on an altogether new footing. Particularly as the English came to inhabit America, which was itself changing almost daily in English eyes and thus seemed the source of every other change, the present appeared to arise more from the discovery than from anything that had preceded it, not excluding the Creation and the rest of the events recorded in the Old and New Testaments. This potentially heretical idea had been suggested a century earlier, in Richard Eden's translation of Pietro Martire: "But not offendynge the reverence due to owre predicessors, what so ever from the begynnynge of the worlde hath byn doone or wrytten to this day, to my iudgement seemeth but little, if wee consyder what . . . [the discoverers] have lefte" (Arber 64). By the middle of the seventeenth century, such sentiments had become routine in English writings, although the authorities disparaged there tend to be more often classical than biblical: "Now let the Antients no Longer Mention Neptune, Minos, [etc.]; to all which Diverse authors Diversly Ascribe the Invention of Navigation," intones *The Present State of Jamaica.* "Missians, Tirrians, Trojans vail your bonnets, strike your Top-sail to this Indian Admiral, that deserveth the Top-sail indeed, by aspiring to the top that sailing could Aim at in Discovering another World" (107–8). Even when English writers attributed the New World to divine creation—pausing only to wonder why God had kept it hidden for so long—its history, and hence that of the present, started with *Columbus.*

It must be said that a good many English writers of the seventeenth century (and earlier) foresaw nothing good in this new history. The very first text to mention the discovery, Alexander Barclay's translation of *Narrenschiff*, repeats Brant's satire on the folly of seeking knowledge outside the soul and then augments that spiritual warning with an epistemological one: the search for knowledge of the world is endless and therefore without ultimate justification. The history that begins with Genesis ends with Revelation; the history that began with *Columbus* is by nature inconclusive and can therefore lead only to greater confusion. As *The Present State of Jamaica* put it, in recording the death of *Columbus*, "This was the end (if ever there can be an end)" (117). Some writers had supposed that discovery did not depart from the scriptural plan. *El Almirante* himself had supposed that he had come to the place where the world began and would end. And just as El Inca Garcilaso de la Vega denied any real division between the Old World and the New (1.9), Edward Hare maintained that the world did not begin again in the West: "we are assured of the contrary by the prophesie of Christ, whereby we gather, that after his word preached throwout the world shalbe the end" (Hakluyt, *Voyages* 6.4). Thomas Scott, on the other hand, merely scoffed at the idea that the discovery had changed anything—"that had not Columbus happely found out the new world in time, there must have beene an end of the old world long before this time" (17); whereas for the Milton of *Paradise Lost*, the departure from God's history to a history authored by *Columbus* could lead nowhere but to endless sin and death.

For every Thomas Scott or John Milton, however, seventeenth-century England produced a score of progressives like Bacon, who counted *Columbus* among his modern prophets in *The New Atlantis* (3.165–166); or Ferdinand Gorges, whose history *America Painted to the Life* (1658) extends from "Columbus his first Discovery, to these later times." John Suckling's *Account of Religion by Reason* (1646) regards with an equal eye the biblical account of the Flood and "reports from the Indians, of a great deluge," demonstrating the impact of the new history upon previously unquestioned authority as he equates Scripture with "the story of *Columbus*" (172). Dryden goes still further in his verse epistle "To My Honor'd Friend Dr. Charleton" (1663). Here, Aristotle gives way to *Columbus*, " . . . the first who shook his throne, / And found a temp'rate in a torrid zone" (17). "Had we still paid that homage to a name," Dryden continues,

> Which only God and nature justly claim,
> The western seas had been our outmost bound,
> Where poets still might dream the sun was drown'd:
> And all the stars that shine in southern skies
> Had been admir'd by none but salvage eyes. (18)

Since the Old World ruled by Aristotle denied America, the New World discovered by *Columbus* and inhabited by Dryden excludes the Stagirite. Even Sir Thomas Browne, who contemplated England's eastern past more often than he did its western future, positioned himself squarely in modern history when he disparaged *Columbus*'s discovery of America by comparing it not to something prior or timeless, to the wisdom of Aristotle or the revelations of Scripture, but to another, even more recent discovery, that of William Harvey concerning the circulation of the blood (6.277).

This tendency to equate stability with a former world and continual change with the world born at the moment of discovery had the effect of removing *Columbus* from the learned past to the experienced present. English writers had always kept *Columbus* abreast of the present by portraying the unforeseen but now known results of his first voyage as his original intentions. Having found "new regions," rather than a new way to old ones, Eden's *Columbus* seeks the support of Ferdinand not for a voyage to Marco Polo's Cataia but for an exploration of "unknowen partes of the worlde" (Arber 28).

And, according to Richard Hakluyt's translation of Antonio Gal-
vano, "In the yeere 1492, . . . Don Ferdinando dispatched one
Christopher Columbus a Genoway with three ships to goe and discover Nova Spagna" (Purchas 10.14). Now that *Columbus* had become identified with emerging America, with continuing discovery,
and with change itself, as imaged in his departure from an Old World
hostile to change and in the alteration of the once timeless New
World, he might occupy the literary imagination as well as historical
memory, acquiring motives, doubts, aspirations, and virtues quite
common to fictional characters but unsupported by any historical
record.

By 1700, more than half a million British subjects lived in America. In the coming century the number of Anglo-Americans would
more than double, hugely increasing both the Anglophone presence
in America and the presence of America in the English-speaking
world as a whole. The latest phase of English history was turning
out, willy-nilly, to be predominantly American; and this new present, so different from any remembered past in its tendency to rapid
change, would attract increasing attention, as the century pro-
gressed, from writers aware of these changes and concerned to plot
the trajectory of England's American history.

This growing concern is reflected in the movement of *Columbus*, after 1700, from the provinces of literature toward its center,
from sporadic appearances in specialized genres read mainly by an
interested coterie to extended runs in most of the popular literary
vehicles of the day. In some cases, the genres in which *Columbus*
had customarily figured were themselves becoming popular as a
result of English activity abroad, especially in America. The growing
need to maintain a connection between the runaway present and the
receding past generated histories galore that, treating developments
of recent urgency, included *Columbus* somewhere among their
most influential human agents. The scope of these histories varied
widely. William Guthrie's twelve-volume *General History of the
World* (1764–67) sought to mend the break between antiquity and
modernity by placing *Columbus* midway on a continuous line running "From Creation to the Present Time." More often, the history
in question begins with *Columbus* and proceeds to some present

aspect of the world born in 1492—whether to all of it, as in Thomas
Salmon's *History of the Modern World* (1724, 1738); to its western
hemisphere, as in William Burke's *Account of European Settlements in America* (1757); to a geographical segment, as in Samuel
Nevill's *History of North America* (1760); to a political segment, as
in Nathaniel Crouch's often reprinted *The English Empire in America* (1685–1728); or to a specific locale, as in *The History of Jamaica*
by Edward Long (1774).

Narratives of travel grew popular for exactly the same reasons,
and multivolume collections of these timely accounts appeared
with increasing regularity during the 1700s. The earliest of these,
John and Awnsham Churchill's four-volume *Collection of Voyages
and Travels* (1704), gave English readers their first look at Fernando
Colón's biography of his father, or rather at Alfonso Ulloa's Italian
translation (1569) of the Spanish original, since lost. Before the century was out, the English-language press produced such anthologies
by the score, at least sixteen of them including some previously
translated, hitherto little-read narratives of the voyages of *Columbus*. That these compendia appealed primarily to readers of "fiction" is clear from the introduction to *A New Collection of Voyages,
Discoveries and Travels* (1767), which distinguishes between the
"antiquary," motivated by historical "curiosity," and "the modern
reader," seeking "pleasure" (iv). That this market was rapidly expanding is evident in the number of times collections were reprinted, in the reappearance of earlier collections under new titles,
and in the compilers' habit of pirating materials from each other.
Upon returning to America after long absence, the narrator of Royall
Tyler's *The Algerine Captive* (1797) is surprised to see the popularity
of religious writings wholly supplanted by a mania for "travels and
novels almost as incredible" (27).

Awareness of England's expanding horizons created a new readership, in the earlier half of the century, for still other genres in
which *Columbus* had commonly appeared without being much no-
ticed. Geographies, like those of Duncan Campbell (1734), John Barrow (1742), and F. Watson (1773), traced the origins of their
knowledge about the world to *Columbus*. Books of curiosities, like
Guido Panciroli's *History of many memorable things lost . . . and*

... *many things found* ... *both natural and artificial* (1715, 1727);
of exotica, like the anonymous *Beauties of Nature and Art displayed in a Tour through the World* (1763); and of modern inventions, like Defoe's *General History of Discoveries and Improvements, in the Useful Arts* (1725–26), all included *Columbus*
among their marvels. Polemics grounded in history, like Charles
Owen's *The danger of the church* ... *from foreigners* (1721) and
Baron Hervey's *Miscellaneous Thoughts on the present posture of
both our foreign and domestic affairs* (1742), looked to *Columbus*
for support.

But of all the genres whose emergence during these years helped
Columbus make his literary weight, none did more than biography.
Offering ample room for the development of individuality—more
than the available data could fill without the aid of invention—
biography went far to speed the transition of *Columbus* from historiography to poetry, fiction, and the stage. *Columbus* had entered
the English-speaking world as the thinnest of biographical subjects,
swaddled in the history of Spanish discoveries. Since 1553, that frail
character had been growing steadily within its historical surroundings, forecasting the emergence of a volume devoted primarily to the
life of *Columbus* and to the discovery of America less as the historical context of that life than as the crowning event in it. Evidence of
this biographical blossoming can be seen as early as 1683, in the *Life
of the Great Columbus*, tacked onto *The Present State of Jamaica*
but related to that subject only by a passing reference to him as the
island's "first Doscoverer" [*sic*] (99).

The next step toward biographical independence came with the
Churchills' inclusion of Fernando's "History of the Life and Actions
of Adm. Christopher Columbus" in their *Collection of Voyages and
Travels* (2.557–688), whose multivolume format provided a sort of
halfway house between historical subordination and biographical
self-sufficency. The model set here would be followed by Samuel
Nevill, who published chapter 1 of his *History of North America* in
the *New American Magazine* (January 1758) under the title "A Life
of Columbus"; as well as by the immensely popular collection *The
World Displayed* (1759–61), whose first volume proceeds immediately from Samuel Johnson's introductory essay to a narrative of

the life and voyages; and by William Burke's *Account of the Spanish Settlements* (1757), part 1 of which is given over to "An Account of the Discovery of America by the Celebrated Christopher Columbus."

Then, in 1741, *Columbus* broke into the open with the anonymous publication of *The History of the Voyages of Christopher Columbus in order to Discover America and the West Indies*, the first free-standing volume in English to give the name top billing and devote itself entirely to that subject. To be sure, the title of this biography retains traces of its generic origins; the *Columbus* named here is still surrounded by *The History of the Voyages . . . to Discover America*. At the same time, the phrase *in order to* effectually subsumes the discovery within the life of the discoverer by construing the outcome of the voyages as the voyager's original intentions. Although the next volume with *Columbus* on the cover lay three decades down the road, the name had arrived as a subject in its own right. By the time Washington Irving sat down to write *The Life and Voyages of Christopher Columbus* (1828), it had dominated the titles of more than thirty English publications. Before the century ran out, this first English monograph on the subject was followed by the first English poem (1756), translated epic (1773), original epic (1787), and play (1792), as well as the first English novel with *Columbus* among its main characters (1798).

Perhaps the most telling of these signs of growing presence—of that presentness which distinguishes literary from antiquarian discourse—is the entrance of *Columbus* into poetry as a principal subject. The discovery, of course, had attracted poetic attention from the beginning. It was in Alexander Barclay's translation of *Narrenschiff* that English readers first learned that

> Ferdynandus that late was kynge of spayne
> Of londe and people hath founde plenty and store
> Of whom the byndynge to us was uncertayne
> No christen man of them harde tell before. (Quinn, *NAW*
> 1.128)

Then, too, of the earliest English promoters of American expansion a disproportionate number were poets, including John Rastell, Matthew Roydon, Thomas Churchyard, Edward Dyer, Henry Roberts, George Gascoigne, Sir Walter Raleigh, Sir Philip Sidney, Andrew Marvell, and John Donne. *Columbus* appeared in an English poem only ten years after the name was introduced.

According to Charles Aleyn's *Historie of Henrie the Seventh* (1638; pp. 127–28), the discoverer himself took heart from the prophecy of a new world in Seneca's *Medea* (3.5), while the voyages, as reported, seem at once to replicate the *Odyssey* and to realize dreams of a golden age and an earthly paradise. Having been inspired by poetry to poetic undertakings, *Columbus* became an associate of writers who, like Thomas Gage, revealed to the world things previously unknown, as well as a source, for future poets, of such themes as the noble savage (Fairchild 34, 362). To Joel Barlow, *Columbus* is an "imperial Homer," one whose epic voyages have spawned happy nations the way "the living lays" of the greatest poet have inspired "unnumber'd bards" (138). To Freneau, only poets have the interests of *Columbus* at heart: rather than "America,"

> Columbia the name was, that merit decreed,
> But Fortune and Merit have never agreed—
> Yet the poets alone, with commendable care,
> Are vainly attempting the wrong to repair. ("Sketches,"
>   82)

Columbus had already appeared in English verse at least a dozen times when Pope asked, rhetorically:

> Who bid the stork, *Columbus*-like, explore
> Heav'ns not his own, and worlds unknown before? (3.102)

But not until Richard Rolt's *On Christopher Columbus, The First Discoverer of America* (1756) did an English poem give *Columbus* the attention that Colón, Colombo, and Colom had been receiving on the Continent since 1493. Rolt's is part of an explosion of Columbian poems in the eighteenth century. Including the translation of Duboccage's *La Colombiade*, in 1773, no fewer than ten English poems took up the subject between 1756 and 1798, when James Lovell Moore published his own *Columbiad*. Continental writers produced another ten: a Latin epic by Ubertino da Carrara (1715);

poems in French by Duboccage (1756), Nicolas Louis Bourgeois (1773), Robert Le Suire (1781), the Chevalier de Langeac (1872) and Pierre Laureau (*en prose*, 1782); an Italian poem by Alvise Querini (1759); a German epic by Johann Bodmer (1753); and one in Spanish by Francisco Vasconcellos (1701).

Whatever may have triggered this international upsurge, the sudden flurry of English poems about *Columbus* reflects the growing semantic force of the name. Thanks to recent translations of Fernando's *Life* (1704), of Herrera (1725) and Muñoz (1797), and of documents ascribed to *Columbus* himself (1785), legends long familiar in other languages became available to English readers, waiting to spring up at the approach of the name and surround it with scenes, stories, and ready-made sentiments. Tales of the fated Beatriz, of *Columbus* before the doctors of Salamanca, of his retreat to the convent of La Rabida, of Isabella's jewels, the rag-tag crew enlisted for the first voyage, the quelling of the mutiny aboard the Santa María, the trumphal return to Barcelona, and the riddle of the egg—such yarns lent *Columbus* that imaginative presence that historical figures achieve only by detaching themselves from their own circumstances and entering into the reader's world.

No less important to the poeticization of *Columbus* is the opposite tendency of eighteenth-century writers to detach the name from the person and use it metaphorically, as a sign of ingenuity, daring, foresight, progress, injustice, and the like. Such eponymous usages, to be sure, depend somewhat upon the reader's prior knowledge of the stories and scenes from which they arise and to which they allude. With enough explanation in context, however, they can serve as the source of those allusions for uninstructed readers. More people today know Hector from the verb than from Homer. It is also true that these usages are endemic to poetry and hence may begin, instead of ending, there. The very first appearance of *Columbus* in English verse (Seall, 1563) also marks the first metaphoric use of the name in the language.

Nonetheless, the associative use of *Columbus* increases in both frequency and ingenuity as the history of British America unfolds. The practice can be seen stirring in seventeenth-century efforts to extract the character from the name. In one of the dedicatory poems for John Smith's *Generall Historie, Columbus* is the "Indies true Christopher" (A5 verso). In the biographical sketch appended to *The Present State of Jamaica* (1683), the narrator pauses to apostrophize: "O name Collon . . . which to the World's end hast conducted Colonies; or may I call thee Collumba, for thy Dove-like simplicity and patience; the true Columna or Pillar whereon the knowledge of the new World is founded; the true Christopher, which with more than Giant-like force and Fortitude, hast carried Christ . . . to unknown lands" (107). By the eighteenth century, *Columbus* had become a metaphorical commonplace, fit for almost any occasion. In 1763, Jonathan Mayhew cried out against Anglican efforts to create a bishopric in America: "Will they never let us rest in peace? Is it not enough that they persecuted us out of the old world? . . . What other new world remains as a sanctuary for us from their oppression . . . ? Where is the Columbus to explore one for, and pilot us to it, before we are consumed by the fame of episcopacy?" (Rossiter, 232). To his European admirers, Benjamin Franklin was "the new Columbus" (Schmitt, 150).

The poeticization of *Columbus* is especially evident in the increasing tendency of writers to abstract his character as often from well-known poems on other subjects as from histories and biographies of *Columbus* himself. By far the most common of these poetic sources was *Paradise Lost*, whose principal dramatis personae provided models for every conception of the discoverer. Joseph Reed's *Columbus*, being "raised above the rest of mankind . . . , approximates to the Deity" (293). As one who drove "a free people . . . from fruitfulness and amenity," condemning them "to labour for the support of life, a prey to despondency, which the recollection of their former happiness sharpened" (36), the *Columbus* of John Payne imitates Satan. Alexander Martin's *Columbus* is the Son, divinely instructed to open a new era of human history that, although long plagued by war and tyranny, will eventuate in a reign of freedom. Joel Barlow's *Columbus* is Adam, consoled for the loss of his new world by an angelic vision of the distant millenium.

Philip Freneau covers all these Miltonic bases in his "Pictures of Columbus" (wr. 1744). Like Adam, the hero is granted a vision of the future, albeit prior to his adventures rather than after them and by a witch instead of an angel. Then, like Satan, he wins over Ferdinand by playing upon the "weak female vanity" (*Poems* 95) of Isabella. As one of the king's courtiers puts it,

> He acts the devil's part in Eden's garden;
> Knowing the man was proof to his temptations
> He whisper'd something in the ear of Eve,
> And promis'd much, but not meant to perform. (99)

To Isabella, *Columbus* then presents himself as the Son, born of woman to regain Paradise:

> As men were forc'd from Eden's shade
> By errors that a woman made,
> Permit me at a woman's cost
> To find the climates that we lost. (102)

Like Satan's flight from Hell to Paradise, however, the voyage of *Columbus* ends with a second fall, with Sin and Death at large in the New World, and the destroyer, chained like Lucifer on the burning lake, lamenting his folly:

> Why was I seated by my prince's side,
> Honour'd, caressed like some first peer of Spain?
> Was it that I might fall most suddenly
> From Honour's summit to the sink of scandal!
> 'Tis done, 'tis done!—what madness is ambition! (120)

The poeticizing of *Columbus* and the semantic effects of that process show up nowhere more clearly than in the writings of Freneau, who may be called the premier Columbian poet of the eighteenth century. He took up the subject when he was still an undergradute at Princeton, and he published an essay called "The Bones of Columbus" more than fifty years later, shortly before he died. In the meantime, he wrote two of the first three original English poems about the discoverer, as well as several other items, verse and prose, in which *Columbus* appears.

All together, these pieces create the impression that *Columbus*

TRANSITION TO IDEA finally interested Freneau less as a historical figure to be celebrated in verse than as a receptacle for his own uncertainties regarding the dual obligations of the poet to society and to the unsettling truths that imagination discovers. Freneau was by no means the only poet of his day to notice this growing conflict; the verses of his contemporaries are full of it. Nor was he the first English writer to recognize the difficulty of reconciling *Columbus* the missionary of Christian civilization with *Columbus* the bigoted destroyer of pagan innocence. He was the first, however, to see the resemblances between these two problems and to analyze the former by transposing it into the terms of the latter.

Freneau's earliest known exercise in this mode is "Columbus to Ferdinand," thought to be a remnant of a historical epic that the poet began at Princeton but later abandoned. Whatever the reasons for that decision, and regardless of whether this dramatic monologue was ever part of the larger work, the poem is unusual among English treatments of the subject in its attention to a single episode in the by now generally familiar story of *Columbus*, and to him as a particular individual rather than as a historical agent. Instead of inviting the reader to regard the visions of *Columbus* in the light of their later validation and present benefical effects, the poem removes him from the long history of the New World to concentrate on the sources of his inspiration, his methods, and the workings of his own mind.

Columbus begins by trying to align his personal obsession with the interests of the Crown. If Ferdinand will support the undertaking, he will "Shine forth the patron and the prince of art" (*Poems* 46). By "art," *Columbus* apparently means the science of navigation, something of value to imperial Spain and its monarch. At the same time, the word suggests something less consensual and rational than scientific skill, something more personal and inspired, for *Columbus* goes on to ground his vision, alternately, in "reason's voice" (47) and in Seneca's poetic prophecy of "a mighty land / Far, far away, where none have rov'd before" (48).

Initially, *Columbus* seems to name these two authorities in order to persuade Ferdinand that he has done his homework and knows what he is about. As the poem proceeds, however, *Columbus* appears less concerned to win the king's support than to persuade himself that his authorities are not in conflict, that reason will verify what the imagination has conceived. Speaking of himself in the third person, as of an enthusiast being subjected to rational judgment, *Columbus* turns the projected voyage into an allegory of daring wedded to reason:

> He fears no storms upon the untravell'd deep;
> Reason shall steer, and skill disarm the gale.
>
> Nor does he dread to lose the intended course,
> Though far from land the reeling galley stray,
> And skies above, and gulphy seas below
> Be the sole objects seen for many a day. (48)

Freneau's next, and longest, poem on the discoverer, "The Pictures of Columbus" (1774), again forsakes historical narrative for dramatic utterance—both soliloquy and dialogue—in order to concentrate still more closely on the relative value of "reason" and "fancy" as sources of knowledge that is both absolutely true and socially beneficial. *Columbus* first reasons that Nature would not tolerate an asymetric geography and then imagines a New World to counterbalance the Old. To confirm the reasonableness of this intuition, he consults an "Inchantress" in her magic cave, where he simultaneously begs her advice and spurns her mumbo-jumbo as delusory. To win over Ferdinand, he plays upon the monarch's superstition, which he does not share, although nearly everyone else considers him a "mad-brain'd enthusiast" (*Poems* 99) whose dreams belie reason (108). Publicly, he rests his belief in the existence of a New World on "antiquity . . . and reason's plainer page" (98), while secretly he fears that the prophecies of the Inchantress "may have represented things untrue, / Shadows and visions for realities" (104). The discovery at first removes these doubts, but when he lies dying, alone and disgraced, they return:

> Were these the hopes deceitful fancy bred;
> And were her painted pageants nothing more
> Than this life's phantoms by delusion led?

Then, just as he is expecting to die "Prais'd by no poet" (121), he is granted a brief vision of the future by none other than "golden fancy" (122), which reassures him that his private imaginings do in fact conduce to the common good.

These doubts of *Columbus* regarding the trustworthiness of the fancy and its ultimate social value raise another question of interest to an aspiring national bard: if the imagination tends to violate reigning opinion, both official and popular, can a true poet also be a republican? When *Columbus* emerges from the Inchantress's cave and publishes the vision she has shown him, everyone—"princes, kings, and nobles" (95), the church (91), and ordinary citizens alike (107)—calls him a "madman" (98). To the populace, he is "A foreigner, an idiot, an impostor, / An infidel" (108). To him, they are "dastards" and "worthless scum" (112), "content to wallow in the mire" (106) of settled belief. "Why," *Columbus* asks Nature,

> hast thou treated those so ill,
> Whose souls, capacious of immense designs,
> Leave ease and quiet for a nation's glory,
> Thus to subject them to these little things,
> Insects, by heaven's decree in shapes of men! (113)

Not until he has been dead for centuries will the world come around to his way of thinking. Meanwhile, to speak for the future, he must speak against the present, denying himself the audience and the fame that justly belong to a public benefactor.

But can such private imaginings, so contrary to public opinion, so dependent on demagoguery for their acceptance, really benefit anyone? The Inchantress tells *Columbus* what will come of his designs:

> The nations at the ocean's end,
> No longer destined to be free,
> Shall owe distress and death to thee!
> The seats of innocence and love
> Shall soon the seats of horror prove. (94)

As for *Columbus* himself, he can expect "hard misfortune . . . cold neglect and galling chains . . . poor solitude . . . Reproach and want"

(93–94). He and the New World will suffer alike, moreover, not because his undertaking is itself misconceived but because, instead of seeking public counsel, he has dared to disturb the "Mistress of the magic spell" (92).

As a sometime progressive and a sometime primitivist, Freneau was ever of two minds regarding the discovery. Did *Columbus* prepare for "The Rising Glory of America" or merely for the extermination of the Aztecs, the Incas, and the Iroquois (86–87)? How can these two very different events be reconciled? Which one realized the vision of *Columbus*? In either case, did those dreams spring from "Nature" or from "Art"; from "the social virtues of the heart" (86) or from individual ambition, greed, curiosity, and the lust for power; from "fierce passions" like those that drove the Indians to tribal warfare and human sacrifice (88) or from the designing reason that invented the compass? "Alas!" Freneau exclaims in his "Sketches of American History":

> how few of all that daring train
> That seek new worlds embosomed in the main,
> How few have sailed on virtue's nobler plan,
> How few with motives worthy of a man! (86)

Was *Columbus* one of these few humane adventurers? Can he be taken as a model for the poet who would serve the public not by versifying its common sentiments but by discovering through the private imagination revolutionary truths that, although apparently dangerous and mad, will prove liberating and universally beneficial in time? By making *Columbus* the bearer of such questions, Freneau greatly enhanced the capacity of the name as a semantic container for current concerns of many sorts—not least the historical and moral legitimacy of the emerging United States.

The New Nation, 1776–1798

Of all the events that make up Anglo-American history, from the English discovery of America in 1510 to the American conquest of English after World War II, none approaches the American Revolution as an influence on the meaning of *Columbus*. Over the previous two centuries, new senses had been added repeatedly to the word in order to keep the discoverer abreast of the ever-changing place he was supposed to have discovered. After the Revolution, this semantic development continued, even accelerated, as countless historians, biographers, novelists, poets, and polemicists wrote back into *Columbus* foreshadowings of each new present in the history of the nation: the *Columbus* of 1992 is as different from that of 1792 as Freneau's is from Richard Eden's. The Revolution itself, however, marks a sudden mutation in the word, for at that point the meaning of *America* changed, from the name for Britain's New World possessions to a short title for the United States, and from a synonym for *empire* to another word for *liberty*. What had been the history of British America became the early or prehistory of the new nation, transforming *Columbus* from the founder of an empire into the first citizen of an independent republic.

This is not to say that the history of British America stops altogether in 1776. It and the Columbus who began it are still intact in *The Present State of the West Indies, . . . together with an authentic account of the first discovery of these islands . . .*, published in London in 1778. Where the British *Columbus* does survive the Revolution, he goes his own way, which is to say not usually in the direction of George Washington. In the anonymous *Interesting account of the early voyages made by the Portuguese, Spaniards, etc. . . . including the voyages of Columbus* (1790), the discoverer's lineage descends straight to the great circumnavigator Captain Cook. Britons like John Williams and Robert Plott, however, seem less resigned to the rebel kidnapping of *Columbus*. There is a distinct odor of sour grapes about the efforts of these writers (1791 and 1777) to revive the slumbering Madoc as the founder of what was left of British America and to dismiss the pretentions of traitorous *Columbus* to that honor.

The unforeseen disruption of British-American history by the Revolution is plainly evident in two monographs that were all but complete when the rebellion broke out. In both W. A. Young's *History of North and South America . . . to which is added an impartial inquiry into the present American disputes* (1776) and William

Russell's *The History of America . . .* , *with an Appendix, contain-ing an account of the rise and progress of the present unhappy con-test between Great Britain and her colonies* (1778), the colonial his-ory begun by *Columbus* finds an altogether unanticipated sequel in the last chapter. Nationalist historians learned to pave over this fissure by predating the birth of the United States some three centu-ries, as in Jedediah Morse's *History of America. Containing . . . A concise history of the late revolution* (1790). But, for imperial histo-rians who had proceeded on the expectation that British America would continue to develop along an unbroken line extending from *Columbus*, through the present, and far into the future, the Revolu-tion threatened their view of the past with instant obsolescence.

William Robertson recognized the heavy impact of the unfore-seen present upon all previous constructions of the past. He had meant to withhold the successive books of his *History of America* until he had finished recounting the betrayal of *Columbus*'s humane New World vision by Spain, its rescue by England, and its ultimate realization in the colonies of British America. When the war broke out, Robertson had brought the history of Spanish America up to the present but had got only as far as 1688 in the history of Virginia and 1652 in that of New England. Divided in his own mind about the justice and wisdom of the Revolution, and unable in any case to predict the "new order of things" that must follow it, Robertson published the chronicle of Spanish America in 1777, promising to complete the narrative of British America, "in which I had made some progress" (3), when its outcome clarified. In the event, how-ever, that "progress" turned out to have been misdirected. Instead of a present with a dark Spanish past and a bright New World future, British America had become the outworn past of a new nation, whose future lay somewhere altogether different and unpredictable. At Robertson's death, his son found among his papers the two books on Virginia and New England, "as carefully corrected as any of his manuscripts which I had ever seen" (388) but still mired in a history whose future had evaporated.

The British *Columbus* and the American one can be examined side by side in the first English play to bear the name, Thomas Morton's *Columbus; or, a World Discovered* (1792), and in the *New*

Scene Interesting to Citizens of the United States that Alexander Martin wrote for Morton's play when it was performed "with applause at the New Theatre in Philadelphia" (t.p.) six years later. Morton's play opens with a verse prologue by one W. T. Fitzgerald, advising the audience that

> Columbus' story patronis'd by you
> Will yield an offering, grateful to his dust—
> A British laurel on a hero's bust.

This patronage will not be unearned. When *Columbus*, upon landing in the New World, asks his crewmen which of them sighted it first, who should step forward but Harry Herbert, an Englishman and, although self-exiled to Spain, "a credit to [his] nation" (4–5). How much a credit Herbert proves by sticking to *Columbus*, in act 2, when the Spanish sailors and their evil officers rebel, and by remaining loyal when the captain is sent back to Ferdinand in chains. After much complication and many crimes against the Indians by the rebels, *Columbus* returns, declaring himself an American rather than a Spaniard with the line, "Oh, my dear country, for I must call thee mine," and lamenting the day he allied himself with Spain: "Had I earlier known that England's monarch would have graced my fortunes with his victorious banner, then would [America's] freedom have been firmly fixed—they only who themselves are free, give liberty to others" (50). The play ends with the defeat of the rebels and an epilogue that equivocates the title of the drama and the name of its hero:

> BRITONS again behold Columbus sue
> To have his fortunes patronis'd by you;
> To your support alone he trusts his course,
> And rests his fame on Englishmen's applause. (52)

The new concluding scene that Alexander Martin wrote for American audiences is a blank-verse dialogue between *Columbus* and "The Genius of America," with a closing "Song" by the "attendant Genii" of the New World. In the dialogue proper, Genius reveals that it was he, not the British spirit of empire, who inspired *Columbus* to seek America, long hidden from grasping Europe, and who guided him to these shores. In order to steel *Columbus* against the injustice and ingratitude he will suffer at the hands of his European rivals, Genius has been sent from heaven with a vision of the future. After describing the extent, the native population, and the natural wealth of the place *Columbus* has found, Genius recounts the Black Legend that will ensue from the discovery, causing *Columbus* to regret his ever having set sail. Repine not, says Genius, for the discovery will awaken England to the existence of America and attract settlers like the freedom-loving William Penn. Better still, when England, envious of the growing wealth and power of the colonies, tries to impose despotic rule upon them, they will form a new nation dedicated to liberty. Could I live to see this happy day, *Columbus* replies, " 'T would all my dangers and my wrongs repay" (8). Genius goes on to name the heroes of the Revolution and the authors of the Constitution and then, with a warning against factionalism, returns to heaven, leaving *Columbus* consoled by the knowledge

> That a great nation yet unborn
> Shall people my new earth, new empires raise
> On Freedom founded, teaching laws and arts,
> And shielding nations from tyrannic sway. (10)

Instead of the BRITONS whom Morton begged to patronize his *Columbus*, Martin's final chorus hails "Columbia," giving America its rightful name and naturalizing its discoverer in a stroke.

These rival *Columbus*es confront each other again in two issues of the *American Museum* published during the tricentennial year. The July number for 1792 carried an excerpt from John Payne's *New and Complete System of Geography* (London 1791), entitled "Some account of Christopher Columbus, with an enquiry into his true character; in opposition to the prevailing opinion which is entertained of it." The "prevailing opinion," evidently, is that *Columbus* was not only a man of "superior fortitude, and . . . steady perseverance" but one "equally distinguished for piety and virtue." In fact, says Payne, he waged unprovoked and unequal war against the Indians during his second voyage, with the result that "five hundred of [them] were sent (or rather brought by Columbus) to Spain, and sold publicly in Seville as slaves" (35). No debunking journalist or revisionist historian of 1992 would be harder on *Columbus* than Payne is here. "Strange contradiction!" he exclaims, "Columbus is celebrated for his humanity and goodness; but should he not rather be considered as a most consummate dissembler, professing moderation while he considered subversion? and . . . renouncing every principle of justice and humanity, when they stopped the career of his ambition?" (36). Let those who would make this villain their Moses do so, Payne implies; "very fortunately for the future wellbeing of the country," Bartholomew's request for English support "met with no success" (33).

Four months later, the *American Museum* displayed an altogether different *Columbus* in "An oration on the discovery of America. Delivered by Mr. Joseph Reed of Philadelphia at the late commencement anniversary held at Princeton, New Jersey." Where Payne's *Columbus* was Satanic, Reed's is positively godlike. "True genius," Reed maintains, "is a ray of divinity, which beams only on the tall and elevated mind. A capacity for bold and original discovery resembles the power of creation; and its possessor . . . approximates to the Deity" (293). "If there be an object truly sublime in nature," Reed continues, "it is Columbus on his first voyage to America! To use the language of antiquity, it is a sight which the gods themselves might behold with pleasure" (294). As a result of this voyage, science and commerce began their march toward the present. And "last, but not least," the discovery "has afforded an asylum to the oppressed of all nations. America, hidden for ages, is laid open to view at the very time when liberty, 'hunted down in the old world,' was panting for the asylum she found in the new." Through the spirit of Liberty, Reed connects *Columbus* directly to the United States: "Hither [Liberty] retired with our stern forefathers—here she preserved her sacred fires—here she beheld her patriot sons grow bold in her cause, till in the fulness of time she announced herself to the world, and established her empire forever" (295–96).

Reed's image of *Columbus* landing on Plymouth Rock represents fairly, if a trifle simplistically, the plan of succession adopted by many nationalist historians after the Revolution. Whereas British-American history had usually included the conquest of Mexico and Peru as an unfortunate, if not very surprising, interlude between the discovery and the settlement of Jamestown, histories of the United States were apt to skip that phase altogether and go straight from *Columbus* to the Puritans. The first volume of Jeremy Belknap's *American Biography* (1794) stands *Columbus* beside the settlers of New England, the leaders of the Revolution, and the framers of the Constitution—all co-authors of American liberty. (To justify this placement, Belknap closes his essay with a detailed rebuttal of Payne's indictment of *Columbus* as the founder of American slavery.) After 1800, this direct association of *Columbus* with America's stern forefathers and patriot sons would be routine. Volume 1 of Richard Snowden's *History of North and South America, From Its Discovery to the Death of General Washington* (1805) deals with *Columbus*, Volume 2 with the War for Independence. In Henry Trumbull's *History of the Discovery of America: of the landing of our forefathers at Plymouth, and of their most remarkable engagements with the Indians in New England* (1802), the colon spans more than a century. The anonymous *American Chronology* (1813) moves in the opposite direction. Instead of bringing *Columbus* forward in time to join the founding fathers, the compiler extends the history of the new nation back to the discovery, providing a *Summary of Events relating to the United States from 1492 to 1813.*

But however the thing was done, naturalizing *Columbus* entailed problems more difficult than the lapse of time between discoverer and discovery. If imperial historians had managed to make *Columbus* more English than Spanish in order to justify the occupation of British America, early national historians traced the origins of the American republic to *Columbus* precisely because, having been rebuffed or ignored by Henry VII, he was not English and so provided the United States with a non-British, even an anti-British, origin. Unfortunately, the less English *Columbus* became, the less he resembled the America he had discovered. To find *Columbia* innate in *Columbus*, and *Columbus* fructified in *Columbia*, national history would first have to explain how a superstitious Spanish agent who enslaved Indians could be considered the founder of a Protestant Anglo-America dedicated to scientific progress, peaceful commerce, and political liberty, and then show how this Columbian spirit was transmitted through generations of conquistadores, buc-

caneers, and colonial warriors to blossom at last in a nation dedicated to life, liberty, and the pursuit of happiness.

Although Joel Barlow's *Vision of Columbus* (1787) is neither the
most original nor the most successful of post-Revolutionary efforts
to connect *Columbus* with the republic, the epic does define the
problem with great clarity. That the birth of the United States
should have been greeted with an epic poem about *Columbus* is
hardly surprising. The literary standing of the genre among readers
and writers schooled in the classics, its association with the founding and emergence of national cultures, and its penchant for dra-
matizing history through the adventures of an individual hero all
recommended the epic to an infant nation concerned to legitimize
itself and display its good breeding in a modern *Aeneid*.

As for *Columbus*, that name came equipped with epic associations, owing to previous treatments by promoters of British America, for whom *Columbus* rivaled Ulysses as a paragon adventurer,
and by continental poets like Madame Duboccage, whose *La Colombiade* (1756) had been translated into English in 1773. What is
more, the *Columbus* whom imperial historians had made the
founder of British America now personified an independent nation
given to styling itself Columbia and everything connected with it
Columbian. When the call went out, then, for an American literature that would at once lend the rebellion historical legitimacy and
show the new nation capable of producing great literature, aspiring
national bards like Freneau, Barlow, and Charles Brockden Brown
quite naturally set about writing Columbiads.

What is surprising is how unsuitable the epic proved, if not to
the facts of American history up through the Revolution, then at
least to the history America wanted for itself and, hence, to the
Columbus it wanted for its founder. Freneau seems to have grasped
this incompatibility among genre, story, and hero early in the game.
The commencement ode that he and Hugh Henry Brackenridge
composed at Princeton in 1771 opens with *Columbus*, as if to trace
"The Rising Glory of America" directly from the discovery. No
sooner is "the hero" (*Poems* 49) introduced, however, than he is
dropped. Since the discovery leads directly to the crimes of Cortés

and Pizarro, the poem would have to navigate a sea of blood in order to arrive at the peaceable present. Whether or not it was this discovery that led Freneau to abandon his projected Columbiad, his decision to treat *Columbus*, in his later poems, as a Hamlet or a Macbeth, rather than as an Aeneas or Ulysses, does avoid the problem of thematic continuity by turning away from the history of the discovery to the psychology of the discoverer.

If Barlow heard this warning, he ignored it. With the help of Moses, Vergil, Milton, Madame Duboccage, and Freneau himself, Barlow solved the formal problem of keeping *Columbus* present throughout the epic action by rendering American history as a vision of the future, granted to console the despondent hero with a very long look at the initially baneful but ultimately glorious results of his discovery. This *Vision of Columbus*, however, turns out to be mostly vision and very little *Columbus*—so little that, after completing the poem, Barlow felt obliged to summarize the life and accomplishments of his hero in the introduction, ostensibly for the benefit of American readers who might not know Robertson's *History* (vii). Throughout the poem itself, *Columbus* is repeatedly called "the hero" (38), "the great Discoverer" (42), and "the Chief" (46). Not once, however, does he do anything to earn these epithets. Insofar as he acts at all, he listens to his seraphic tutor, watches the vision unfold, asks set questions calculated to evoke prepared answers, and responds—whenever Barlow remembers whose vision it is—with a distinctly unheroic tear (63) or sigh (130).

Heroic deeds are performed entirely by others—Manco Capac, Raleigh, Wolfe, Washington, General Lincoln—men less given than *Columbus* to repining at ill fortune and longing for release from this troubled life. His purportedly "venturous soul" (55) finds its tongue once, early in the poem, in a wish to reenter the history of discovery, but is quickly silenced by the Angel:

> Though still to virtuous deeds thy mind aspires,
> And heavenly visions kindle new desires;
> Yet hear with reverence what attends thy state,
> Nor pass the confines of eternal fate. (38)

From then on, *Columbus* sits passively on the sidelines of the poem, visible only as a pronoun and a verb ("He saw") and sometimes disappearing altogether for whole books at a stretch. Not for nothing is he called "the great Observer" (168).

The history *Columbus* observes is glorious enough in the epic sense but distinctly inglorious when viewed from the pastoral present to which it has supposedly led. From the discovery to the Revolution, that history is an uninterrupted parade of wars: among native tribes, between Europeans and Indians, among the several invading nations, between Britain and the rebel colonies. On the other hand, the *Columbus* who initiates all this bloodshed and the America that somehow emerges from it are both devoted to peace. He left Spain in search not of military conquest but of "peaceful triumph o'er this newfound world" (31), and his vision of the liberal, harmonious society that will finally realize his pacific design opens with a hymn to returning peace (199–200). Where, then, has peace been hiding in the meantime?

"Too long," the poet laments, shouldering the Angel aside:

Too long the groans of death, and battle's bray
Have rung discordant through the unpleasing lay. (199)

That is, the poem has been an epic, all right, but unfortunately "a regular Epic" (xxi), an American *Iliad* or *Aeneid* rather than a *Columbiad*. Evidently sensing the discrepancy between his hero and his epic story, Barlow has the Angel reverse "the flight of time" (201), in book 7, and rehearse the entire history of America in a quasi-pastoral mode, as a course of imperial husbandry rather than warfare. Then, in book 8, Barlow suspends the vision altogether, while the Angel explains to *Columbus* why the progress of reason is so slow and so frequently interrupted by strife. From this rationalization, there emerges an idea for a new sort of epic, one more appropriate to modern conditions. In ancient times, the Angel muses,

When pride and rapine held their vengeful sway,
And praise pursued where conquest led the way,
Fair nature's mildest grace, the female mind,
By rough-brow'd power neglected and confined,

Unheeded sigh'd, mid empire's rude alarms,
Unknown its virtues and enslaved its charms.
. . . .
Blest Science then, to rugged toils confined,
Rose but to conquer and enslave mankind. (222)

In this advanced age, however,

A happier morn now brightens in the skies,
Superior arts, in peaceful glory, rise;
While softer virtues claim their guardian care,
And crowns of laurel grace the rising fair. (222–23)

As a result of this feminine influence, masculine activities—
commerce, agriculture, industry, government, even war, but, most
important, the exploration of "unknown worlds" (223)—all conduce to domestic tranquillity:

Then, while the daring Muse, from heavenly quires,
With life divine the raptured bard inspires,
With bolder hand he strikes the trembling string,
Virtues and loves and deeds like thine [i.e., *Columbus*'s]
    to sing. (224)

Barlow took a swipe at this "trembling string" when he turned
The Vision into *The Columbiad* (1807). In the meantime, James
Lovell Moore, master of the Free Grammar School in Hertford, England, tried his hand at explaining how the precursor of Cortés and
Pizarro could also be the sire of George Washington. Moore—one of
those "American" Englishman, like William Lisle Bowles, James
Montgomery, Samuel Rogers, and George Waddington, who celebrated *Columbus* in verse—saw in the Revolution a great leap toward the ideals of individual freedom and social harmony that guide
historical progress; and his *Columbiad*, like Barlow's *Vision*, struggles mightily to discover the sources of enlightened America in its
shady past. Moore's narrator attempts the first connections between
Spanish then and Anglo-American now in book 4 by pausing at each
island *Columbus* raises during the second voyage to recount England's future battles with Spain and France for their possession. In

book 6, Moore abandons narrative hindsight for divine foresight, as Raphael descends from heaven to inspire *Columbus* with a vision of Britain's eventual conquest of North America. Then, in book 7, *Columbus* is visited by the genius loci of the Orinoco, who unveils the coming Revolution and prophesies the future glory of the new nation. In book 11, an angel arrives to quell the mutiny in Hispaniola and, by reassuring *Columbus* of God's favor, to prepare him for the trial that awaits him back in Spain.

Like the vision Barlow gave *Columbus*, these reveal, more or less, what will happen in the centuries to come without explaining how it will do so or what it all means. Moore himself seems to have been perfectly aware of this failing. Instead of pressing on to show how the actions and fate of *Columbus* generate the future events that the narrator has recounted and the three spirits have revealed, Moore's narrative loops back, in book 12, to rehash the action of the preceding three books in the form of *Columbus*'s testimony at his trial. Persuaded by his eloquence, Ferdinand orders the admiral back to America to estabish a prosperous and just colony that will lay the foundations for the distant republic. But since Moore knew perfectly well that nothing of the sort actually happened, and makes no effort to invent a mythical substitute for what did happen, his *Columbus* sails off into an empty fiction utterly devoid of either historical or poetic conviction. The epic insists that he is headed straight for Philadelphia, but any reader not totally uninformed would have known that *Columbus* was in for some unpleasant surprises.

Given these repeated failures by historians and poets to make *Columbus* a plausible founder of the United States, one can only wonder at the force and persistence of their felt need to do so. What was there in that name to inspire amateurs like Barlow and Moore to prodigies of versification in the quixotic hope of turning *Columbus* into a Yankee? Why did they not simply dismiss the project as unworkable, not to say unnecessary, and seek their historical legitimation somewhere less anomalous? The only explanation for an aim so seemingly irrational must lie in the history of the word *Columbus* itself, in the meanings it had acquired over two centuries of increasing use by Anglophones preoccupied with the discovery of America and its unceasing impact on every arrangement of life, from the largest to the most immediate and ordinary. *[cause + effect?]*

To say that, however, is merely to displace the question without quite answering it. Why, of all the names available, did *Columbus* become the English synonym for *America* and *discovery?* Vespucci entered the language earlier and shared his name with the place. Cabot—to say nothing of Madoc—was in every way less obstinately foreign. Drake, Raleigh, and Smith were not only English but names, unlike *Columbus*, borne by persons actually known to those who first wrote and read about their crucial roles in the establishment of British America. As for *Columbus*, no English speaker ever laid eyes on a man so called. Whatever information English writers attached to the name came from foreign sources and was sketchy, conflicting, and unverifiable. Of English commentaries on the discovery, plenty doubted the priority or the ultimate importance of *Columbus*, and their arguments were no weaker, certainly, than those they questioned. If Anglo-America demanded a history beginning in a single, identifiable, individual human action, how did *Columbus* get chosen over other, seemingly sounder alternatives as the site for this elaborate construction?

It is a mystery. Like Barlow and Moore, the historian of *Columbus* can chronicle the documented events, but their cause and rationale remain elusive. The answer may lie in the problem itself. What favored *Columbus* may well have been its semantic emptiness, its initial paucity of reference and settled meaning, combined with its seeming specificity of denotation. As a proper name, *Columbus* said "fact." As a word referring solely to other words, *Columbus* lent itself to endless redefinition. The published letters of Vespucci limited the adaptability of that name; the absence of contemporary documents deprived Madoc of empirical weight. But *Columbus* was at once something specific, a supposed historical personage concerning whom some things were true and others not, and almost anything one might desire—including the father of American independence.

The trick, it seems, lay in neither adhering so closely to the already written history of *Columbus* that the word resisted adaptation to one's designs nor departing so far from that archive that one's invention lost all semblance of historicity. Barlow could not make Robertson's *Columbus* a plausible source of domestic tranquillity, while the *Columbus* who sets out in Moore's closing verses to found a humane colony in the New World lacks even the pretense of factuality. The necessary equipoise of history and invention, apparently, could not be attained in the epic. Saddled with defining conventions, the genre had become too artificial to convey the empirical authority required of modern history and too formally inelastic for the demands of modern fiction. The place to "dream strange things, and make them look like truth," as Hawthorne put it (1.36), was the novel, the genre that, born from the unbelievable truths and plausible lies of New World voyagers, had by 1800 perfected the art of obscuring the boundaries between history and invention. Before Barlow got around to feminizing his epic, and even as Moore was writing his, Susanna Rowson was supplying the wants of both of these writers by the simple expedient of transferring the story of *Columbus* from the epic to the novel.

Comprising "History, Poetry, Fiction and Truth, blended so soft as to relieve each other" (265), *Reuben and Rachel* (1798) employs the formal conventions of the domestic romance to reconcile both the heroic and the pastoral themes that Barlow's epic would not accommodate without a good deal of generic overhaul. Already fully feminized, the domestic romance required no tinkering. With its conventional story of a protagonist's departure from an imperfect home and discovery, by way of manifold adventures, of a new, perfect one, the genre welcomed those "virtues" of humanity and benevolence, those "deeds" of heroism, and, not least, those "loves" that had been denied to Barlow's *Columbus*. Better still, the organic connection between *Columbus* and Columbia that had eluded historians and epic poets came to the domestic romance automatically along with its central metaphor of the family tree. Observing that "the generality of books intended for students [of history] are written for boys" and deciding to write one, instead, "for my own sex only" (iv), Rowson recounted the history of America as the adventures of a single family during their three-hundred-year removal from the Old World to the New—a family descended directly from *Columbus.*

Ostensibly concerned with its titular characters—siblings in pre-Revolutionary Philadelphia—*Reuben and Rachel* devotes the first of its two volumes to explaining how they came to be Americans. The genealogy begins three centuries earlier, when *Columbus* marries one Beatina, the widow of a Spanish nobleman, and adopts her son, Ferdinando. Accompanying his stepfather on the third voyage, Ferdinando marries Orabella, daughter of the king of Peru. Their only surviving child, Isabelle, marries Sir Thomas Arundel, moves to England, and raises her daughter, Columbia, as a Protestant. Columbia marries Sir Egbert Gorges, by whom she has five children: Edward, who sails with Drake and dies in the assault on Santo Domingo; Jane, who dies in infancy; a second Beatina, who marries a Penn; Elizabeth, who marries a Dudley and bears one son, Henry; and a second Ferdinando, who marries a conveniently unnamed "lady of family and fortune" (126) and fathers yet another Isabelle. This latest Isabelle and her cousin Henry wed secretly. Their son, Edward, marries Arabella Ruthven and takes her to America, where their first son, William, marries a Narragansett princess named Oberea. These two produce a son, William, Jr., who grows up to marry Cassiah Penn, a direct descendent of Beatina Gorges Penn, from three generations back. Their two children are Reuben and Rachel, the "[l]ong look'd for come at last" (161) in volume 2.

No slumbering spirit of liberty or supernatural visions here: Reuben and Rachel are at once related to *Columbus*, through no fewer than three of his great-granddaughter Columbia's five offspring, and at home in America by virtue of having renounced their rights to English titles and raised their own "sons as true-born Americans" (363). What is more, the spirit of the patriarch has remained evident throughout the generations and all their changes of religion, nationality, and political allegiance. "Undaunted spirit of my ancestor," cries Columbia on reading the discoverer's letters to his wife, "may you ever inhabit the bosoms of his descendants" (17). Sir Ferdinando Gorges has "[t]he spirit of his great and enterprizing ancestor" (125). Edward Dudley "almost unperceptibly imbibed the enterprizing spirit that had characterized his ancestors" (138). As a boy, Reuben was "open, generous, unsuspecting, and possessed of a firmness of temper, almost approaching to obstinacy" (174); and as a young man, he is "[s]purred on by the native impulse of his mind, which incited him to activity, and inspired him with the most sanguine presentments of future prosperity" (210). Of Reuben and Rachel it can be said quite literally what Barlow could say of his fellow Americans only metaphorically, that they are *Columbus*'s "brave children" (162).

However "enterprizing," the transmitted spirit of *Columbus* is even more domestic. "Whilst I search this vast globe for unknown worlds," he writes to his bride, "I would have the fame, the glory of the discovery all your own . . . ; for you inspired the thought, prompted the searches, and are the magic charm that actuates all my endeavours" (13). Indeed, his sole motive for the undertaking is to restore the status she has lost by marrying him and to seek "in the new world a kingdom of which my Beatina shall be queen" (16). A model family man, *Columbus* labors, as he says, "not to my own advantage, but for the advantage of those so nearly, so dearly connected with me" (14). Imprisonment bothers him only for their sakes, "for of what consequence would the smiles or frowns of princes be to me, were not my wife and children [*sic*] to be involved in my disgrace" (34). Outside his family, Queen Isabelle alone commands his loyalty. To her he owes "the means of making the great attempt" (14). Although she calls him her "invincible hero" (41), it is she who rescues him from his detractors; he worships her, and dies soon after hearing of her death. As for the New World itself, *Columbus* says that "no man should ever claim a right to govern it" (16), for one woman inspired the discovery, and another financed it. To Queen Isabelle he proposes that the place be called *Columbia*, a nominal wedding of *Columbus* and Beatina (20).

Inspired by his wife and sustained by his queen in the discovery of a land named for his marriage, *Columbus* makes love the basis of his dealings with the Indians. "Go, valiant chief," Queen Isabelle commands, "and reign over a people you have conquered by practicing humanity, not the arts of war" (37). Ideally, *Columbus* himself should marry an Indian princess to domesticate the conquest. The trope had been around for some time, most recently in the story of Alonzo and Cora as told, successively, by Marmontel, Kotzebue, Sheridan, and Thomas Morton—any of whose plays Rowson could have seen on the American stage. (*Columbus*'s granddaughter Isabelle has an Indian servant named Cora, and both Orabella and Oberea seem to be variant forms of that name.) This voyager already has a Penelope, however, and since a Dido or a Circe would neither suit his domestic character nor serve his foreign policy, the office of marrying the New World falls to his "only son" (23).

Unfortunately, while *Columbus* is establishing domestic relations with Peru, the evil Roldan institutes a reign of "war, rapine, and destruction" in Hispaniola (26). And while the admiral and his family recuperate in Spain after the third voyage, the pirate Garcias takes over in Peru. Antagonists to *Columbus* the homemaker, these homewreckers seduce the daughters of his Indian friends and dispossess "thousands of innocent families" (46). "I sought not new worlds for conquest or for power" (26), *Columbus* insists, whereas Garcias, when asked by what right he commands Peru, replies, "by conquest; not by a ridiculous family compact with a savage" (43).

The language of domesticity, clearly, can sharpen the moral contrast between the benevolent designs of *Columbus* and the wicked behavior of his adversaries yet still permit him to perform heroic deeds in defense of his family. That idiom can also explain how his ideals, although not much in evidence throughout the three centuries of murder, rapine, and destruction that constitute American history, manage to survive within the family circle until they emerge with the Declaration of Independence to become the law of the land. The United States of America is the home *Columbus* sought when he set out from Spain to discover a place where his declassée bride could be a queen; and, like all the mothers and fathers of domestic fiction, he resides there in the persons of his descendants. For Richard Eden's *Columbus*, home lay back in monarchical Spain, which rewarded his American sojourn with the "glorious tittles" he coveted. Reuben and Rachel "renounce them; they are distinctions nothing worth, and should by no means be introduced into a young country" (2.363). *Columbus* has come a long way since Eden urged his readers to follow that "Gentleman of Italie" across the perilous ocean rather than to remain with the romancers, "in soft beddes at home, among the teares and weping of women" (6).

To be sure, the domestication of *Columbus* comes at some cost to the historical sources, including those that Rowson herself used. To spruce up the irregular domestic affairs of the historical *Columbus*, she gives her discoverer one wife, who survives him, rather than a wife who dies before his first voyage and a mistress who bears him a son; and gives him only one son, adopted, rather than two, the second illegitimate. To keep family matters at stage center, Beatina goes along on the third voyage, which ends up in Peru, a more likely spot than Hispaniola for Ferdinando to find a suitable bride. Then, it is Garcias, not *Columbus*, who exacts tribute from the Indians; and the Diego who shares command of the Hispaniola colony is Roldan's lieutenant, not *Columbus*'s brother. Princess Orabella seems to speak for Rowson when, about to regale her Peruvian friends with the wonders of Spain, she says, "[O]nly that they know my lips abhor falsehood, they would think that some of the strange things I have to relate were nothing more than fictions" (42).

In its slight regard for the historical record, of course, *Reuben and Rachel* really is nothing more than fiction. The domestic romance may have enabled Rowson to solve problems created by historians and funked by epic poets, but the form imposed demands of its own that violated history as much as the epic did. *Columbus* had his origin, his very being, in historiography. That was his native element, and he has to this day seldom breathed comfortably in any other medium. Never mind that the histories themselves were little more than fictions; those fictions had been couched in the forms, the vocabulary, the grammar, and the semantics of historiography; and it would not do merely to extract the fictions of *Columbus* from their natural habitat and allow them to propagate without check. Rowson was a facile romancer and a quick study, but she was no historian; and so her *Columbus*, in entering the reader's presence, leaves his own past behind. Not until Washington Irving did *Columbus* find a writer equally competent in both history and fiction. *The Life and Voyages of Christopher Columbus* (1828) contains more "stretchers" than Rowson, Barlow, and Moore put together. But, believing them himself, Irving put his fictions into a history rather than his history into a novel. In doing so, he made the distant past as present to his readers as Eden had made a far more recent past to his. There, the accumulated "History, Poetry, Fiction and Truth" of *Columbus* really would be "blended so soft as to relieve each other" and complete the definition of the word that ministered to Emerson's mind.

5

Franklin in His Element: The End of Early American Literature

Benjamin Franklin wrote the last install- ment of his autobiography in 1790. That same year, William Blake completed "The Marriage of Heaven and Hell." Just seven years later, Jane Austen began the novel we know as *Northanger Abbey*. As acknowledged classics of their respective genres, all written in the same language in the same decade, these three works, despite their obvious differences, would seem to belong in the same chapter of En- glish literary history. Indeed, had they been written in almost any other lan- guage—in French, say, or Spanish—or at some other time—before the American Revolution or after the First World War— they would doubtless have appeared side by side in the literary histories of their era. But because they were written in En- glish after 1776, when writings in the lan- guage supposedly divided into two separate national streams, and before 1918, when the two streams supposedly rejoined in the international current of English modernism, they are almost never spoken of in the same breath.

Franklin's *Autobiography*, being the work of an American, is considered an American work, on the assumption that anything done by an American is itself American, no matter how few other Americans or how many non-Americans have done something similar. Although begun when Franklin was still a loyal British subject; written in English, not in American; modeled avowedly on the styles of Bunyan and Defoe and on the

genre of advice to apprentices; prompted initially by demands from
London editors; composed largely in Europe; and published first in a
French translation, in Paris, the *Autobiography* belongs to American literary history—somewhere between Cotton Mather, whose
most fundamental beliefs (in divine revelation and infant depravity,
for example) Franklin utterly rejected, and Henry Thoreau, to whom
Franklin's beliefs (in civic conformity and the economic basis of
virtue) were equally repellant. Blake's poem and Austen's novel, on
the other hand, belong to the history of "English" literature—which
is to say, the literature of England. "The Marriage of Heaven and
Hell" occupies the "Romantic" phase of that history, alongside the
writings of Byron, whom Blake detested; and *Northanger Abbey*,
being expressly anti-Romantic despite its having been written
squarely in the "Romantic era," is ordinarily assigned to the "Victorian period," which would not arrive, even nominally, until Austen
was in her grave.

The customary distribution of these three linguistically and
chronologically related works into American, Romantic, and Victorian subcategories fairly typifies the fragmentation of English literary history between the closing decades of the eighteenth century
and the opening decades of the twentieth that has made this
period—although a good deal shorter and, arguably, more of a piece
than those we so blithely name the Middle Ages and the Renaissance—virtually incomprehensible to students, not to say experts,
in the field. No such uncertainty attends our conception of the periods that precede or follow this one. Rightly or wrongly, we entertain quite clear and distinct ideas of what the Eighteenth Century
means:

> Whether amid the gloom of night I stray,
> Or my glad eyes enjoy revolving day,
> Still Nature's various face informs my sense
> Of an all-wise, all-pow'rful Providence. (Gay 203)

Here John Gay displays a sensibility that is felt to be typical of the
period. Speaking ostensibly in his own voice, the poet addresses an
audience of persons essentially like himself, not to tell them something they don't know, but to proclaim himself one of them by

restating, in a recognizably poetic idiom, their shared beliefs and sentiments regarding the rationally intelligible organization of a world, at once vast and luminous, that exists independent of the words used to describe and celebrate it.

Similarly, we have little difficulty in framing for ourselves a literary idea of the Twentieth Century:

> Call the roller of big cigars,
> The muscular one, and bid him whip
> In kitchen cups concupiscent curds.
> . . . .
> Let be be finale of seem.
> The only emperor is the emperor of ice-cream. (Stevens,
> *Poems* 64)

An unidentifiable speaker—certainly not the poet—addresses someone equally obscure, someone apparently inside the poem, rather than the reader. This voice issues strange commands in an altogether unusual language and a tone at once jocular and desperate, creating in the process a populated scene whose existence depends entirely on the words used to describe it—words whose uncertain import tends to deepen, rather than to pave over, the differences between the withdrawn poet and his unaccommodated reader.

Regarding the literary landscape that stretches between these two very different but equally familiar locales, however, our historical imaginations entertain no such unitary picture, whether true or false. Instead of a single, coherent Nineteenth Century, we see three more or less discrete images: a Romantic era, followed by a Victorian period, with American literature lying off to one side. Nor can we form a composite image of the whole by combining these three pieces. Although carved out of the whole, they cannot possibly be reassembled to give us a vision of the period, for each is constructed on a different basis: Romantic literature according to how it is written, Victorian literature according to when it was written, and American literature according to where it was written. Worse yet, although they were created to distinguish among ostensibly different sorts of writing, because these categories are formed on differing principles they necessarily overlap, raising no logical barriers against our designating, say, Whitman's "As I Ebb'd With the Ocean of Life" at once Romantic in manner, Victorian in date, and American in provenance.

In addition to frustrating our efforts to see this period of English literature whole, the impossibility of either putting its parts together or keeping them apart has effectively prevented us from describing the literary development that runs through it, connecting its preceding period to the one that follows it. Instead of a single, coherent history of literature in English between the Enlightenment and Modernism, we have two incoherent histories: one British, the other American. The former comprises, in bewildering succession, the late eighteenth-century twilight of receding Neoclassicism and approaching Romanticism; the revolutionary but inexplicably short-lived Romantic era, whose label identifies only one of its various literary ingredients; the Victorian period, artificially unified under the name of the reigning monarch; and then, at the turn of the century, the Edwardians and Georgians, who somehow manage to be Romantic, Victorian, and Modern all at once. Over on the American side, running parallel to, but apart from, Britain's spasmodic literary history, the nineteenth century opens with the Early National period, named after its political circumstances, and then proceeds through three more or less distinct eras—the belatedly Romantic "American Renaissance," the "Rise of Realism," and "Naturalism"—named after the literary predilections of some, but by no means all, of the writers working at those times.

Incoherent in themselves and unrelated to each other, these two national literary histories cannot do, either singly or together, what history is supposed to do: explain in retrospect the relations of the past to the present. They were devised, early in the twentieth century, to explain what literary historians of the time thought was happening or wanted to happen—moral, economic, and social progress, on the one hand, and the realization of national literary independence on the other. Fashioned to those purposes, they cannot possibly explain what in fact happened: the somewhat tardy entrance, around the time of the First World War, of English letters as a whole into the international current of literary Modernism with the writings of such nationally displaced persons—British, American, and Irish—as Henry James, Joseph Conrad, Gertrude Stein, James Joyce, T. S. Eliot, Ezra Pound, D. H. Lawrence, and Samuel Beckett.

Like most historical developments, this one discredited the historical schemes that preceded it, and demanded a new literary history written from its own point of view. Owing to political interests, academic as well as national, however, this demand has never really been met. Even though studies of English Modernism have regularly acknowledged its international character by lumping the work of its major figures together in expatriate congress, studies of the preceding era have, with very few exceptions, gone on dividing it into British and American strands, ignoring the readily available evidence of widespread transatlantic literary commerce throughout the century and trying vainly to make each of these national strains produce international Modernism all by itself, whether by extending the Romantic movement up through the Victorian, Edwardian, and Georgian periods or by tracing Modernism back through the American Renaissance to the Puritans.

To the extent that these revisionary histories have recognized the Modern literary situation and allowed it to condition their critical point of view, they have managed to identify those writings of the period, both British and American, which, speaking most eloquently to contemporary ears, seem to constitute a Modern literary tradition. By continuing to separate these proto-Modern texts into Romantic, Victorian, and American compartments, however, they have obscured the relations, both literary and historical, among them and, hence, the very literary past that the Modern point of view at once demands and discloses. Instead of a coherent, intelligible literary period connected at one end to the Enlightenment and at the other to Modernism, we have a collection of Romantic, Victorian, and American masterworks united only by their common appeal to contemporary critical taste.

Since the proper subject of literary history is literature—those past texts in which an age discovers its own origins—the presently recognized classics are the materials with which a truly literary history of the period must deal. But a literary history must also be a history—an account of changes occurring in some continuous, unchanging entity—if it is not to be simply a chronology of essentially isolated events. To be at once literary—as opposed to, say, political or social or intellectual—and historical—rather than merely chronological—literary history must find in successive literary texts a temporally continuous, essentially literary property that will allow the differences among them to be seen and treated as developments, changes in that constant element.

As I have said before, the only thing that will meet all these requirements of a truly literary history is the particular language in which the literary texts in question are written—English in the case at hand. Like all languages, this one is historical, having changed markedly over the centuries without ceasing to be English. As the basis for the production and reception of all writing in the language, it is also essential to literature. Most important of all, it is the ground on which history and literature interact to produce a literary definition of history—the pattern of changes induced in the language by writing—and a historical definition of literature—past writings whose contribution to the development of the language lends them an air of presentness, an appearance of having helped to create the linguistic situation in which they are received.

The feature of languages that makes them especially useful to the business of literary history is their continuous temporal existence. But languages have another dimension that is equally important to literary history—their geographical extension. The common language that connects the *Canterbury Tales* to *The Waste Land* across the centuries also conjoins *Bleak House* and *The House of the Seven Gables* across the Atlantic. The literary historian in search of writings that have markedly influenced the development of English must regard these two dimensions of the language—chronological and geographical—as inseparable. For, just as a literary event can occur at any time in the history of the language, such an event can occur in any place where the language is written. Any subdivision of this linguistic geography along political or physical lines is apt to obscure the history of English no less than would a division of its temporal line at some arbitrary point. Insofar as our ability to construct a literary history that will be both literary and historical depends upon our preserving its linguistic foundation intact, keeping in view all of the times and places where writing may have given the evolution of the language a significant turn, we must avoid any political temptation to interfere with its temporal and spatial integrity.

To catch a glimpse of what a literary history grounded in language rather than in nationality might look like, we may reconsider the three texts used earlier to illustrate the problems of conventional histories of the period. By removing Franklin's *Autobiography*, "The Marriage of Heaven and Hell," and *Northanger Abbey* from their respective compartments—American, Romantic, and Victorian—and thinking about all three together as English writings of the 1790s that readers in the 1990s agree to call literature, we may see them at once as productions, however various, of their linguistic moment and as contributors to the linguistic present in which we receive them and recognize them as our authors.

The differences between Franklin's *Autobiography* and "The Marriage of Heaven and Hell" may seem so numerous and so essential as to justify the usual placement of these two works in separate literary histories. Franklin writes prose; Blake writes poetry. Franklin tells a story; Blake utters incantatory fragments in seemingly random succession. The events Franklin describes are of a sort familiar to the reader, while the ones in Blake's poem are utterly strange. Franklin's words are to be understood as referring to actual, historical events, or at least to his recollection of those events. The things that happen in Blake's poem, on the other hand, are imagined rather than remembered, fictional rather than true. Whereas Franklin's subject and language are consciously contemporary, Blake's are no less intentionally archaic. Franklin speaks directly to his readers, translating his personal experience into communal principles and explaining the public value of his private life. Blake's esoteric pronouncements seem to address someone other than the reader, perhaps the speaker himself, in an unknown or forgotten tongue, seeking not so much to impart truths to the audience as to awaken truths slumbering unnoticed in the reader's heart. Franklin narrates his story in retrospect from the stable viewpoint of achieved universal Reason, organizing the energetic actions of his past life into a coherent moral design. Blake's words are themselves symbolic actions, a dance performed in the continuing, ever-changing present to a melody which the reader cannot quite grasp.

Stark as they are, these differences are less essential than they may appear. Although Franklin writes prose and Blake writes poetry, Franklin himself would not have recognized "The Marriage of Heaven and Hell" as poetry, mainly because it seems actively to avoid, rather than to seek, those forms of doubling—rhymes, measures, and stanzas—that Franklin's favorite poets had taught him to associate with the genre. Except for occasional rhetorical doublings, like anaphora, and an apparent pervasiveness of semantic doubling, like that of allegory, Blake's poem offers little that would have enabled Franklin to distinguish it from prose; and even the rhetorical doublings might have seemed to him closer to the Bible than to verse, while Blake's polysemous usages might have struck him as unreliable poetic signs, insofar as the "other," nonliteral meanings of these figures remain obscure and, hence, perhaps illusory. Franklin's recollection of learning to write by translating passages from the *Spectator* into verse and then back into prose suggests that he equated poetry with versification, a pleasurable but finally impractical exercise that, pursued for its own sake, tends to divert the writer from his proper business, the direct transmission of socially useful knowledge. To Blake, on the other hand, poetry meant truth—not meters, as Emerson would put the case, but a meter-making argument (225). What most people, including Franklin, called poetry was to Blake merely versified prose, social discourse in fancy dress. True poetry breaks through all conventional forms to an immediate vision of the real, which, being unavailable to common sense, necessarily expresses itself in strange, seemingly disordered figures, often formally indistinguishable from prose and yet lacking the immediately graspable meanings that prose normally conveys.

The difference between these two works, in sum, lies not so much in their respective forms—the one prose, the other poetry—as in their authors' understanding of these terms. But even here, we find points of significant agreement. Both Franklin and Blake considered prose to be a public language, a currency minted to facilitate the exchange of information among individuals engaged in social commerce. And both regarded poetry as a more private speech—not the language of a man in society, as Hawthorne would say (9.6), but the discourse of a solitary man with his own mind and heart. Where Franklin and Blake part company, then, is in their very different evaluations of these two registers. For Franklin, poetry tended to isolate its speakers instead of socializing them and thus to confirm, rather than to correct, those selfish instincts which mark the barbaric youth of the individual and the race alike. These instincts must be transformed, through maturation, into enlightened self-interest if mankind is ever to arrive at that perfect state of rational civility where self-interest and the common interest are one. Concurring in this diagnosis of the poetic tendency, Blake was determined to pursue its inward, regressive drift away from the light of common day and the increasingly artificial forms of social life to the dark, primitive source of those creative energies from which all things derive their true being and in which they can discover their absolute relations to each other.

But even this qualified distinction requires further qualification. If Blake's idea of poetry generates a form sometimes indistingishable from prose, his words also aim at a condition of general comprehensibility very much like the one Franklin associates with prose. Although unavoidably cryptic at this early stage of the poet's solitary quest for that absolute ontology called "the marriage of Heaven and Hell," his idiosyncratic language will become universal once its symbolic action has discovered the eternal laws that have guided it—as they do all virtuous actions—from the beginning. Then those syballine utterances that now alienate Blake's readers will unite them with the poet in a true community of shared understanding.

Nor is Franklin's narrative, for all its prosaic intentions, utterly bereft of poetry in the Blakean sense. Although his primary motive for writing the story of his life is to provide a model for public conduct, he also sees his task as an opportunity to relive the past in words, for his own pleasure. In order to realize his public aim, he writes prose, translating his personal experiences into general propositions that can be applied to other lives. The fulfillment of his private, nostalgic motive, however, requires a language of imagined experience, whose meaning and value lie in its own symbolic action and cannot be abstracted in the form of publicly useful advice. Like Blake's, this deeply personal discourse makes few concessions to common sense. The reader who would follow it must take up the writer's peculiar point of view and see things through his uniquely privileged eyes.

This ground of fundamental agreement beneath the apparently contradictory ideas of Franklin and Blake regarding the purposes and methods of writing can, with a little digging beneath the surface, be seen to underlie all the other differences between the *Autobiography* and "The Marriage of Heaven and Hell." Franklin does recount a sequence of past events, whereas Blake seems to produce a random series of disconnected fragments. As Blake's opening and concluding verses indicate, however, these anecdotes and gnomic catalogs are to be understood as present events in a historical sequence announced in the prefatory "Argument": "Once . . . Then . . . Till . . . Now . . ." (33). This sequence leads directly to the body of the poem and, through it, to a conclusion that, although foreseen in "A Song of Liberty," remains far distant and as yet unrealized.

The general design of this history, moreover, closely resembles the one Franklin relates. Both retell the familiar Christian myth of an original estate lost through ambition and desire, which leads at first to suffering and then, through the purification of desire, to a final redemption that justifies the initial act of rebellion and all of its tumultuous consequences. The difference between these two redactions of the myth lies primarily in the points of view from which they are told. Franklin stands at the end of the completed process and shows how the ambition that prompted him to rebel against his brother has brought him, through struggle and error, to a position in the new republican order so eminent that he is virtually identified with it. Blake, in contrast, stands in the midst of this as yet uncompleted history, after the fall but before the realization of that perfect human society in which individual desire and communal laws are no longer in conflict. Or, rather, because he has not yet reached that "point marked out by Heaven," as Wordsworth was to call it (225), which is the object of his desires, he cannot stand still and complacently survey, in the light of achieved wisdom, the purblind gropings, false starts, and lucky breaks that have brought him there. He must press on in words, as the young Franklin did in life, trying one thing and another to see what will serve, finding his way by going.

But even this difference grows less distinct upon closer inspection. Although Franklin professes to know the outcome of the story he is telling, that story never arrives at the point from which he tells it, partly because he is repeatedly interrupted by present business, partly because each time he resumes his narrative he finds himself in a different situation with a longer, even more eventful, and in certain respects quite different story to tell. Part 1, written in England in 1771, when Franklin was Pennsylvania's colonial agent in London, covers the years from his birth, in 1706, to his marriage, in 1730, and tells the story of his rise from poverty and obscurity to wealth and reputation. Part 2, written in France thirteen years later, when he had become an international celebrity, advances the history only a year or two, through 1731. In 1788, then retired from public life, Franklin brought the record up to 1757; and two years later, in his final illness, he managed a last brief entry, leaving more than forty years, the most important period in his public life, unaccounted for.

In an apparent effort to maintain a consistent attitude toward his project and some coherence in the narrative itself, Franklin makes very little of these abrupt shifts in point of view, merely noting at the beginning of each installment the passage of time since the previous one. The changes in point of view are nonetheless quite evident in the selection and treatment of remembered details and in his identification of his audience; and these alterations create the impression of a writer moving in and through his text, very much as Blake does, trying to bring his writing to its desired, dimly seen, but endlessly receding conclusion. As time goes on, and the number of events to be recorded and explained multiplies, Franklin seems to despair of ever completing his chronicle, let alone comprehending its ultimate design. Parts 3 and 4 seem less concerned to select and arrange remembered events according to some known, communicable principle than to get everything down, so that some future historian, knowing their outcome, will be able to judge the relative consequence of these bewildering affairs and give them their proper weight and order. Like Blake's cryptic outbursts, it seems, these timely chronicles must discover their eternal meaning in due time, when the universal pattern of particular things has finally made itself clear.

If Franklin's story seems familiar, immediately recognizable, while Blake's seems strange, we must recall that the facts of Franklin's life became known for the first time only with the publication of his memoirs, and the lesson he draws from those facts, concerning the moral and social value of personal ambition, was still a revolutionary one in 1790. Blake's story, on the other hand, asks to be seen as timeless, ancient, the recitation of a once-familiar but now-forgotten legend. If we maintain that the events in the *Autobiography* are true, remembered, while those in Blake's poem are made up, imagined, we must also admit that Franklin fictionalizes his life to make it serve his public lesson, leaving out those experiences which were either not "fit to be imitated" (1) or by nature inimitable and simplifying the rest to suit the general needs and lesser capacities of his audience. Blake's imaginings, on the other hand, are conceived— and meant to be taken—as true. Indeed, the *Autobiography* verified Blake's assertion that today's accepted truths are yesterday's imaginings (36) when Franklin's early biographers used the fictional account of his boyhood as the source of their historical facts. And although we cannot ignore the difference between the modes of representation that Franklin and Blake chose for telling their truths—verisimilar realism in the one case and mysterious symbolism in the other—neither can we forget that both modes are ultimately allegorical, attempts to express something beyond themselves: that unconditional ground of conditioned things, in Emerson's words (46), which previous ages seem to have known but, in these rapidly changing times, can only be faintly discerned through the dark, enigmatic glass of remembered or imagined figures.

As for Franklin's concern to enclose his youthful appetites within the circle of mature Reason and Blake's efforts to liberate creative desire from the constraints of false Reason, these represent opposite approaches to the same fundamental problem: the relative priority—ontological, moral, and aesthetic—of those collective forms and individual energies that, Blake and Franklin agreed, together constitute reality. In one respect, these two approaches are irreconcilable. Franklin represents the very system of secular, rational empircism against which Blake is rebelling, while Blake embodies those disruptive, potentially anarchic energies that Franklin had seen at work in the Revolution and was now determined to bring under the rule of law.

In certain equally important respects, however, these two positions lie very close together. If Blake seems to speak for the rebellious impulses that Franklin wants to control, that is because the political revolution—the one, indeed, through which Franklin rose to eminence and power—provided much of the inspiration for Blake's message, as well as one of its recurrent metaphors. What is more, although the *Autobiography* imposes the form of mature Reason upon the energies of youth, in the life story itself youthful impetuosity precedes and, somehow, produces mature Reason—thus appearing to support at least one meaning of Blake's dictum "Reason is the bound or outward circumference of Energy" (34).

This question concerning the relation between human action and the forms of meaning preoccupies Franklin throughout the *Autobiography*. He wants to believe—or at least asks his reader to believe—that Reason exists prior to, and independent of, its acquisition by any individual, governing the actions even of unreasonable persons and directing the course of human history from benighted barbarism to enlightened civility. Having discarded revelation as a way of knowing the absolute form of the world and having made this knowledge dependent on maturity, however, he cannot clearly distinguish Reason from achieved reasonableness or explain how that frame of mind can arise from the irrational desires of youth. All he can say is that, somehow—whether by luck or providentially, with the help of foresight or hindsight—his life has brought him to Reason and may therefore serve to guide others toward that desirable end. And even if Reason is not the justifying form of human action a priori, it will constitute such a form in effect, once enough people have decided to follow the fortunate path of his experience rather than the uncertain course of their own desires. With none of the old maps to direct him, he has made his way, by trial and error, through the mirror-maze of life to the place of wealth and wisdom; and he can now see which turns were right and which were dead-ends or regressions. Knowing the way, he can even reenter the labyrinth in imagination and run through it again, this time with pleasure instead of anxiety regarding its outcome. Above all, by laying down a direction for the ambitions of future generations, he can forestall the fatal errors to which desire naturally tends and so bring posterity, through the strait gate of his text, to a true community of reasonable men essentially like himself.

Blake, too, aims to chart a course for individual desire that will arrive at its justifying conclusion in a perfect society. Where Franklin plots each stage of the voyage in relation to the fixed celestial point of universal Reason, however, Blake navigates by dead reckoning, measuring his progress and plotting the next leg of the journey from each new position attained. This uncertain procedure lends the prospective voyage an air of risk, especially when compared to Franklin's reassurances concerning the trustworthiness of ambition and desire. And yet Blake's admonitions to leave the known world and set sail for unknown waters bespeak an optimism, a capacity for belief in the rightness of desire, that is largely absent from Franklin's cautionary advice to wandering mariners. Blake seems never to doubt that these are, in Whitman's phrase, "all the seas of God" (421), diabolical though they may appear to the timid landsman's eye. In order to survive, we must drown; to rise, we must fall, for the way up is downward; true sanity lies in madness; what is called reality is only a dream from which we must awake.

Measured by these standards, Franklin's reputed optimism begins to look deeply skeptical if not downright despairing. Although unaccountably fortunate in his own case, individual ambition cannot normally be relied upon to discover or produce Reason all by itself. If selfish desire is to culminate in the perfect society, where self-interest and the common interest are identical, rather than in anarchy, where individual desires are in ceaseless conflict with each other, then desire must take instruction from Reason. And since Reason exists, so far as Franklin can tell, only in the minds of those who, like himself, have stumbled upon it, that instruction must come from the voyager safe in port, not from one still adrift on the seas of desire with his finger in the wind.

While it is true, then, that Franklin's celebration of social, political, and economic ambition sounds a distinctly modern note, his doubts concerning the ultimate reliability of unregulated desire as a guide to Reason and his consequent efforts to put Reason in charge of desire generate a discourse that is closer to John Gay's than to Wallace Stevens's, as well as a narrative form that, in its resemblance to Augustine's *Confessions*, is essentially medieval. Even though Franklin's present wisdom seems much indebted to his past foolishness, Reason retains its absolute authority over desire, identifying the "errata" of individual experience as if, like Gay's and Augustine's knowledge of universal truth, it owed nothing to that experience. "The Marriage of Heaven and Hell," in contrast, seems, for all its archaic mannerisms, altogether modern in its reluctance to distinguish general meanings from the particular actions that realize them. It is perhaps too much to say that for Blake, as for Stevens, desire is "the only emperor." Still, Blake does give desire ultimate authority, not only over the conduct of life but over that of his poem as well, which enacts the writer's life immediately, as a mode of being, instead of reshaping the memory of it to represent general principles, in a form of seeming.

In a still deeper sense, however, it is Franklin rather than Blake who anticipates the Modernist sensibility expressed in Stevens's bleak and lovely poem. Blake can say that individual desire is the only emperor, not because, as Stevens maintains, that is all there is, but because he believes unquestioningly that desire arises from, surely manifests, and tends inevitably toward an eternal, unchanging form of reality in which all things and persons, scattered in time and space, exist together in absolute, divine being. Although a writer of fictions, he is a true believer.

There is in Franklin's true story, on the other hand, a degree of intentional artifice that bespeaks a deep skepticism regarding the universal scheme of things he calls Reason. Unable to say how his ambitions and follies happened to culminate in happiness, wealth, and fame rather than in misery, poverty, and infamy, he cannot be certain that universal Reason really is the emperor of desire, that his mature, reasonable self was always there, as it is in his narrative, presiding over his youthful enthusiasms and directing them to their eternally appointed end. To initiate the reign of Reason, therefore, he must transform his peculiar luck into a universal lesson, portraying what was in fact the blind evolution of a most remarkable and inimitable man as a model for the conduct of ordinary men. The resulting narrative is a veritable dream of Reason, an "idea of order" or "supreme fiction" (Stevens, *Poems* 128, 380) invented to enthrone in human society the king who once reigned in Heaven and thus to forestall the otherwise inevitable anarchy of natural desire. Modernism may find in Blake a source of its own poetic forms and idiom, but it must look to Franklin for that "abdication of belief" (Dickinson 646) which is its spiritual legacy.

The winding way that leads among all these differences and similarities debouches at a point of fundamental identity: both Franklin and Blake are engaged in a project of life-writing. To be sure, they employ different generic forms for this purpose. Franklin shapes his life upon a historiographical model in order to turn the disconnected experiences he has selected from memory into a coherent story of rising fortunes and justified ambitions. Instead of writing about his life, Blake lives it in writing, choosing poetry as the only true, justifiable form of human conduct. These two models, furthermore, employ different orders of language, which locate the value of life in very different realms. The language of historiography refers to human actions that exist prior to, and independent of, the words that describe them, and discovers the significance of those actions in their cumulative moral design. The meanings of poetry, on the other hand, and hence the value of the life it records, lie in the words themselves, in symbolic actions rather than in static moral forms.

Nevertheless, the subject of both the *Autobiography* and "The Marriage of Heaven and Hell" is the writer's own experience. It constitutes the motive for writing, the main object of textual attention, the sole source of all information regarding the ultimate form in which experience is supposed to occur, and the ground of authority for all explanations and judgments. Both Franklin and Blake aspire to, and sometimes presume, a possession of absolute truths about their own experiences and about human history in general. For both, however, that comprehension depends entirely on what they themselves have seen, done, and imagined. No other source of knowledge—theological, historical, or institutional—exists to answer the questions that experience raises; and those established authorities that profess to do so—revelation in Franklin's case, science and the church in Blake's, the monarchy in both—are summarily rejected as forms of oppression. Franklin reasons from his experience; Blake imagines his. For both, the value of that experience lies not in its corroborations of received truths but in its own cognitive powers—its ability to recover truths once known but lost in the course of history, or to discover truths that, while eternal, have never been known before, or even to create truths that may in time become eternal.

Franklin and Blake write because their experiences have removed them from the worlds in which they began life and in which their contemporaries still live. The game, they see, has changed; the old rule book has become obsolete. Ambition, curiosity, and disdain for established authority have won Franklin wealth, social station, and even a species of immortality rather than disgrace or damnation. God did not create us, Blake has learned; we created the God who now tyrannizes over us and are free to create another, better one, a deity responsible to sanctified human desires. Arising entirely from their own unique experiences, these revolutionary discoveries have set Franklin and Blake apart from their contemporaries, who either go on playing the old game as if nothing had changed or else find themselves caught up in the new one, "blundering on in the dark," as Benjamin Vaughn wrote to Franklin, "almost without a guide" (67). But, however isolating, these unique experiences have potential meaning and value for modern society at large. They have given their subjects a glimpse into the rules of the new game, and though these may not yet be codifiable, they can at least be adumbrated in the language of the experiences that discovered them. By recounting their experiences, Franklin and Blake aim to contribute a chapter to the new rule book demanded by the new game, and thus repair the fissure that experience has opened up between them and their readers.

In certain significant respects, these two preliminary rule books for modern life could not be more different. The complex code of

REASON vs. SUPERSTITION: A
CARICATURE

values that Franklin lumps together under the heading of Reason
and seeks to substitute for all forms of enslaving superstition is the
very one that Blake rejects in the name of imagination and a liberating spirituality. Nonetheless, both are writing a new scripture for a
new age, a book of revelation arising entirely from their own experiences and communicable only in terms of the experiences that produced and contain them. While both are explicit in identifying the
bankrupt systems they seek to supplant—metaphysics in Franklin's
case, physics in Blake's—neither of them wishes merely to write off
the past as hopelessly benighted. On the contrary, both aspire to the
discovery of a historical scheme that will explain the past and the
present and, by incorporating these seemingly irreconcilable times
in a single design, recover the now rapidly vanishing past and unveil
the future. But just as their initial discovery that the game has
changed came to them in playing it, this ultimate discovery of its
still imperfectly graspable rules must emerge gradually from continued play and ceaseless reflection upon the significance and value of
every maneuver. With nothing but his own actions and their consequences to teach him the rules, the player must be at once "in and
out of the game," as Whitman says (32), simultaneously playing it
and watching himself play, in anticipation of that day when he and
all the other players will finally know who they are and what they
are doing (Emerson 226).

CF.
PROGRESSIVE
NATURE OF
ART.

PROCESS

The introduction of *Northanger Abbey* into this literary company
would appear to detach Franklin altogether from Blake and to form
with the *Autobiography* an anti-Romantic alliance that fairly represents the minority status of anything like "The Marriage of Heaven
and Hell" among English writings of the 1790s. Where Blake con-
cocts a language and a mythology of his own to express the most
personal of otherworldly visions, Franklin and Austen adopt the
ordinary idioms of public discourse to tell the most familiar of secular stories, the progress of wayward youth through experience to
social maturity. Addressing persons essentially like themselves,
readers who already entertain their most basic assumptions, they
caution repeatedly against extremes of any sort—luxury or poverty,
tyranny or anarchy, personal idiosyncrasy or servitude to fashion,

irrational superstition or spiritless materialism. To a readership utterly unlike himself, Blake preaches revolution of the most thoroughgoing sort—political, social, epistemological, linguistic, and metaphysical. Where they seek lucidity and coherence in order to make generally available their lessons on present conduct, he risks obscurity and formlessness in a quest for timeless wisdom. To them a symptom, if not a principal cause, of error, poetry is to him the only source of truth.

Indeed, "The Marriage of Heaven and Hell" might be said to epitomize the evils of those popular romances that Austen is at such pains to deride. Like the gothic novels that so mislead Catherine, Blake's poem unsettles the mind, violates all common sense, and calls into question the evidence of our own eyes. It engages supernatural characters in obscurely motivated, seemingly portentous actions, seducing its readers from all customary human relations and isolating them in the dark, subterranean passages of their own buried passions. It, too, emits an odor of archaic religiosity, like some foul but perversely irresistible exhalation from a recently opened crypt. As unnatural and nonsensical as any *Udolpho*, it is the embodiment of Austen's signature pejoratives: fanciful, enthusiastic, curious, unsteady, wandering, and, all together, un-English.

This immediate inclination to see Austen leagued with Franklin against Blake is, of course, too simple. On the one hand, none of the writers constructed by these texts would have much sympathy for either of the other two. If to the Austen of *Northanger Abbey* Blake would seem irrational, Franklin would appear altogether too ready to sacrifice principle to social expediency. Franklin would regard Austen's fable as only slightly less fanciful, more true to actual modern life, than Blake's; whereas Blake would consider Franklin and Austen equally materialistic, given their shared conviction that virtue rests on economic independence rather than material poverty. As for their hearts' respective homes, Franklin would deem Blake's Eden an untamed wilderness and Austen's favorite suburbs merely inert; while she would equate Philadelphia with Isabella's Bath, the Orcian underworld with Catherine's imagined abbey; and Blake would consider both Franklin's city and Henry

Tilney's Woodston the commercial and ecclesiastical foundries of our mind-forged manacles.

There are, on the other hand, qualities essential to these three texts that, rather than distinguishing them from each other, prove them varieties of a single literary species. Although Franklin's is an autobiography, Blake's a poem, and Austen's a novel, all three claim for themselves an unusually close relation to truth by detaching themselves, explicitly or implicitly, from conventional forms that they associate with fiction—poetry in Franklin's case, ordinary prose in Blake's, and in *Northanger Abbey* those popular romances which, being grossly false to actual life, must be tempered by historical study, sound judgment, and good taste if they are not to lead their reader into regions of error where no sensible person would wish to go. Whatever is discursive meat to one of these writers is rhetorical poison to the others. Still, the object of writing is the same for all three: the apprehension and conveyance of the truth.

The motive or occasion for this truth-finding and truth-telling also appears to be the same for all three: things have changed. The forms and modes of explanation that once described reality, governed human conduct, and illuminated the course of history will no longer do so. For a century or more, it seems, a reservoir of learning and experience has been accumulating behind the dam of received wisdom, which has now broken, inundating modern society in a flood of novel ideas, unprecedented opportunities, and drastically altered relations that must be understood anew if this accelerating current is not merely to deliver human history to purposeless extinction in the annihilating sea. Irreversible, these changes involve a loss of something valuable—shared belief, self-knowledge, predictable consequences—evoking in their victims feelings of nostalgia for the past and anxiety regarding the future. But even if the old, the original, condition could be restored, no one would wish it, for these changes are also liberating. They provide a freedom of personal choice, a range of social opportunities, a latitude of possible experience that makes the past seem stifling and the future a cause for enthusiastic optimism.

Like Franklin and Blake, Austen contemplates the altered pre-

sent with mingled sensations of loss and gain. Where Franklin cele-
brates the liberation of individual ambition but fears the anarchy to
which self-interest points, and Blake laments the decay of religious
myth but looks forward to the new, eternal myth to be discovered by
the unshackled imagination, Austen detests the falsity and in-
stability of fashionable society but recognizes that if things had
remained as they were when the abbey, rather than Bath, ruled England, Catherine would never have spoken to Henry Tilney, let alone
have married him. Isabella may not know her place, but the difference between her ambitions and Catherine's is, as General Tilney
demonstrates, not one that the old order would have recognized.

Insofar as these wholesale changes in the conditions of life entail a loss of something valuable, their benefits are shadowed by guilt
and must be redeemed—not merely rationalized in terms of their
immediate advantages but absolutely justified, as the disobedience
of Adam and Eve had been, by the revelation of a new covenant that,
although unveiled in time, would prove true for all time, binding
lost past, unsettled present, and uncertain future in a single eternal
scheme. Rather than a series of fatal errors removing humankind
ever farther from its original, divinely ordained condition, the successive acts of rebellion against church and king that mark the
course of modern history must be seen as steps leading upward from
darkness to light—a progress to an otherwise unreachable Jerusalem, Philadelphia, or Woodston.

If these three place names seem to play a descending scale on the
harp of human aspirations, that fairly betokens the relative scope of
the worlds to which these three texts refer—Blake's cosmos, Franklin's modern civilization, and Austen's middle-class England—as
well as that of the mental faculties which discover these destinations and are embodied there: visionary imagination, universal Reason, and "good sense." This diminishing resonance also reflects the
shift in tonal balance from Blake's enthusiasm flecked with irony
("Enough! or Too Much," 37), to enthusiasm and irony in about
equal proportions in the *Autobiography* ("So convenient a thing it is
to be a reasonable creature, since it enables one to find or make a
reason for everything one has a mind to do," 32), to the relentlessly
ironic treatment of every enthusiasm in *Northanger Abbey*.

But however circumscribed Woodston may appear when set alongside the telos of action in "The Marriage of Heaven and Hell" or even in the *Autobiography*, it is no less the place of complete being and true community that satisfies all the desires which have propelled the action and redeems all the errors committed along the way. Indeed, the justifying goal of Catherine's journeyings more closely resembles that of Blake's imagined adventure, both being figured as a marriage, than it does that of Franklin's remembered career, in which marriage constitutes merely a stage on the road to success. And though it might be too much to call Catherine's union with Henry Tilney a marriage of Heaven and Hell, that wedding does reconcile a personification of disruptive desire with one of repressive duty, extravagant energy with its "outward bound" of reason, in a final form that is at once eternally static, since the pair presumably live "happily ever after," and endlessly dynamic, since they will presumably produce Catherines of their own. In achieving this state of completeness, however, *Northanger Abbey* outstrips Blake's poem, which ends before the envisioned marriage takes place, as well as Franklin's *Autobiography*, whose action stops before the remembered protagonist has merged with the remembering narrator to close the circle of Reason drawn by desire.

To pursue this line of inquiry is to observe a striking resemblance among the thematic structures of these three texts. Beneath their undeniable differences in texture, tone, and manner, all three begin in an original condition that has apparently prevailed unaltered up to this point and is portrayed as a youth at home: Catherine at Fullerton, Franklin apprenticed to his brother in Boston, and the "son of fire" in heaven with the "starry king" (44, 43). Impelled by desire—to see the world, find a mate, throw off constraint, realize themselves—these children depart from home and the ancient laws it represents, an act at once "natural" and rebellious. As a result of this transgression, they suffer the discomforts, if not the outright terrors, of isolation, uncertainty, and self-division until, by some happy agency or other, they are brought to—or at least closer to—a new condition that recovers all the virtues of the original one but leaves behind the conflicts and shortcomings that motivated the departure in the first place.

Described this way, Blake's, Franklin's, and Austen's stories all dramatize the reason for their own existence: their authors' perception that the old forms of belief will not explain or justify modern aspirations and conduct, that these must discover, somehow, new forms of justification essentially like the old ones but immune to any further historical change. New stories of new modes of life in a new time, they nonetheless recapitulate the form of the outmoded scripture they would supplant: the tale of original innocence, temptation, a fall, suffering, repentance, absolution, and redemption. Unfortunate, foolish, or wicked when construed as a departure from the old home, change becomes progress, a movement away from the beginning to an end that is the beginning come again in a new and perfect form.

According to the moral design of this action, error lies not in movement itself, as the old order maintained, but in any waywardness that does not bring the voyager closer to the redeeming goal or, equally bad, in an attempt to reverse the direction of inescapable movement and go back to the past. By pushing ahead on a spiritual rather than a material track, Blake finds himself speaking in the original tongue. Arrived at Reason, Franklin discovers a new value in his unreasonable youth: its crucial function in a life fit for general imitation. In attempting to revisit the vanishing past, however, Catherine loses sight of her proper goal, possession of the abbey through marriage to its eventual owner, and finds herself at once possessed and excluded by it, exactly as her lowborn ancestors were.

Surviving only as a memory, the past can be revisited only in imagination, which obscures the evident, external world and turns the mind inward to become, once again, the victim of its own superstitious terrors. Just as Franklin's desire to relive his life requires him to reenact all his former mistakes and invites him to include in his narrative events that not only defer its conclusion but threaten to complicate its intended portrait of an imitable career, Catherine's backward flight from the prosaic, dispirited present to the romantic world—a world that began to disappear when her forebears learned to read and that she herself knows entirely from her reading—delays her progress to Woodston and immures her in a fictional dungeon of her own imagining. The difference, of course, is that whereas the uniquely remarkable life that Franklin would relive in writing is, like Blake's poetic inventions, truer than the exemplary career he devised for public instruction, Catherine's true life lies in the consensual daylight world, with families old and new, while her unreality lies in the solitudes of her regressive fancy.

Given the ineluctable fact of change, as well as the impossibility of stopping or reversing it, the energies responsible for it must be recontained within a moral form essentially like the one they left behind. But whereas that ancient form had revealed itself through suprahuman, supranatural sources, knowledge of the new form—"the coming revelation," as Hawthorne would call it (1.263)—will have to arise in due time, from human action itself. In *Northanger Abbey*, as in Franklin's *Autobiography* and "The Marriage of Heaven and Hell," the speaker is the sole authority for all explanations and judgments concerning the human actions recounted, not a mouthpiece for some prior, transpersonal authority. The Bible explains *Paradise Lost*, but Blake's poem explains the Bible. Even those ostensibly universal forms for which Franklin, Blake, and Austen speak—Reason, imagination, good sense—are entirely their own, grounded upon their own experiences and couched in their own words.

When the actions motivated by natural, human energy are the source of the absolute forms that purportedly enclose them, a question arises regarding the relation between action and form: which one is ontologically prior and absolute, which one subsequent and contingent? According to Franklin, his impetuous actions led in time to Reason, which in the order of composition precedes and governs his actions. In "The Marriage of Heaven and Hell," composition is itself a temporal action, leading to the eventual discovery, or invention, of its eternal form. Austen, however, seems far less sanguine than Blake—less so even than Franklin—concerning the ability of individual actions, guided only by desire, to arrive at the form that will justify them. Blake has no doubt that his poetic energies will eventually discover or produce their eternal, outward bound of reason, and Franklin maintains that his ambitions and curiosity have already done so. But Catherine must be turned out of the course she is pursuing and taught good sense by Henry Tilney if she is to acquire that necessary property of the true society. Were she to go on in the way of her romantic inclinations she would end up God knows where—married to some spectre bridegroom, perhaps, but certainly not to the Reverend Tilney.

Blake, to be sure, would advise her to hold her course along the path of desire and not let herself be dissuaded by this horse of instruction from her poetic inquest into the subterranean secret of things. As for Franklin, he might join Tilney in advising Catherine to look about her and notice where she is, in the enlightened modern world; but he might also express some surprise, both at the apparent inutility of her experience and at the presence in her world of someone who already occupies the goal toward which she has been blindly groping. Whether by providential plan or by sheer luck, Franklin came to Reason through his own actions, bad as well as good, not through the lectures of some reasonable contemporary who showed him that his life to that point had all been a foolish mistake. Although the very words suggest that "good sense" is developed through personal experience in the world, rather than revealed or innate, it comes to Catherine entirely from outside herself; and when it does, it discredits her previous life as thoroughly as Saint Paul's thunderbolt and Augustine's *tolle lege* did theirs. Franklin can look back upon his errata with mingled contempt and affection because, bad as they may have been, they brought him closer to his present happy estate. Catherine's mistakes, by comparison, are merely embarrassing, although when seen from the viewpoint of good sense, to which they have contributed nothing, they fill her with shame.

This utter discreditation of Catherine's gothic fancies is particularly remarkable because, like the sado-masochistic tales from which they are derived, they seem a displaced form of the same erotic energies that lead to marriage. As Blake might have told her, the catacomb beneath the ancient church seems an infernal pit only until the judging angel departs; then it turns into an Edenic pasture. Henry, of course, has no such faith in the fundamental sanctity of our darkest desires. Even so, as Catherine's prospective husband, he might have suggested that, while not bad in themselves, her energies would be better invested in him than in the phantoms of Northanger

Abbey. In that case, her desires would be justified by a conclusion that is at once, like Blake's marriage, wholly a product of individual desire; like Franklin's success, a socially approved condition; and, like one of the lost mysteries of the ruined abbey, a sacrament linking the individual and society, past and present, heaven and earth. Instead, Catherine's marriage seems to require the virtual extinction of all desire, especially that extravagant strain which once set her rummaging through an imagined netherworld much like Blake's and which, had she been a man, might have made her as rich and powerful as Franklin but must now be tamped well down if she is to become a suitable companion to Henry's "pleasing manners and good sense" (1205). Accordingly, it is not passion that brings them together, not even love, so much as admiration on her side and, on his, a delight in her admiration of him. As the narrator puts it, "there are some situations of the human mind in which good sense has very little power" (1199), and since erotic energy seems to be the chief of these, it must depart if good sense is to prevail.

If Woodston seems to descend upon Catherine like a god from the machine instead of arising organically, the way Blake's and Franklin's justifying forms do—or will—as a sublimation of incipiently anarchic desire, the artificiality of this conclusion does not escape Austen's notice. Indeed, the narrator calls attention to it in one of her closing paragraphs, acknowledging that her readers "will see in the tell-tale compression of the pages before them, that we are all hastening together to perfect felicity" (1206). Far from attempting to paper over the yawning gap between Catherine's outlandish experiences and her domestic fate by pretending that the former have discovered the latter, Austen seems to be saying that if what we want is "perfect felicity" of the sort once imaged in the sacraments, we will not find it, as Blake and Franklin suppose, along the path of human desire. On the contrary, that road—as Coleridge's wedding guest was even then so sadly but wisely discovering—leads away from marriage, or any such final form, to further wanderings whose only conclusion is the cessation of desire in death. To borrow Melville's words, "wedding-bells peal . . . in the last scene of life's fifth act" (141) for Catherine because Austen cynically jumps to the conclusion that Blake and Franklin are still anticipating when their narratives leave off. If we are to have such conclusions, *Northanger Abbey* suggests, we must have them in fictions, for only there do "parental tyranny" and "filial disobedience" (1207) conspire to produce marriages of Heaven and Hell or Benjamin Franklins.

When we contemplate the literary past, as we cannot avoid doing, from the standpoint of our own evolved linguistic situation, that past arranges itself not in parallel national lines, American and British, or in disconnected clumps, Romantic and Victorian, but in a single, unbroken sequence of English writings, each of which we value literarily according to how clearly it seems to point our way, to discover our verbal origins. Along this continuous line that leads from the earliest English text to this morning's newspaper, we erect arbitrary period markers in order to signal our perception of sharp differences between such chronologically separated points as those occupied by John Gay's "Contemplation of Night" and Wallace Stevens's "Emperor of Ice-Cream." Between these two points, we conclude, the way of writing poems in English changed significantly; and this change occurred in a continuous, unchanging thing, the fundamental English grammar that enables us to read both of these otherwise very different poems.

In order to acknowledge this difference and to bracket the course of change that leads from the earlier poem to the later one, more than one Modernist has defined the intervening era as a single literary period with its own beginning and ending. To Wallace Stevens, the French Revolution marked "the end of one era in the history of the imagination and the beginning of another" (*Necessary Angel* 21–22). Gertrude Stein agreed. "The eighteenth century finished with the French Revolution," she decided, completing her definition of the literary period lying between the Enlightenment and Modernism by giving it a terminal boundary: "[T]he nineteenth century [ended] with the world war, but in each case the thing had been done the change had been made but the wars made everybody know it" (*Narrative* 1).

I myself prefer to date this literary period from the American Revolution, rather than the French, if only for metaphorical reasons.

The American Revolution happened where the literature in question did, in the English-speaking world. In more than one sense of the word, the American Revolution anticipated the French one. It also marks the point where writings in English by Americans are generally supposed by literary historians to have departed from writings in English by Britons to form an independent branch called American literature, just as the First World War marks the point where the British and American lines are supposed to have reunited in transatlantic Modernism. Most important of all, by choosing an American event for the beginning of this period, we remind ourselves of America's central role in the development of English since the early sixteenth century—the time, as it happens, of both the English discovery of America and, according to historians of the language, the dawn of modern English.

This American system of periodization can be applied to the entire history of written English as it appears from our linguistic vantage point in the fully Americanized English-speaking world of the late twentieth century. In the American history of English, the medieval period ends and the Renaissance begins with the earliest appearance of the word *America* in the language, around 1510. The Renaissance gives way to the Enlightenment early in the seventeenth century, with the transportation of English, already partially Americanized by a century of writings about the New World, to America in the hands and mouths of the first British-American colonists. What we may call the Nineteenth Century, for want of a better term, opens with the Declaration of Independence, which begins the transfer of linguistic control from England to America. The period closes with the completion of that transfer, reflected in the removal of the demographic and stylistic center of the English-speaking world to North America, and with the counterinvasion of England by American heiresses, soldiers, and writers around the time of the First World War. As Gertrude Stein put it, America invented the twentieth century, and Henry James, "being an American," was "the only nineteenth century writer who . . . felt the method of the twentieth century" (*Writings* 73). That these periods roughly coincide with those ordinarily in use suggests that literary historians have been following the American plan all along, without knowing—or perhaps wanting to know—what it was they were observing.

Located in this American history of English literature, rather than in their customary national compartments and generic or stylistic subcompartments, Franklin's *Autobiography*, "The Marriage of Heaven and Hell," and *Northanger Abbey* can be seen to register a common consciousness of change, of alterations in the customary arrangements of life and thought so thoroughgoing as to touch upon the supposedly unchanging forms of all such arrangements. The changes themselves, of course, had long been under way, having begun with the first appearance of America upon the horizon of the English medieval world and having accelerated with the steady growth of that conceived place both as a source of domestic wealth and as an open field for human adventure of every sort—material and spiritual, individual and collective. What sets writings like those of Franklin, Blake, and Austen apart from those of their predecessors and most of their contemporaries is the authors' consciousness of change—an awareness fixed upon the unbridled human energies of their day and concerned to discover in these outrunning forces unchanging, intelligible principles like those that had governed and explained all human action until human action discredited them by finding things undreamt of in all their cosmologies. Earlier English writing had recorded the steady expansion of the New World within the language, whether as a cause for celebration or alarm. Franklin, Blake, and Austen grasped the full potential of those changes both for good and for ill and sought to provide their readers with the means of understanding them.

As connoisseurs of change, these three writers stand at the threshold of the Nineteenth Century, that period in the American history of English literature during which the energies emanating from the New World would gradually displace the fixed forms of the Old World until change itself became the accepted ground of reality, and the forms of understanding and judgment became themselves changing things, subject to the actions they were once thought to command. Located at this turning point, Franklin, Blake, and Austen may be said to mark the end of Early American Literature in

English—of writings we call literature because, in recording the earliest incursions of America into the vocabulary, grammar, and semantics of the language, they seem to us responsible in part for the linguistic world in which we receive them. The dividing line, of course, is largely arbitrary, merely a way of saying that Franklin, Blake, and Austen share our vision of the world and employ the idioms of that vision more than do Richard Eden, John Smith, Milton, and Susanna Rowson. At the same time, there is in the *Autobiography*, "The Marriage of Heaven and Hell," and *Northanger Abbey* a clear sense that the center of the world is moving rapidly from England to America, that rather than something on the distant horizon, to be contemplated or ignored at will, America is the cause and adequate symbol of the present and future condition of the English-speaking world, hence a thing to be dealt with—whether rationalized, embraced, or suppressed.

Besides, Early American Literature, being early, must stop somewhere so that American literature proper can arrive on the historical scene. According to the scheme of periodization proposed here, Early American Literature has spanned the Renaissance and the Enlightenment, nearly three hundred years. By the end of the eighteenth century, *America* and its countless verbal appurtenances had become an essential ingredient—in many respects, the most essential—of every serious English writer's language. That it was so is owing to the persistent efforts of writers who, sensing the expressive powers latent in the word, had taught their readers to say *America* and to see the horizon open at the sound upon a New World of endless possibilities and punishments for the enaction of human desire.

Afterword

The Early American Literature glimpsed in the foregoing chapters is a good deal larger (chronologically and geographically) and a good deal richer (literarily) than the one that usually flashes upon the inward eye at the sound of those words. It is, nonetheless, only part of the subject that those three words imply. A historical atlas that charted the growth of English in the newfound lands of the Western Hemisphere after 1500, and the linguistic changes accompanying that growth, would show a simultaneous development, geographical and stylistic, in all the other European languages—Dutch, French, German, Spanish, and Portuguese—that began their respective voyages from medievalism to modernity by discovering America.

The American histories of these languages differ greatly, to be sure. The tenure of Dutch was both short and narrow. French has survived in Quebec, Haiti, and some of the Leeward Islands, but its territories have shrunk drastically since the eighteenth century. German, the second most common language of United States citizens in 1900 and a significant presence in Mexico and Central America until the Second World War, is now virtually defunct. Portuguese has an uninterrupted history only in Brazil; Spanish, on the other hand, has spread throughout the Americas and, after something of a rollback in the nineteenth and early twentieth centuries, now threatens to unseat English as the first language of the United States.

The linguistic effects of these differing American histories have, no doubt, been equally various. German has nothing like the lexical appetite for foreign words that makes English so adaptable to new surroundings. French resists neologisms and stylistic impurities with paranoiac fury, even as it gathers to its bosom French writers of every nationality. The development of Luso-Brazilian seems to have removed it from European Portuguese rather than to have affected the language as a whole, the way American usage has changed English. The impact of America on Spanish, however, appears to have been as deep and as broad as it has upon English. In both cases, more writings in the language now come from America than from Europe, including the ones that carry off the international literary prizes; and Latin American literature is rapidly acquiring the status in our departments of Romance languages that Anglo-American literature enjoys in English studies.

Whether these various linguistic evolutions all display an essential similarity that would permit us to talk about a single, polyglot American literature is anybody's guess. My own hunch is that the European languages involved in the discovery all underwent, to some degree, the same process of Americanization—by which I mean a course of stylistic change leading to the modern conception of the world and of human history as things being made, and endlessly remade, by human action rather than created before time was, by divine decree. If so, the Early American Literature in each of these languages will comprise those writings that, having begun this process, discover to modern readers the origins of their modernity.

But this is just a guess—a way of suggesting how large and various the subject of Early American Literature becomes once we remove it from the disfiguring context of American nationalism and restore it to the linguistic grounds from which it sprang and in which it remains inextricably rooted. There are many Early American Literatures, each in its own language, all written during the three centuries before the New World produced its first nation. Whether they are fundamentally alike (as I suppose) or radically different, that discovery lies a long way off, beyond a comparative study of American literary histories that has not yet even begun. Nor can it begin until we understand what, if anything, happened to each of these languages when its writers forced it originally to recognize America.

For those of us who profess to profess English, our part in this larger comparative project is as plain as it is daunting. We need to know what America did to the language—lexically, semantically, syntactically. We need to know which of these changes have survived in English usage to condition our own linguistic world, the circumstances in which we receive all writing. We must learn to recognize the texts responsible for these innovations and for their general adoption—the writings we call Early American Literature because, in discovering America, they helped to create us. To do this work, we will have to learn things about the language that few of us know, especially the dynamics and the tendency of those changes that constitute its history. On this linguistic ground alone can America, literature, and history come together to produce an idea of America that is literary as well as historical, an idea of literature both American and historical, and an idea of history at once American and literary.

Discovering this ground, should anyone think the task worth the labor, is the proper business of American literary history. I myself can hardly imagine that a scholar interested in early American writing and convinced of its present value would not prefer such an undertaking, no matter how much boning up it required, to a life sentence on the rock pile of Early American Literature heaped up by Samuel Lorenzo Knapp. We are what we are, see things as we do, and value some texts more than others in large measure because our language is what it is. And modern English is what it is, in equal measure, because certain English writers of the Renaissance and the Enlightenment reshaped it again and again to keep pace with the endlessly unfolding idea of America. These are the early American authors, the ones whose writings, transmitted to us through the language they helped to invent, we recognize by calling them literature.

Bibliographical Note

This note aims only to identify those titles most responsible for the shape and tendencies of my argument. Although seldom cited in my text, they stand behind it, breathing audibly. Full bibliographic entries for the items noted here can be found in "Works Cited."

The development of Early American Literature as an academic subject is involved in the history of English studies and of American literary studies as a whole. The rise of English studies in the United States is traced, wholly or in part, by Phyllis Franklin, Gerald Graff, Karl Kroeber, William Riley Parker, Frederick Rudolph, Myron Tuman, and Laurence Veysey. For the origins of the subject in England, see D. J. Palmer and René Wellek's *Rise of English Literary History*. The history of "American literature" can be traced from the origins of the idea, after the Revolution, to the academic enshrinement of the subject, after the Second World War, in Jonathan Arac, Nina Baym, Merle Curti, Alan Golding, Howard Mumford Jones's *Theory of American Literature*, Fred Louis Pattee's *Colophon* essay, Richard Ruland's *Rediscovery*, Benjamin T. Spencer, Willard Thorp, Kermit Vanderbilt, and chapter 3 of Robert Weimann's *Structure and Society*. The beginnings, development, and present state of Early American Literature itself are outlined by Wesley Craven, R. M. Cutting, Philip Gura ("The Study of Colonial American Literature"), David Hall, Michael Lofaro, and Bruce Tucker.

Among the many writers on the general problem of literary history, the most useful to me have been F. W. Bateson, the contributors to Ralph Cohen's collection, Paul de Man, Claudio Guillén, Josephine Miles, D. W. Robertson, Robert Weimann, René Wellek, and, above all, Michael Riffaterre.

The problem of American literary history is variously formulated by Sacvan Bercovitch, Peter Carafiol, Raymond Dolle, Emory Elliott, Hans Galinsky, Franz Link, Richard Ruland ("Mission"), Gary Stonum, and myself (*Mirror*). The place of colonial writings in this history gets attention from the contributors to James McIntosh's special issue of *Texas Studies*, from David Laurence, from Richard DeProspo ("Marginalizing"), and from my review essays "Puritan Influences" and "Unanswered Questions."

Critiques of nationalist historiography are general in John Hurt Fisher, David Potter, and Walter P. Webb; imperialist in Charles M. Andrews, George L. Beer, Lawrence Gipson, and H. L. Osgood (their debate with exceptionalist historians is outlined by A. S. Eisenstadt); and Pan-American in Herbert E. Bolton, Gustavo Firmat, Lewis Hanke, Max Savelle, and Silvio Zavola. Antinationalist proponents of an undivided Atlantic culture include Marcus Cunliffe, Norman Fiering, Michael Kraus, and Ian K. Steele. The comparatist alternative to American nationalism is advanced by Owen Aldridge, Wayne Falke, Earl Fitz, W. P. Friederich and Clarence Gohdes, Howard Mumford Jones ("European Background"), John McCormick, René Wellek (*Confrontations*), and the essays in C. Vann Woodward's collection. New-historicist critiques of the national narrative appear in Bercovitch (after *Puritan Origins*), Emory Elliott, and the volume edited by Jack P. Greene and J. R. Pole, *Colonial British America*.

General histories of English that pay some attention to the effects of America upon the language include those by Albert C. Baugh, Robert Burchfield, Brian Foster (esp. chap. 1), Dick Leith (esp. chap. 7), and Mario Pei (esp. 77–81). Pertinent studies of English in the period of Britain's American expansion are by Charles Barber, Murray Cohen, and Susie Tucker (*English Examined*). The Americanization of English is considered by Randolph Quirk in his own volume (chaps. 1 and 2) and in his joint venture with Albert Markwardt. M. L. Samuels formulates a detailed theory of linguistic evolution and (92ff) examines the role of foreign contact on linguistic change.

The impact of the discovery on European culture is generally surveyed by Germán Arciniegas and Anthony Grafton; considered in relation to the Renaissance by Hans Baron, William Bousma, R. R. Cawley, Federico Chabod, the contributors to Fredi Chiappelli's two volumes, John H. Elliott, James Gillespie, Hugh Honour, and Tzvetan Todorov (Conquest); traced through the Renaissance and the Enlightenment by Percy Adams, William Brandon, and Peter Hulme; and examined during the Enlightenment alone by J. B. Botsford and R. W. Frantz.

The English discovery of America is the concern of Gustav Blanke, Richard Dunn, Barbara Lewalski, Franklin McCann, Jarvis Morse, John Parker, G. B. Parks, Boies Penrose, David B. Quinn (England), A. L. Rowse, Colin Steele, and Lyon Tyler.

On English prose style in the era of the overseas expansion, see Joan Webber and Maurice Croll. On the prose style of John Smith, see Percy Adams (Travel Literature 251–52), Richard Beale Davis (Intellectual Life 19, 74, 1318; and "Gentlest Art" passim), Everett Emerson (Captain John Smith 52–53), Richard Gummere (31–36), and Edwin Rozwenc.

The archive of English writings about Columbus lies buried in the larger bibliographies of John Alden and Dennis Landis, E. G. Cox, Sterg O'Dell, and Clifford Shipton and James Mooney; the short-title catalogues of A. W. Pollard and G. R. Redgrave and of Donald Wing; the checklist of Americana in the Short Title Catalogue by Jackson Boswell; Oscar Wegelin's Early American Plays; the Notes of Henry Harrisse; and the Bibliografía Colombina. Previous efforts at extracting this archive were by Claudia Bushman and Kirkpatrick Sale, whose studies, along with that of Kenneth Silvermann, overlap mine in a number of respects. The history of histories relating to Columbus is surveyed by Edward Bourne (82–83, 322–28) and by A. K. Manchester.

For model semantic histories, see Susie Tucker ("enthusiasm"), Wilcomb Washburn ("discovery"), and René Wellek ("romanticism").

That American literature should not restrict itself to writings in English is an argument made thirty years ago by Gerhard Friederich and fifty years ago by Thomas Pearce. Only recently, however, have Americanists even begun to shake the habit of monolinguism. See the polemic of Marie Harris and Kathleen Aguero; the Modern Language Association publications by Houston Baker, King-Kok Cheung and Stan Yogi, Robert DiPietro and Edward Ifkovic, and A. L. B. Ruoff and Jerry Ward; and the study by Ramón Saldivar. The work of these scholars still lies outside the American Literature Section of the MLA, however. And while a multilingual American literature would seem to undermine the nationalist idea beyond repair, the linguistically expanded subject continues to draw its materials almost entirely from writings by citizens, actual or honorary, of the United States.

Works Cited

Abbot, George. *A brief description of the whole worlde*. London: T. Judson for John Browne, 1599.

Adams, Percy G. "The Discovery of America and European Renaissance Literature." *Comparative Literature Studies* 13 (1976): 100–115.

———. *Travelers and Travel-Liars, 1600–1800*. Berkeley and Los Angeles: University of California Press, 1962.

———. *Travel-Literature and the Development of the Novel*. Lexington: University Press of Kentucky, 1983.

Alden, John E., and Dennis C. Landis, eds. *European Americana: A Chronological Guide to Works Printed in Europe Relating to the Americas, 1493–1776*. Vols. 1, 2, 5, and 6. New York: Readex Books, 1980–88.

Aldridge, A. Owen. *Early American Literature: A Comparatist Approach*. Princeton, N.J.: Princeton University Press, 1983.

Aleyn, Charles. *The historie of . . . Henrie . . . the seventh, King of England*. London: T. Cotes for W. Cooke, 1638.

Allibone, Samuel A. *A Critical Dictionary of English Literature and British and American Authors. . . .* 3 vols. Philadelphia: J. B. Lippincott, 1858–71.

American Chronology; or a Summary of Events relating to the United States from 1492 to 1813. Philadelphia: N.p., 1813.

American Literary Scholarship: An Annual. Edited by James Woodress et al. Durham, N.C.: Duke University Press, 1965–.

Andrews, Charles M. *The Colonial Period of American History*. 4 vols. New Haven, Conn.: Yale University Press, 1935–38.

Works Cited

Arac, Jonathan. "Afterword" to *The Yale Critics*, 185–86. Edited by Jonathan Arac, Wlad Godzich, and Wallace Martin. Minneapolis: University of Minnesota Press, 1983.

———. "F. O. Matthiessen: Authorizing an American Renaissance." In *The American Renaissance Reconsidered: Selected Papers from the English Institute, 1982–1983*, edited by Walter Benn Michaels and Donald Pease, 90–112. Baltimore: Johns Hopkins University Press, 1985.

Arber, Edward. *The First Three English Books on America*. London: Archibald Constable, 1895.

Arciniegas, Germán. *America in Europe: A History of the New World in Reverse*. Translated by Gabriela Arciniegas and R. V. Arana. San Diego, New York, and London: Harcourt Brace Jovanovich, 1986.

Armstrong, Paul B. "Pluralistic Literacy." In *Profession 88*, edited by Phyllis Franklin, 29–32. New York: Modern Language Association of America, 1988.

Ascham, Anthony. *A lytle treatyse of astronomy*. London: William Powell, 1552.

The Atlantic Club-book. 2 vols. New York: Harper and Bros., 1834.

Augustine, Saint. *The Confessions*. Translated by Rex Warner. New York: New American Library, 1963.

Austen, Jane. "Northanger Abbey." In *The Complete Novels of Jane Austen*, 1061–1207. New York: Modern Library, n.d.

Bacon, Francis. *Of the Advancement of Learning*. 5th ed. Edited by William A. Wright. Oxford: Clarendon Press, 1920.

———. *Works*. 14 vols. Edited by James Spedding, Robert Ellis, and Douglas Heath. London: Longman, 1857–74.

Baker, Houston, ed. *Three American Literatures: Essays in Chicano, Native American, and Asian-American Literature for Teachers of American Literature*. New York: Modern Language Association of America, 1982.

Barber, Charles Laurence. *Early Modern English*. London: Deutsch, 1976.

Barbour, Philip L. *The Three Worlds of Captain John Smith*. Cambridge, Mass.: Harvard University Press, 1964.

Barclay, Alexander, trans. *The shyp of folys of the worlde*. London: R. Pynson, 1509.

Barfield, Owen. *History in English Words.* London: Methuen, 1926.

Barlow, Joel. *The Vision of Columbus.* Hartford, Conn.: Hudson and Goodwin, 1787.

Baron, Hans. "The Querelle of the Ancients and the Moderns as a Problem for Renaissance Scholarship." *Journal of the History of Ideas* 20 (1959): 3–22.

Barrow, John. *A new geographical dictionary. . . .* 2 vols. London: J. Cooke, 1742.

Bateson, F. W. *English Poetry and the English Language.* 2d ed. New York: Russell and Russell, 1961.

Baugh, Albert C., and Thomas Cable. *A History of the English Language.* 3d ed. Englewood Cliffs, N.J.: Prentice-Hall, 1978.

Baym, Nina. "Early Histories of American Literature: A Chapter in the Institution of New England." *American Literary History* 1 (1989): 459–88.

The Beauties of Nature and Art displayed in a Tour through the World. 14 vols. London: For J. Payne, 1763.

Beer, George L. *The Old Colonial System, 1660–1754.* New York: Macmillan, 1912.

——. *The Origins of the British Colonial System, 1578–1660.* New York: Macmillan, 1908.

Beers, Henry A. *An Outline Sketch of American Literature.* New York: Chatauqua Press, 1887.

Belknap, Jeremy. *American Biography. . . .* 2 vols. Boston: Isaiah Thomas and E. J. Andrews, 1794–98.

Berchet, Guglielmo. *Fonti Italiane per la Storia della Scoperta del Nuovo Mondo.* Rome: Ministero della publica instruzione, 1892–93.

Bercovitch, Sacvan. "America as Canon and Context: Literary History in a Time of Dissensus." *American Literature* 58 (1986): 99–108.

——. "The Problem of Ideology in American Literary History," *Critical Inquiry* 12 (1986): 631–53.

——. *The Puritan Origins of the American Self.* New Haven, Conn.: Yale University Press, 1975.

Bercovitch, Sacvan, ed. *Reconstructing American Literary History.* Cambridge, Mass.: Harvard University Press, 1986.

Works Cited

Bibliografía Colombina: Enumeración de Libros y Documentos Concernientes a Cristobal Colón y sus Viajes. La Real Academia de la Historia (Madrid). Madrid: Establecimiento Tipográfico de Fortanet, 1892.

Blake, William. *The Poetry and Prose.* . . . Edited by David V. Erdman. Garden City, N.Y.: Doubleday, 1965.

Blanke, Gustav H. *Amerika im Englischen Schriftum des 16. und 17. Jahrhunderts.* Bochum-Langendreer: Pöppinghaus, 1962.

Blankenship, Russell. *American Litrature as an Expression of the National Mind.* New York: Henry Holt, 1931.

Bodmer, Johann Jakob. *Die Colombona: Ein Gedicht in fynf Gesängen.* Zurich: C. Orell, 1753.

Bolton, Herbert E. *Wider Horizons of American History.* New York: D. Appleton, 1939.

Boswell, Jackson C. "A Checklist of Americana in the STC." *Early American Literature* 9, Supplement (1974): 2–124.

Botsford, J. B. *English Society in the Eighteenth Century as Influenced from Oversea.* New York: Macmillan, 1924.

Bourgeois (de la Rochelle), Nicolas Louis. *Christophe Colomb, ou l'Amerique découverte, Poème en 24 chants par un Américain.* Paris: Chez Moutard, 1773.

Bourne, Edward Gaylord. *Spain in America, 1450–1580.* New York: Harper and Bros., 1904.

Bouterwek, Friedrich. *Gedichte der Poesie und Berendsamkeit dem Ende der dreizehnten Jahrhunderts.* 12 vols. Göttingen: J. F. Röwer, 1801–19.

Bowles, William Lisle. *The Spirit of Discovery, or the Conquest of the Ocean. A Poem in Five Books.* Bath: R. Crutwell, 1804.

Bowsma, William J. "The Renaissance and the Drama of Western History." *American Historical Review* 84 (1979): 1–15.

Brandon, William. *New Worlds for Old: Reports from the New World and Their Effect on the Development of Social Thought in Europe, 1500–1800.* Athens, Ohio: Ohio University Press, 1986.

Bronson, Walter C. *A Short History of American Literature.* 1900. Rev. ed. Boston and New York: D. C. Heath, 1919.

Brooks, Cleanth. "Literary History vs. Criticism." *Kenyon Review* 2 (1940): 403–12.

Brooks, Cleanth, and Robert Penn Warren. *Understanding Poetry.* New York: H. Holt, 1938.

Brooks, Van Wyck. "On Creating a Usable Past," *Dial* 64 (1918): 337–41.

———. *The Ordeal of Mark Twain.* New York: Dutton, 1920.

Browne, Sir Thomas. *Works.* 6 vols. Edited by Geoffrey Keynes. London: Faber and Faber, 1931.

Budd, Louis J., and E. H. Cady, eds. *Toward a New American Literary History.* Durham, N.C.: Duke University Press, 1980.

Burbank, Rex, and Jack B. Moore, eds. *The Literature of Early America.* Columbus, Ohio: Charles E. Merrill, 1967.

Burchfield, Robert. *The English Language.* New York: Oxford University Press, 1985.

Burke, William. *An Account of the European Settlements in America. In six parts.* London: For J. and R. Dodsley, 1757.

Bushman, Claudia L. *America Discovers Columbus.* Hanover, N.H.: University Press of New England, 1992.

Camden, William. *Annales.* London: For B. Fisher, 1625.

Campbell, Duncan. *Time's telescope universal and perpetual . . . : with a general view of the four parts of the world.* London: J. Wilcox, 1734.

Canby, Henry Seidel. *Classic Americans.* New York: Harcourt Brace, 1931.

Carafiol, Peter C. *American Ideal: Literary History as a Worldly Activity.* New York: Oxford University Press, 1991.

Carrara, Ubertino da, S.J. [Endosso Pauntino]. *Columbus carmen epicum eminentissimo. . . .* Rome: Rocchi Bernabò, 1715.

Cassirer, Ernst. *An Essay on Man.* New Haven, Conn.: Yale University Press, 1944.

Cawley, R. R. *Milton and the Literature of Travel.* Princeton, N.J.: Princeton University Press, 1951.

———. *Unpathed Waters: Studies in the Influence of the Voyagers on Elizabethan Literature.* Princeton, N.J.: Princeton University Press, 1940.

———. *The Voyagers and Elizabethan Drama.* London: Oxford University Press, 1938.

Chabod, Federico. "The Concept of the Renaissance." Translated by David Moore. In *Machiavelli and the Renaissance,* edited by F. Chabod, 149–200. New York: Harper and Row, 1965.

Chaloner, Thomas. Dedicatory poem to Thomas Gage. In Gage, *The English-American.* London: R. Coates, 1648.

Cheever, George Barrell. *The American Commonplace Book of Prose.* Boston: S. G. Goodrich, 1828.

Cheung, King-Kok, and Stan Yogi, comps. *Asian-American Literature: An Annotated Bibliography.* New York: Modern Language Association of America, 1988.

Chiappelli, Fredi, ed. *First Images of America: The Impact of the New World on the Old.* 2 vols. Berkeley and Los Angeles: University of California Press, 1976.

Churchill, Awnsham, and John Churchill, eds. *A Collection of Voyages and Travels.* 4 vols. London: H. C. for A. and J. Churchill, 1704.

Clarke, Samuel. *A Geographicall Description of all the Countries of the Known World.* London: R. I. for Thomas Newbery, 1657.

———. *The Marrow of Ecclesiastical Historie.* London: W. Dugard, 1650, 1654.

Cobb, Lyman. *North American Reader.* Philadelphia: Desilver, Thomas, 1836.

Cohen, Murray. *Sensible Words: Linguistic Practice in England, 1640–1785.* Baltimore: Johns Hopkins University Press, 1977.

Cohen, Ralph, ed. *New Directions in Literary History.* London: Routledge and Kegan Paul, 1974.

Colacurccio, Michael. "Does American Literature Have a History?" *Early American Literature* 13 (1978): 110–31.

Coleridge, Samuel Taylor. *Samuel Taylor Coleridge.* Edited by H. J. Jackson. New York: Oxford University Press, 1985.

[Columbus, Christopher]. *The "Diario" of Christopher Columbus's First Voyage to America, 1492–1493.* Edited and translated by Oliver Dunn and James E. Kelley, Jr. Norman and London: University of Oklahoma Press, 1988.

Columbus, Christopher. *Four Voyages to the New World.* Translated and edited by R. H. Major. London: Hakluyt Society, 1847. Repr. New York: Corinth Books, 1961.

[Columbus, Christopher]. "A Letter from Christopher Columbus [Jamaica 1503] to the King of Spain." *Gentleman's Magazine* (London) 4 (1785): 30–32.

Cooper, James Fenimore. *Notions of the Americans: Picked Up by a Travelling Bachelor.* Philadelphia: Carey, Lea, and Carey, 1828.

Cornelius, Peter. *Languages in Seventeenth- and Early Eighteenth-Century Imaginary Voyages.* Geneva: Librairie Droz, 1965.

Cox, Edward G. *A Reference Guide to the Literature of Travel.* 2 vols. Seattle: University of Washington Press, 1935–38.

Craven, Wesley Frank. *The Legend of the Founding Fathers.* New York: New York University Press, 1956.

Croce, Benedetto. *History: Its Theory and Practice.* Translated by Douglas Ainslie. New York: Russell and Russell, 1960.

Croll, Morris. *Style, Rhetoric, and Rhythm.* Edited by J. Max Patrick et al. Princeton, N.J.: Princeton University Press, 1966.

Crouch, Nathaniel. *The English Empire in America.* 1685. 6th ed. London, 1728.

Cunliffe, Marcus. "Americanness." *Southern Review* 4 (1968): 1093–98.

Cunningham, William. *The cosmographical glasse. . . .* London: J. Day, 1559.

Curti, Merle. *The Growth of American Thought.* 2d ed. New York: Harper and Bros., 1943.

Cutting, R. M. "America Discovers Its Literary Past: Early American Literature in Nineteenth-Century Anthologies." *Early American Literature* 9 (1975): 226–51.

Dante Alighieri. *The Divine Comedy.* Translated by John Ciardi. New York and London: Norton, 1970.

Davis, Richard Beale. "The Gentlest Art in Seventeenth-Century Virginia." *Tennessee Studies in Literature* 2 (1957): 151–63.

———. *Intellectual Life in the Colonial South.* 3 vols. Knoxville: University of Tennessee Press, 1978.

Defoe, Daniel. *A general history of discoveries and improvements in the useful arts.* . . . Parts 1–3. London: J. Roberts, 1725. Part 4. London: W. Mears, 1726.

de Man, Paul. "Literary History and Literary Modernity." In *Blindness and Insight,* 142–65. New York: Oxford University Press, 1971.

DeProspo, Richard C. "Marginalizing Early American Literature." *New Literary History* 23 (1992): 233–65.

———. *Theism in the Discourse of Jonathan Edwards.* Newark, Del.: University of Delaware Press, 1985.

Dickinson, Emily. *Complete Poems.* Edited by T. H. Johnson. New York: Little, Brown, n.d.

Digges, Sir Dudley. *Of the circumference of the earth: or, a treatise of the northeast passage.* London: W. W. for J. Barnes, 1612.

Dionysius Periegetes. *The surveye of the world.* London: Henrie Bynneman, 1572.

Di Pietro, Robert, and Edward Sfkovic, eds. *Ethnic Perspectives in American Literature: Selected Essays on the European Contribution.* New York: Modern Language Association of America, 1983.

DiSalvo, Jackie. " 'In narrow circuit strait'n'd by a Foe': Puritans and Indians in Milton's *Paradise Lost.*" In *Ringing the Bell Backward,* edited by R. G. Shafer, 19–34. Indiana, Pa.: Indiana University of Pennsylvania, 1982.

Dolle, Raymond F. "The New Canaan, the Old Canon, and the New World in American Literature Anthologies." *College Literature* 17 (1990): 196–208.

Douglass, William. *A Summary, History and Political,* . . . *of the British Settlements in North-America.* 2 vols. Boston: Rogers and Fowle, 1747–52.

Drayton, Michael. *Works.* 2 vols. Edited by J. William Hebel. Oxford: Basil Blackwell, 1931.

Dryden, John. *The Poetical Works* . . . : *Student's Cambridge Edition.* Boston: Houghton Mifflin, 1909.

Duboccage, Madame [Marie-Anne Le Page, Madame Fiquet du Boccage]. *The Columbiad.* [Translation of *La Colombiade, ou la foi porteé au nouveau monde.* Paris: Chez Durand, 1756]. London, 1773.

Dunn, Richard S. "Seventeenth-Century English Historians of America." In *Seventeenth-Century America,* edited by J. M. Smith. Chapel Hill, N.C.: University of North Carolina Press, 1959.

Duyckinck, George L., and Evert A. Duyckinck. *Cyclopedia of American Literature.* New York: Charles Scribner's Sons, 1855.

Earle, Alice M. *Customs and Fashions in Old New England.* New York: Charles Scribner's Sons, 1893.

Eden, Richard, ed. and trans. *The decades of the new world or West India, by Pietro Martire d'Anghiera.* London: W. Powell, 1555.

Eisenstadt, A. S. *Charles McLean Andrews: A Study in American Historical Writing.* New York: Columbia University Press, 1956.

Eliot, George. *The Mill on the Floss.* Edited by Gordon S. Haight. Oxford: Clarendon Press, 1980.

Elliott, Emory. "New Literary History: Past and Present." *American Literature* 57 (1985): 611–21.

———. "The Politics of Literary History." *American Literature* 59 (1987): 268–76.

Elliott, Emory, ed. *The Columbia Literary History of the United States.* New York: Columbia University Press, 1988.

Elliott, John H. *The Old World and the New, 1492–1650.* 1970. Repr. 1992. Cambridge: Cambridge University Press, 1970.

Emerson, Everett. *Captain John Smith.* Boston: Twayne Publishers, 1971.

———. "John Smith." In *American Writers Before 1800: A Critical and Biographical Dictionary,* edited by J. A. Levernier and D. R. Wilmes, 3:1333. Westport, Conn.: Greenwood Press, 1983.

Emerson, Everett, ed. *The Major Writers of Early America.* Madison: University of Wisconsin Press, 1972.

Emerson, Ralph Waldo. *Selections.* Edited by Stephen E. Whicher. Boston: Houghton Mifflin, 1960.

Emerson, Ralph Waldo, ed. *Parnassus.* Boston and New York: Houghton Mifflin, 1874.

Fairchild, Hoxie Neal. *The Noble Savage.* New York: Columbia University Press, 1938.

Falke, Wayne. "The Necessity for Internationalism in American Literary Study." *University College Quarterly* 19 (1973): 23–32.

Feidelson, Charles. *Symbolism in American Literature.* Chicago: University of Chicago Press, 1953.

Femia, Joseph V. "An Historicist Critique of 'Revisionist' Methods for Studying the History of Ideas." *History and Theory* 20 (1981): 113–34.

Fiedler, Leslie. "Literature as an Institution: the View from 1980." In *English Literature: Opening Up the Canon: Selected Papers from the English Institute, 1979.* Edited by Leslie A. Fiedler and Houston A. Baker, Jr., 73–91. Baltimore and London: Johns Hopkins University Press, 1980.

Fiering, Norman. "The Transatlantic Republic of Letters: A Note on the Circulation of Learned Periodicals to Eighteenth-Century America." *William and Mary Quarterly,* 3d ser., 33 (1976): 642–60.

Firmat, Gustavo Perez, ed. *Do the Americas Have a Common Literature?* Durham, N.C.: Duke University Press, 1990.

Fisher, John H. "Nationalism and the Study of Literature." *American Scholar* 49 (1979–80): 105–10.

Fitz, Earl E. *Rediscovering the New World: Inter-American Literature in a Comparative Context.* Iowa City: University of Iowa Press, 1991.

Foerster, Norman, ed. *The Reinterpretation of American Literature.* New York: Harcourt Brace, 1928.

Foster, Brian. *The Changing English Language.* New York: St. Martin's Press, 1968.

Framton, John, trans. *Joyfull newes out of the newe founde worlde,* by Nicolas Monardes. London: J. Norton, 1577.

Franklin, Benjamin. *The Autobiography and Other Writings.* Edited by Russell B. Nye. Boston: Houghton Mifflin, 1958.

Franklin, Phyllis. "English Studies: The World of Scholarship in 1883." *PMLA* 99 (1984): 356–70.

Frantz, R. W. *The English Traveller and the Movement of Ideas, 1600-1732.* Lincoln: University of Nebraska Press, 1934.

Freneau, Philip. "The Bones of Columbus." *True American* (Trenton, N.J.), August 17, 1822.

———. *The Poems. . . .* Vol. 1. Edited by Fred Louis Pattee. Princeton, N.J.: University Library, 1902.

———. "Sketches of American History." In *The Columbian Muse: A Selection of American Poetry . . .* , 80–88. New York: J. Carey for M. Carey, 1794.

Friederich, W. P., and Clarence Gohdes. "A Department of American and Comparative Literature." *Modern Language Journal* 33 (1949): 135–37.

Friedrich, Gerhard. "The Teaching of Early American Literature." *English Journal* 49 (1960): 387–94.

Fuller, Thomas. *The History of the worthies of England.* London: J. G. W. L. and W. G., 1662. New 2 vol. ed., edited by John Nichols. London: for F.C. & J. Rivington, 1811.

Gage, Thomas. *The English-American, his Travail by Sea and Land, or a new survey of the West India's. . . .* London: R. Coates, 1648.

Galinsky, Hans. "Literary Criticism in Literary History: A Comparative View of the 'Uses of the Past' in Recent American and European Histories of American Literature." *Comparative Literature Studies* 1 (1964): 31–40.

Garcilaso de la Vega ("el Inca"). *Royal Commentaries of the Incas.* 2 vols. Translated by H. J. Livermore. Austin: University of Texas Press, 1966.

Garrison, Joseph M., Jr. "Teaching Early American Literature: Some Suggestions." *College English* 31 (1970): 487–97.

Gay, John: *Poetical Works.* Edited by G. C. Faber. London: Oxford University Press, 1926.

Gilbert, Sir Humphrey. *A discourse of a discoverie for a new passage to Cataia.* London: Henry Middleton for Richard Jhones, 1576.

Gillespie, James E. *The Influence of Oversea Expansion on England to 1700.* New York: Columbia University Press, 1920.

Gipson, Lawrence H. *The British Empire Before the American Revolution.* 15 vols. Caldwell, Idaho: Caxton Printers, 1936–70.

Gohdes, Clarence. "The Study of American Literature in the United States." *English Studies* 20 (1938): 61–66.

Golding, Alan C. "A History of American Poetry Anthologies." In *Canons,* edited by Robert von Hallberg, 279–308. Chicago: University of Chicago Press, 1984.

Golding, Arthur, trans. *The rare and singuler worke of Pomponius Mela. . . .* London: For Thomas Hacket, 1590.

Goodall, Baptist. *The tryall of travell.* London: J. Norton, 1630.

Gorges, Ferdinand. *America Painted to the Life. The true History of the Spaniards' Proceedings . . . from Columbus his first Discovery, to these later Times.* London: For Nathaniel Brook, 1658–59.

Gough, John. *The strange discovery: a tragi-comedy.* London: E. Griffin for W. Leake, 1640.

Grabo, Norman. "Puritan Devotion and American Literary Theory." In *Themes and Directions in American Literature.* Edited by Ray B. Browne and Donald Pizer, 6–21. Lafayette, Ind.: Purdue University Press, 1969.

———. "The Veiled Vision: The Role of Aesthetics in Early American Intellectual History." *William and Mary Quarterly* 19 (1962): 493–510.

Graff, Gerald. *Professing Literature: An Institutional History.* Chicago: University of Chicago Press, 1987.

Grafton, Anthony, with April Shelford and Nancy Siraisi. *New Worlds, Ancient Texts: The Power of Tradition and the Shock of Discovery.* Cambridge, Mass.: Belknap Press of Harvard University Press, 1992.

Greene, Jack P., and J. R. Pole, eds. *Colonial British America: Essays in the New History of the Early Modern Era.* Baltimore: Johns Hopkins University Press, 1984.

Griswold, Rufus W., ed. *Poets and Poetry of America.* Philadelphia: Carey and Hart, 1842.

———. *Prose Writers of America.* Philadelphia: Carey and Hart, 1846.

Guicciardini, Francesco. *The historie of Guicciardin . . . Reduced into English by Geffray Fenton.* London: T. Vautrollier, 1579.

Guillén, Claudio. *Literature as System: Essays Toward a Theory of Literary History.* Princeton, N.J.: Princeton University Press, 1971.

Gummere, Richard M. *The American Colonial Mind and the Classical Tradition.* Cambridge, Mass.: Harvard University Press, 1963.

Gura, Philip. "John Who? Captain John Smith and Early American Literature." *Early American Literature* 21 (1986–87): 260–67.

———. "The Study of Colonial American Literature, 1986–1987: A Vade Mecum." *William and Mary Quarterly,* 3d ser., 45 (1988): 305–42.

Guthrie, William. *General History of the World, from the Creation to the present time. . . .* 12 vols. London: J. Newbery, 1764–67.

Hakluyt, Richard, ed. *Divers voyages touching the discovery of America.* London: Thomas Dawson for Thomas Woodcocke, 1582.

————. *The Principall navigations, voyages, and discoveries of the English nation.* London: George Bishop and Ralph Newberrie, 1589.

————. *The principal navigations, voiages, traffiques and discoveries of the English nation. . . .* London: George Bishop and Ralph Newberrie, 1598.

————. *Voyages.* 8 vols. London: J. M. Dent, 1907.

Hall, David D. "On Common Ground: The Coherence of American Puritan Studies." *William and Mary Quarterly*, 3d ser., 44 (1987): 193–229.

Halleck, R. P. *History of American Literature.* New York: American Book, 1911.

Hanke, Lewis. *Do the Americas Have a Common History? A Critique of the Bolton Theory.* New York: Knopf, 1964.

Harris, Marie, and Kathleen Aguero. *A Gift of Tongues.* Athens, Ga.: University of Georgia Press, 1987.

Harrisse, Henry. *Notes on Columbus.* Cambridge, Mass.: Riverside Press, 1865.

Hart, John S. *Manual of American Literature.* Philadelphia: Eldridge, 1873.

————. *Class Book of Poetry.* Philadelphia: Butler and Williams, 1845.

————. *Class Book of Prose.* Philadelphia: Butler and Williams, 1845.

Hawthorne, Nathaniel. *The Centenary Edition of the Works.* 20 vols. Edited by William Charvat et al. Columbus: Ohio University Press, 1962–88.

Hellowes, Edward, trans. *A booke of the invention of the art of navigation,* by Antonio de Guevara. London: Ralph Newberrie, 1578.

Herbert, Sir Thomas. *A relation of some years travaile.* London: W. Stansby and J. Bloome, 1634.

Herrera y Tordesillas, Antonio de. *The general history of the vast continent and islands of America. . . .* Translated by Capt. John Stevens. 8 vols. London: J. Batley, 1725–26, 1740.

Hervey, John, Baron. *Miscellaneous thoughts on the present posture both of our foreign and domestic affairs.* London: J. Roberts, 1742.

Works Cited

Heylyn, Peter. *Cosmographie in Foure books. . . .* London: A. Seile, 1652.

———. *Microcosmus.* Oxford: J. Lichfield for J. Short, 1621.

Higginson, Thomas Wentworth, and Henry W. Boynton. *A Reader's History of American Literature.* Boston: Houghton Mifflin, 1903.

The History of the voyages of Christopher Columbus in order to discover America and the West Indies. Glasgow: Robert Urie, 1741.

Holinshed, Ralph. *Chronicles.* London: J. Harrison, 1578.

Honour, Hugh. *The European Vision of America.* Cleveland: Cleveland Museum of Art, 1975.

Howes, Edmund. *Annals.* London: R. Meighen, 1631.

Hubbell, Jay B. *Who Are the Major American Writers?* Durham, N.C.: Duke University Press, 1972.

Hulme, Peter. *Colonial Encounters: Europe and the Native Caribbean, 1492–1797.* London: Methuen, 1986.

An Interesting account of the early voyages made by the Portuguese, Spaniards, etc. . . . including the voyages of Columbus. London: Printed for the proprietors and sold at Stalker, 1790.

James, Henry. *The American.* Edited by W. C. Spengemann. New York: Penguin Books, 1982.

Jayne, Cecil, ed. *Select Documents Illustrating the Four Voyages of Columbus.* 2 vols. London: Hakluyt Society, 1930, 1932.

Jones, Howard M. "The European Background." In *The Reinterpretation of American Literature,* edited by Norman Foerster, 62–82. New York: Harcourt Brace, 1928.

Jones, Howard Mumford. *The Theory of American Literature.* 2d ed. Ithaca: Cornell University Press, 1965.

Josselyn, John. "Chronological Observations of America. . . ." 1674. In John Josselyn, *Colonial Traveler,* edited by Paul J. Lindholt. Hanover, N.H.: University Press of New England, 1988; 148–97.

Kallich, Martin, comp. *British Poetry and the American Revolution.* 2 vols. New York: Whitston, 1988.

Keats, John. *Complete Poems.* Edited by Jack Stillinger. Cambridge, Mass.: Harvard University Press, 1982.

Keese, John. *The Poets of America.* 2 vols. New York: S. Coleman, 1840–42.

Kettell, Samuel. *Specimens of American Poetry.* 3 vols. Boston: S. G. Goodrich, 1829.

Knapp, Samuel Lorenzo. *Lectures on American Literature, with Remarks on Some Passages of American History.* New York: E. Bliss, 1829.

Kotzebue, August von. *Die Spanier in Peru, oder Rollas tod.* Leipzig: P. D. Kummer, 1796.

Kraus, Michael. *The Atlantic Civilization.* Ithaca: Cornell University Press, 1949.

———. "Literary Relations Between Europe and America in the Eighteenth Century." *William and Mary Quarterly,* 3d ser., 1 (1944): 210–34.

———. *The North Atlantic Civilization.* Princeton, N.J.: D. Van Nostrand, 1957.

Kroeber, Karl. "The Evolution of Literary Study, 1883–1983." *PMLA* 99 (1984): 326–39.

Langeac, Égide Louis Edme Joseph de Lespinasse, Chevalier de. *Colomb dans les fers. . . .* London: A. Jombert, 1782.

La Peyrère, Isaac de. *Men Before Adam.* London: N.p., 1656.

Laureau de Saint André, Pierre. *L'Amérique découverte.* Autun: Dejussieu, 1782.

Laurence, David. "Jonathan Edwards as a Figure in Literary History." In *Jonathan Edwards and the American Experience,* edited by Nathan O. Hatch and Harry S. Stout, 226–45. New York: Oxford University Press, 1988.

Lawrence, D. H. *Studies in Classic American Literature.* New York: T. Seltzer, 1923.

Lawry, Jon S. "Response [to Jackie DiSalvo]." In *Ringing the Bell Backward,* edited by R. G. Shafer, 34–36. Indiana, Pa.: Indiana University of Pennsylvania, 1982.

Leith, Dick. *A Social History of English.* London: Routledge and Kegan Paul, 1983.

Lemay, J. A. Leo. *The American Dream of Captain John Smith.* Charlottesville: University Press of Virginia, 1991.

———. "Captain John Smith." In *The History of Southern Literature,* edited by Louis D. Rubin, Jr., 26–33. Baton Rouge, La.: Louisiana State University Press, 1985.

Le Suire, Robert Martin. *Le Nouveau Monde, ou Christophe Colombe.* Paris: Chez Quillau, 1781.

Levin, David. *In Defense of Historical Writing.* New York: Hill and Wang, 1967.

Levin, Harry. *The Power of Blackness.* New York: Knopf, 1958.

Lévi-Strauss, Claude. *Tristes Tropiques.* New York, 1979.

Lewalski, Barbara Kiefer. "English Literature at the American Moment." In *The Columbia Literary History of the United States,* edited by Emory Elliott, 24–32. New York: Columbia University Press, 1988.

Lewisohn, Ludwig. *Expression in America.* New York: Harper and Bros., 1932.

Link, Franz H. *Amerikanische Literaturgeschictesschreibung, ein Forschungsbericht.* Stuttgart: Metzler, 1963.

Lofaro, Michael A. "A Colloquium on the Present State of Colonial American Literature and the Contributions of Richard Beale Davis to This Study." *Tennessee Studies in Literature* 26 (1981): 1–47.

Long, Edward. *The History of Jamaica.* London: T. Lowndes, 1774.

Lowell, James Russell. *The Literary Criticism.* Edited by Herbert F. Smith. Lincoln: University of Nebraska Press, 1969.

McCann, Franklin T. *English Discovery of America to 1585.* New York: King's Crown Press, 1952.

McCormick, John O. "Notes on a Comparative American Literary History." *Comparative Literature Studies* 5 (1968): 167–79.

McIntosh, James, ed. "The Puritan Imagination in Nineteenth- Century America." Special Issue of *Texas Studies in Language and Literature* 25 (1983): 1–178.

Manchester, A. K. "Columbus: An Historical Note on the Literature." *South Atlantic Quarterly* 59 (1960): 278–83.

Mandeville, Sir John. [*Travels*]. London: Richard Pynson, 1496.

Marckwardt, Albert H., and Randolph Quirk. *A Common Language: British and American English.* London: Cox and Wyman, 1964.

Marmontel, Jean François. *Les Incas, ou la destruction de l'empire du Pérou.* Paris: Lacombe, 1777.

Martin, Alexander. *Columbus: A New Scene Interesting to the Citizens of the United States, Additional to the Historical Play of Columbus* [by Thomas Morton]. Philadelphia: Franklin Bache, 1798.

Martire d' Anghiera, Pietro. *De orbe novo . . . decades.* Alcalá de Henares: A. G. de Brocar for A. de Nebrija, 1516.

Matthews, Brander. "What is American Literature?" *Bookman* 44 (1916–17): 218–23.

May, Caroline, ed. *The American Female Poets.* Philadelphia: Lindsay and Blakeston, 1848.

Mela, Pomponius. *The worke . . . concerning the situation of the worlde.* Translated by Arthur Golding. London: Thomas Hackett, 1585.

Melville, Herman. *Pierre.* Edited by Harrison Hayford et al. Evanston and Chicago: Northwestern University Press and the Newberry Library, 1971.

Mencken, H. L. "Puritanism as a Literary Force." In *A Book of Prefaces,* 197–283. New York: Knopf, 1917.

Miles, Josephine. *Eras and Modes in English Poetry.* Rev. ed. Westport, Conn.: Greenwood Press, 1964.

Miller, Perry. "Jonathan Edwards to Emerson." *New England Quarterly* 13 (1940): 589–617.

———. *The New England Mind.* 2 vols. New York: Macmillan, 1939, 1953.

Miller, Perry, and Thomas H. Johnson, eds. *The Puritans.* New York: American Book, 1938.

Milton, John. *Paradise Lost.* Edited by Scott Elledge. New York and London: Norton, 1975.

Montaigne, Michel de. *The Complete Works. . . .* Translated by Donald M. Frame. Stanford, Calif.: Stanford University Press, 1958.

Montgomery, James. *The West Indies. . . .* London: Longman, Hurst, Rees, and Orme, 1810.

Moore, Rev. James Lovell. *The Columbiad: An Epic Poem on the Discovery of America and the West Indies by Columbus, in twelve Books.* London: F. and C. Rivington, 1798.

More, Paul Elmer. "The Origins of Poe and Hawthorne," *Independent* 54 (1902): 2453–60.

More, Thomas. *A fruteful and pleasant worke . . . called Utopia.* Translated by Ralph Robinson. London: S. Mierdman for A. Veale, 1551.

———. *Libellus . . . de optimo reip. statu, deque nova insula Utopia.* Louvain: T. Martens, 1516.

Morse, Jarvis. *American Beginnings.* Washington, D.C.: Public Affairs Press, 1952.

Morse, Jedediah. *The History of America in two books. Containing, I. A general history of America. II. A concise history of the late revolution.* Philadelphia: Thomas Dobson, 1790.

Morton, Thomas. *Columbus: or, a World Discovered: An Historical Play. As it is performed at the Theatre-Royal, Covent-Garden.* London: W. Miller, 1792, 1796.

Muñoz, Juan Bautista. *The History of the New World.* [Anon. trans. of his *Historia del nuevo mondo,* 1793.] London: G. G. & J. Robinson, 1797.

Münster, Sebastian. *Cosmographiae universalis.* Basel: H. Petri, 1550.

Murdock, Kenneth B. *Literature and Theology in Colonial New England.* Cambridge, Mass.: Harvard University Press, 1949.

Nashe, Thomas. *Quaternio, or a fourefold way to a happie life.* London: J. Dawson, 1633.

Neal, John. *American Writers. . . .* [1824–25]. Edited by Fred Louis Pattee. Durham, N.C.: Duke University Press, 1937.

[Nevill, Samuel]. *The History of North-America, from the first discovery thereof . . . By Sylvanus Americanus.* 2 vols. Woodbridge, N.J.: James Parker, 1760, 1766.

———. "A Life of Columbus." *New American Magazine* 1 (January 1758).

A New Collection of Voyages, Discoveries and Travels. 7 vols. London: J. Knox, 1767.

Newcomer, Alphonso G., ed. *Three Centuries of American Poetry and Prose.* 1917. Rev. ed. Chicago: Scott, Foresman, 1929.

Nichol, John. *American Literature: An Historical Sketch.* Edinburgh: A. and C. Black, 1882.

Nichols, Thomas, trans. *The pleasant historie of the conquest of the West India,* by Francisco López de Gómara. London: Henry Bynneman, 1578.

Nicolson, Marjorie Hope. *The Breaking of the Circle.* Evanston, Ill.: Northwestern University Press, 1950.

Nye, Russell. *American Literary History, 1607–1830.* New York: Knopf, 1970.

O'Dell, Sterg. *A Chronological List of Prose Fiction in English Printed in England and Other Countries, 1475–1690.* Cambridge, Mass.: MIT Press, 1954.

O'Gorman, Edmundo. *The Invention of America.* Bloomington: Indiana University Press, 1961.

Oldmixon, John. *The British Empire in America.* London: J. Nicholson and B. Tooke, 1708.

Onderdonk, James L. *A History of American Verse, 1610–1897.* Chicago: A. C. McClurg, 1901.

Osgood, H. L. *The American Colonies in the Eighteenth Century.* New York: Columbia University Press, 1924.

———. *The American Colonies in the Seventeenth Century.* 3 vols. New York: Macmillan, 1904–7.

Otis, William B. *American Verse, 1625–1807.* New York: Moffat, Yard, 1909.

Oviedo y Valdez, Gonzalo Fernández de. *Coronica delas Indias.* Salamanca: J. de Junta, 1547.

Owen, Charles. *The danger of the church from foreigners.* London: For the author, 1721.

Page, Evelyn. *American Genesis: Pre-Colonial Writing in the North.* Boston: Gambit, 1973.

Palmer, D. J. *The Rise of English Studies.* London and New York: Oxford University Press, 1965.

Panciroli, Guido. *The history of many memorable things . . . both natural and artificial.* London: A. Ward, 1715. Reiss. 1727.

Parker, John. *Books to Build an Empire: A Bibliographical History of English Overseas Interests to 1620.* Amsterdam: N. Israel, 1965.

Parker, William Riley. "Where Do English Departments Come From?" *College English* 28 (1967): 339–51.

Parks, G. B. *Richard Hakluyt and the English Voyagers.* New York: American Geographical Society, 1952.

Parrington, Vernon Louis. *Main Currents of American Thought.* Vol. 1: *The Colonial Mind, 1620–1800.* New York: Harcourt Brace, 1931.

Parry, J. H., ed. *The European Reconaissance: Selected Documents.* London and Melbourne: Macmillan, 1968.

Patee, Fred Louis. "Anthologies of American Literature Before 1861." *Colophon* 16 (1934): N.p.

———. *A History of American Literature.* Boston and New York: Silver, Burdett, 1896.

Payne, John. *A New and Complete System of Universal Geography.* . . . 2 vols. London: J. Johnson and C. Stalker, 1791–92. Rev. ed. J. Hardie. New York: Low, 1798–1800.

Pearce, Roy Harvey. *The Continuity of American Poetry.* Princeton, N.J.: Princeton University Press, 1961.

Pearce, Thomas M. "American Traditions and Our Histories of Literature." *American Literature* 14 (1942): 277–84.

Peckham, Sir George. *A true reporte of the late discoveries . . . , by Sir Humfrey Gilbert.* London: J. C. for J. Hinde, 1583.

Pei, Mario. *The Story of English.* New York: Lippincott, 1952.

Penrose, Boise. *Travel and Discovery in the Renaissance.* Cambridge, Mass.: Harvard University Press, 1952.

Person, David. *Varieties: or, a surveigh of rare and excellent matters.* London: R. Badger, 1635.

Phillips, Edward. *The New World of English Words.* London: E. Tyler for N. Brooke, 1658.

Plinius Secundus, Caius. *A summarie of the antiquities, and wonders of the worlde.* London: Henry Denham for Thomas Hacket, 1566.

Plott, Robert. "An Account of the Discovery of America by the Welsh, more than 300 years before the Voyage of Columbus." In *British Remains,* by Rev. Nicholas Owen. London: For J. Bew, 1777.

Pocock, J. G. A. "Languages and Their Implications: The Transformation of the Study of Political Thought." In *Politics, Language and Time: Essays on Political Thought and History*, pp. 3–41. New York: Atheneum, 1971.

Pollard, A. W., and G. R. Redgrave, comps. *A Short-Title Catalogue of Books Printed . . . 1475–1640.* 2 vols. 2d ed. London: Bibliographical Society, 1976.

Pope, Alexander. *The Poems. . . .* Edited by John Butt. New Haven, Conn.: Yale University Press, 1963.

———. *Selecta poemata Italorum qui latine scripserunt. . . .* London: J. and P. Knapton, 1740.

Potter, David M. "The Historians' Use of Nationalism and Vice Versa." *American Historical Review* 67 (1962): 924.

The Present State of Jamaica with the Life of the Great Columbus The First Discoverer. . . . London: Fr. Clark for Tho. Malthus, 1683.

The Present State of the West Indies, . . . together with an authentick account of the first discovery of these islands. London: For R. Baldwin, 1778.

Purchas, Samuel. *Hakluytus Posthumous or Purchas his Pilgrims.* 1613–26. 20 vols. Glasgow: James MacLehose, 1905–7.

Querini, Alvise. *L'Ammiraglio dell' Indie . . . poema di Ormildo Eremessio, pastor [pseud.].* Venice: F. Pitteri, 1759.

Quinn, David Beers. *England and the Discovery of America, 1481- 1620.* New York: Knopf, 1974.

Quinn, David Beers, ed. *New American World: A Documentary History of North America to 1612.* 5 vols. New York: Arno Press, 1979.

Quirk, Randolph. *The English Language and Images of Matter.* London: Oxford University Press, 1972.

Raleigh, Sir Walter. *The discoverie of the large, rich, and bewtiful empyre of Guiana.* London: R. Robinson, 1596.

Ramusio, Giovanni Battista. *Navigationi et viaggi.* Venice: Heirs of L. Giunta, 1550.

Ransom, John Crowe. *The New Criticism.* Norfolk, Conn.: New Directions, 1941.

Rastell, John. *A new interlude and a mery of the nature of the iiij [four] elements.* London: J. Rastell, 1520.

Read, Thomas Buchanan, ed. *The Female Poets of America.* Philadelphia: Butler, 1848.

Reed, Joseph. "An oration on the discovery of America. Delivered . . . at the late anniversary commencement held at Princeton, New Jersey." *American Museum* 12 (1792): 293–96.

Rees, Robert, and Earl Harbert, eds. *Fifteen American Authors Before 1900.* Madison: University of Wisconsin Press, 1971.

Richards, Ivor A. *Practical Criticism.* London: K. Paul, Trench, Trubner, 1929.

———. *Principles of Literary Criticism.* New York: Harcourt Brace, 1924.

Richardson, Charles Francis. *American Literature.* 2 vols. New York: G. P. Putnam's Sons, 1886–88.

Riffaterre, Michael. "A Formal Approach to Literary History." In *Text Production*, translated by Terèse Lyons, 90–110. New York: Columbia University Press, 1983.

———. "The Stylistic Approach to Literary History." In *New Directions in Literary History*, edited by Ralph Cohen, 147–64. London: Routledge and Kegan Paul, 1974.

Riley, Isaac Woodbridge. *American Philosophy, From Puritanism to Pragmatism.* New York: H. Holt, 1915.

———. *American Thought from Puritanism to Pragmatism and Beyond.* New York: H. Holt, 1923.

Roberts, Henry. *A most friendly farewell . . . to . . . sir Frauncis Drake.* London: W. Mantell & T. Lawe, 1585.

Robertson, D.W. "Some Observations on Method in Literary Studies." *New Literary History* 1 (1969): 21–33.

Robertson, William. "The History of America." 1777. In *Robertson's Historical Works*, edited by John Frost, 1:17–539. New York: J. and J. Harper, 1831.

Rogers, Samuel. *The Voyage of Columbus: A Poem.* London: T. Cadell and W. Davis, 1810.

Rolt, Richard. *On Christopher Columbus, the First Discoverer of America.* London, 1756.

Rossiter, Clinton. *Seedtime of the Republic.* New York: Harcourt Brace, 1953.

Rowse, Alfred L. *The Elizabethans and America.* London and New York: Harper, 1959.

Rowson, Susanna Haswell. *Reuben and Rachel, or Tales of Old Times.* Boston: Manners and Loring, 1798.

Royse, N. K. *Manual of American Literature.* Philadelphia: Coppertwhait, 1872.

Rozwenc, Edwin C. "Captain John Smith's Image of America." *William and Mary Quarterly* 16 (1959): 27–36.

Rudolf, Frederick. *Curriculum: A History of the American Undergraduate Course of Study Since 1636.* San Francisco: Jossey-Bass, 1977.

Ruland, Richard. "The Mission of American Literary History." In *The American Identity,* edited by Rob Kroes, 46–64. Amsterdam: Amerika Instituut, University of Amsterdam, 1980.

————. *The Rediscovery of American Literature.* Cambridge, Mass.: Harvard University Press, 1967.

Ruland, Richard, ed. *The Native Muse: Theories of American Literature from Bradford to Whitman.* New York: Dutton, 1976.

Ruoff, A. L. Brown, and Jerry W. Ward, eds. *Redefining American Literary History.* New York: Modern Language Association of America, 1990.

Russell, William. *The History of America, from its Discovery to the Conclusion of the Late War, with an Appendix, containing an Account of the Rise and Progress of the Present Unhappy Contest between Great Britain and her colonies.* 2 vols. London: For Fiedling and Walker, 1778.

Saldivar, Ramón. *Chicano Narrative: The Dialectics of Difference.* Madison: University of Wisconsin Press, 1990.

Sale, Kirkpatrick. *The Conquest of Paradise.* New York: Knopf, 1990.

Salmon, Thomas. *Modern History.* 5 vols. London: G. Grierson, 1724–38.

Samuels, M. L. *Linguistic Evolution: With Special Reference to English.* Cambridge: Cambridge University Press, 1972.

Savelle, Max, and Darold D. Wax. *A History of Colonial America.* 3d ed. Hinsdale, Ill.: Dryden, 1973.

Schlesinger, Arthur, Sr. "Social History in American Literature." *Yale Review* 18 (1928): 135–47.

Schmitt, Albert R. *Herder und Amerika.* The Hague: Mouton, 1967.

Scott, Thomas. *The Belgicke pismire: stinging the slothfull sleeper.* London: n.p., 1622.

Seall, Robert. *A commendation of the adventurous viage of the wurthy captain M. Thomas Stutely . . . towards the land called Terra Florida.* London: John Alde, 1563.

Sears, Lorenzo. *American Literature in the Colonial and National Periods.* Boston: Little, Brown, 1902.

Sensabaugh, George. *Milton in Early America.* Princeton, N.J.: Princeton University Press, 1964.

Shea, Daniel, Jr. *Spiritual Autobiography in America.* Princeton, N.J.: Princeton University Press, 1968.

Sheridan, Richard Brinsley, trans. *Pizarro . . . from the German Drama of Kotzebue.* London: J. Ridgway, 1799.

Sherman, Stuart Pratt. "Hawthorne: Puritan Critic of Puritanism." In *Americans.* New York: Charles Scribner's Sons, 1922; pp. 122–52.

Shipton, Clifford K., and James E. Mooney, comps. *National Index of American Imprints Through 1800.* 2 vols. Worcester, Mass.: American Antiquarian Society, 1969.

Silverman, Kenneth. *A Cultural History of the American Revolution.* New York: Thomas Y. Crowell, 1976.

Simpson, David. *The Politics of American English, 1776–1850.* New York: Oxford University Press, 1986.

Sismondi, Jean Charles Leónard Simonde de. *Historia de la literatura española. . . .* Translated by José Lorenzo Figuero. Seville: Alvarez, 1841–42.

Skinner, Quentin. "Meaning and Understanding in the History of Ideas." *History and Theory* 8 (1969): 3–53.

Smith, Adam. *Wealth of Nations.* 1776. Edited by Edwin Cannan. London: University Paperbacks, 1961.

Smith, John. *The Complete Works . . . in Three Volumes.* Edited by Philip Barbour. Chapel Hill: University of North Carolina Press, 1986.

————. *The Generall Historie of Virginia, New England and the Summer Isles*. London: I. D. and J. H. for Michael Sparks, 1624.

Snowden, Richard. *The History of North and South America, from its Discovery, to the Death of General Washington*. Philadelphia: Jacob Johnson, 1805.

Solinus, Caius Julius. *The excellent and pleasante work of . . . Polyhistor*. London: J. Charlewood for Thomas Hackett, 1587.

Spencer, Benjamin T. *The Quest for Nationality*. Syracuse, N.Y.: Syracuse University Press, 1957.

Spender, Stephen. *Love-Hate Relations*. New York: Random House, 1974.

Spengemann, William C. "American Literary History: Some Still Unanswered Questions." *Early American Literature* 23 (1988): 90–100.

————. *A Mirror for Americanists: Reflections on the Idea of American Literature*. Hanover, N.H., and London: University Press of New England, 1989.

————. "Review Essay: Puritan Influence in American Literature." *Early American Literature* 16 (1982): 176–86.

Spiller, Robert E. "Value and Method in American Studies: The Literary Versus the Social Approach." *Journalism Quarterly* 4 (1959): 11–24.

Spiller, Robert E., et al., eds. *The Literary History of the United States*. New York: Macmillan, 1948.

[Springer, Balthasar]. *Of the newe landes and of the people found by the messengers of the kynge of Portygale named Emanuel*. Antwerp: Jan van Doesborch, 1510.

Stavely, Keith W. F. *Puritan Legacies: "Paradise Lost" and the New England Tradition*. Ithaca, N.Y.: Cornell University Press, 1988.

Stedman, Edmund C. *The Poets of America*. Boston and New York: Houghton Mifflin, 1885.

Stedman, Edmund C., and Ellen M. Hutchinson, eds. *A Library of American Literature*. 11 vols. New York: C. L. Webster, 1888–90.

Steele, Colin. *English Interpreters of the Iberian New World from Purchas to Stevens, 1603–1726*. New York: Oxford University Press, 1975.

Steele, Ian K. *The English Atlantic, 1675–1740*. New York: Oxford University Press, 1986.

Stein, Gertrude. *Narration: Four Lectures*. . . . Chicago: University of Chicago Press, 1935.

———. *Selected Writings*. Edited by Carl Van Vechten. New York: Vintage Books, 1972.

Stevens, Wallace. *Collected Poems*. New York: Knopf, 1965.

———. *The Necessary Angel*. New York: Knopf, 1951.

Stillwell, Margaret B. *Incunabula and Americana, 1450–1800*. New York: Cooper Square, 1931.

Stone, Lawrence. "The Revival of Narrative: Reflections on a New Old History." In *The Past and the Present*, 74–96. London: Routledge and Kegan Paul, 1981.

Stonum, Gary. "Undoing American Literary History," *Diacritics* 11 (1981): 2–12.

Stovall, Floyd, ed. *Eight American Authors: A Review of Research and Criticism*. New York: Modern Language Association of America, 1956.

Stow, John, and Edmund Howes. *The Annales, or a Generall Chronicle of England*. London: A. Mathewes for R. Meighen, 1631.

Strachey, William. *Historie of Travell into Virginia Britania*. 1612. Edited by L. B. Wright and V. Freund. London: Hakluyt Society, 1953.

Suckling, John. *Account of Religion by Reason*. London: Ralph Raworth, 1646.

Tasso, Torquato. *Godfrey of Bulloigne, or the recoverie of Jerusalem. Done into English heroicall verse by Edward Fairefax*. London: A. Hatfield for J. Jaggard and M. Lownes, 1600. Repr. Carbondale: University of Southern Illinois Press, 1962.

Taylor, John. *Works of John Taylor the Water Poet*. Manchester: Spenser Society, 1869.

Thevet, Andre. *The new found worlde, or Antarctiche*. London: H. Bynneman for T. Hacket, 1568.

Thorp, Willard. "Exodus: Four Decades of Scholarship in American Literature." *Modern Language Quarterly* 26 (1965): 40–61.

Tiraboschi, Girolamo. *Storia della letteratura italiana*. Florence: Domengo Marzi, 1774–81.

Todorov, Tzvetan. *The Conquest of America.* Translated by Richard Howard. New York: Harper Colophon Books, 1984.

———. "Literary History." In *The Encyclopedic Dictionary of the Sciences of Language,* edited by T. Todorov and Oswald Ducrot, 144–48. Baltimore and London: Johns Hopkins University Press, 1972.

Trent, William P. *A History of American Literature, 1607–1865.* New York: D. Appleton, 1903.

Trent, William P., and Benjamin Wells, eds. *Colonial Prose and Poetry.* 3 vols. New York: Thomas Y. Crowell, 1901.

Trent, William P., et al., eds. *The Cambridge History of American Literature.* Vol. 1. New York: G. P. Putnam's Sons, 1917.

Trilling, Lionel. "Reality in America." In *The Liberal Imagination,* 15–32. Garden City, N.Y.: Anchor Books, 1953.

Trumbull, Henry. *History of the Discovery of America: of the landing of our forefathers at Plymouth, and of their most remarkable engagements with the Indians in New-England.* Brooklyn: Grant and Wells for J. W. Carew, 1802.

Tucker, Bruce. "Early American Intellectual History After Perry Miller." *Canadian Review of American Studies* 13 (1982): 145–57.

Tucker, Susie J. *Enthusiasm: A Study in Semantic Change.* Cambridge: Cambridge University Press, 1972.

Tucker, Susie J., comp. *English Examined: Two Centuries of Comment on the Language.* Cambridge: Cambridge University Press, 1961.

Tuckerman, Henry T. "Sketch of American Literature." In *Outlines of English Literature,* by Thomas B. Shaw. Philadelphia: Lea and Blanchard, 1849.

Tuman, Myron. "From Astor Place to Kenyon Road: The NCTE and the Origin of English Studies." *College English* 48 (1986): 339–49.

Tyler, Lyon Gardiner. *England in America, 1580–1652.* New York and London: Harper Bros., 1904.

Tyler, Moses Coit. *History of American Literature, 1607–1765.* 2 vols. New York: G. P. Putnam's Sons, 1878.

Tyler, Royall. *The Algerine Captive.* Edited by Don L. Cook. New Haven, Conn.: College and University Press, 1970.

Underwood, Francis H. *Handbook of English Literature: American Authors.* Boston: Lee and Shepard, 1872.

Vanderbilt, Kermit. *American Literature and the Academy.* Philadelphia: University of Pennsylvania Press, 1986.

Van Doren, Carl. "Toward a New Canon." *Nation* 134 (1932): 429–30.

Vasconcellos, Francisco Botehlo de Moráes e. *El nuevo mundo: Poemma heroyco.* Barcelona: I. P. Marti for Francisco Barnola, 1701.

Veysey, Laurence. *The Emergence of the American University.* Chicago: University of Chicago Press, 1965.

Vigo, Giovanni de. *The most excellent workes of chirurgerye.* Translated by B. Traheron. London: E. Whytchurch, 1543.

Waddington, George. *Columbus: A poem which obtained the chancellor's medal at the Cambridge commencement, July 1813.* Cambridge: N.p., 1813.

Waggoner, Hyatt H. *The American Poets.* Boston: Houghton Mifflin, 1968.

Warton, Thomas. *The History of English Poetry.* London: J. Dodsley, 1774–81.

Washburn, Wilcomb E. "The Meaning of 'Discovery' in the Fifteenth and Sixteenth Centuries." *American Historical Review* 68 (1962): 1–21.

Watson, Henry, trans. *The shyppe of fooles.* London: W. de Worde, 1509.

Webb, Walter P. *The Great Frontier.* Boston: Houghton Mifflin, 1952.

Webber, Joan. *The Eloquent I: Style and Self in Seventeenth-Century Prose.* Madison: University of Wisconsin Press, 1968.

Wegelin, Oscar. *Early American Plays, 1714–1830.* 2d ed., rev. New York: Literary Collector Press, 1905.

Weimann, Robert. "Past Significance and Present Meaning in Literary History." *New Literary History* 1 (1969): 91–109.

———. *Structure and Society in Literary History.* Charlottesville: University Press of Virginia, 1976.

Weisbuch, Robert. *Atlantic Double-Cross: American Literature and British Influence in the Age of Emerson.* Chicago: University of Chicago Press, 1986.

Wellek, René. "The Concept of Evolution in Literary History." In *Concepts of Criticism*, edited by Stephen G. Nichols, Jr., 37–53. New Haven, Conn.: Yale University Press, 1963.

———. "The Concept of Romanticism in Literary History." In *Concepts of Criticism*, 130–146.

———. *Confrontations: Studies in the Intellectual and Literary Relations Between Germany, England, and the United States in the Nineteenth Century.* Princeton, N.J.: Princeton University Press, 1965.

———. "Literary History." In *Literary Scholarship: Its Aims and Methods*, ed. Norman Foerster, 91–130. Chapel Hill: University of North Carolina Press, 1941.

White, Greenough. *Sketch of the Philosophy of American Literature.* Boston: Ginn, 1891.

Whitman, Walt. *Leaves of Grass. Comprehensive Reader's Edition.* Edited by H. W. Blodgett and Sculley Bradley. New York: New York University Press, 1965.

Whittier, John Greenleaf. *Songs of Three Centuries.* Boston: J. R. Osgood, 1876.

Whorf, Benjamin Lee. *Language, Thought, and Reality: Selected Writings. . . .* Edited by John B. Carroll. Cambridge, Mass.: Technological Press of MIT, 1956.

Williams, John. *An Enquiry into the truth of the tradition concerning the discovery of America by Prince Madog ab Owen Gwynedd, about the year 1170.* London: J. Brown, 1791.

Wimsatt, William K. "History and Criticism: A Problematic Relationship." In *The Verbal Icon: Studies in the Meaning of Poetry.* Lexington: University of Kentucky Press, 1954; 253–65.

Wing, Donald, comp. *Short-Title Catalogue . . . , 1641–1700.* 3 vols. New York: Modern Language Association of America, 1972.

Woodward, C. Vann, ed. *The Comparative Approach to American History.* New York: Basic Books, 1968.

Wordsworth, William. *The Prelude: 1799, 1805, 1850.* Edited by Jonathan Wordsworth, M. H. Abrams, and Stephen Gill. York: Norton, 1979.

Wright, Louis B. *Middle-class Culture in Elizabethan England.* Chapel Hill: University of North Carolina Press, 1935.

———. "Toward a New History of American Literature." *American Literature* 12 (1940–41): 283–87.

Wright, Louis B., ed. *The Elizabethans' America.* Cambridge, Mass.: Harvard University Press, 1965.

Wright, Thomas G. *Literary Culture in Early New England.* New Haven, Conn.: Yale University Press, 1920.

Yale University. *Needs of the University.* New Haven, Conn.: n.p., 1871.

———. *Report on the Course of Instruction in Yale College.* New Haven, Conn.: H. Howe, 1828.

Young, W. A. *History of North and South America, containing an account of the first discoveries of the New World. . . . To which is added an impartial inquiry into the present American disputes.* 2 vols. London: J. Whitaker, 1776.

Zavala, Silvio. "A General View of the Colonial History of the New World." *American Historical Review* 66 (1961): 913–29.

Index

Abbey, Edwin Austin, 8

Abbot, George: *Briefe description of the whole worlde*, 135, 139

Aldridge, Owen, 24

Aleyn, Charles: *Historie of Henrie the Seventh*, 152

Allibone, Samuel G., 4

America: and national literary history, 23–33; and English language, 33–50, 91–93, 205–6, 210; British views of, 56–57, 60–63, 97; Healey's vision of, 56–57; Smith's vision of, 56–57, 59–64, 77–78, 87–88; early books on, 60–63, 97, 134–39; in Smith's *True Relation of Virginia*, 67–84, 77–78, 87–88; Milton's lack of interest in, 97–101; in Milton's *Paradise Lost*, 98–101, 106–8, 116–17; Vespucci on, 103–4; Hakluyt on, 104; Montaigne on, 104–5; Frobisher on, 106; association with Satan's project in Milton's *Paradise Lost*, 107–10; love-hate relationship with Great Britain, 115–17; Melville on, 115; Stein on, 115; discovery of, 119, 120–21, 126–34, 144; origin of term, 119; in Eden's *Treatyse of the newe India*, 120–21, 126–34, 135, 137; changes in meaning of, 125; invention of British America (1555–1607), 133–40; first English reference to, 137, 205; settlement of British America (1607–1776), 140–59; number of British in, by 1700, 148; as new nation (1776–1798), 159–77; Revolutionary War in, 159–61, 204–5; as essential ingredient of English writer's language, 207. *See also Columbus*; and specific American authors

American Chronology (1813), 165

Index

American Literature (journal), 21
American Museum (journal), 163–65
Andrews, Charles, 24
Archer, Gabriel, 63
Arciniegas, Germán, 24, 43, 107
Armstrong, Paul, 44
Ascham, Anthony: A lytel treatyse of astronomy, 127
Atlantic Clubbook (1834), The, 9
Augustine: Confessions, 192
Austen, Jane: Northanger Abbey, 178, 179, 195–204, 206–7

Bacon, Francis, 47; The Advancement of Learning, 143; Novum Organum, 143; The New Atlantis, 146–47
Bacon, Nathaniel, 16
Barclay, Alexander, 134, 146, 151
Barlow, Joel, 9, 152, 154, 174; Vision of Columbus, 166–69, 170, 172, 176
Barrow, John, 149
Bateson, F. W., 37, 38, 115
Beauties of Nature and Art (1763), 150
Beckett, Samuel, 182
Beer, George, 24
Beers, Henry, 7
Belknap, Jeremy: American Biography, 165
Berchet, Guglielmo: Fonti Italiane per la Storia della Scoperta del Nuovo Mondo, 123
Bercovitch, Sacvan, 22; The Puritan Origins of the American Self, 19
Blackwood's Magazine (1824–25), 27
Blake, William: "America," 29; "The Marriage of Heaven and Hell," 178, 179, 184–204, 206–7
Blankenship, Russell: American

Literature as an Expression of the National Mind, 18
Bodmer, Johann, 153
Bolton, Herbert E., 24
Booker, John, 143
Boughton, George: The Puritans Going to Church, 8
Bourgeois, Nicolas Louis, 153
Bouterwek, Friedrich, 27, 29
Bowles, William Lisle, 169
Boynton, Henry W., 5, 6
Brackenridge, Hugh Henry, 166–67
Bradford, William, 7, 20, 31, 32
Bradstreet, Anne, 4, 7, 9, 20, 96; "Contemplations," 16, 50, 116; "Epitaph," 16
Brandt, Sebastian: Narrenschiff, 127, 146, 151
Britain. See Great Britain
British America. See America
Brooks, Cleanth: Understanding Poetry, 15; "Literary History vs. Criticism," 17
Brooks, Van Wyck, 14; "On Creating a Usable Past," 17
Brown, Charles Brockden, 20, 166
Browne, Sir Thomas, 147
Brownson, Orestes, 5
Bryant, William Cullen, 2, 7, 31, 51; Selections from the American Poets, 9
Bunyan, John, 82, 178
Burbank, Rex: The Literature of Early America, 21
Burke, William: Account of European Settlements in America, 149; Account of the Spanish Settlements, 151
Byrd, William, 20

Cabot, John and Sebastian, 120, 127, 136, 138, 141, 171
Calvin, John, 44

Index

Index